"True For You, But Not For Me"

"True For You, But Not For Me"

DEFLATING THE SLOGANS THAT LEAVE CHRISTIANS SPEECHLESS

PAUL COPAN

BETHANY HOUSE PUBLISHERS
MINNEAPOLIS, MINNESOTA 55438

Published by Bethany House Publishers
A Ministry of Bethany Fellowship International
11400 Hampshire Avenue South
Minneapolis, Minnesota 55438
www.bethanyhouse.com

Printed in the United States of America by
Bethany Press International, Minneapolis, Minnesota 55438

Library of Congress Cataloging-in-Publication Data

Copan, Paul.
    True for you, but not for me : deflating the slogans that leave Christians
speechless / by Paul Copan.
       p. cm.
    ISBN 0-7642-2091-8 (pbk.)
    1. Apologetics. 2. Relativity—Controversial literature. 3. Religious
pluralism—Controversial literature. I. Title.
    BT1211.C67 1998
    239—ddc21

                                                97-45477
                                                  CIP

This book is dedicated
to my precious wife,

Jacqueline,

who restrains excesses,
corrects errors,
and always encourages and inspires.

PAUL COPAN is a pastor and scholar well-versed in answering the real-world questions of both students and adults. He is an adjunct professor at Trinity Evangelical Divinity School and a Ph.D. student at Marquette University. He makes his home with his wife and children in Wisconsin.

Acknowledgments

I appreciate the encouragement of Kevin Johnson at Bethany House Publishers, who has been enthusiastic about this book from the outset. I am also indebted to those who read through various chapters of my manuscript and offered helpful suggestions: Craig Blomberg, Larry Lacy, Scot McKnight, and Stan Wallace. I am particularly grateful to Doug Geivett, who patiently read through the entire manuscript and offered incisive comments that resulted in a stronger book.

Finally, I owe so much to my wonderful wife, Jacqueline, who has been my delight these nine years of marriage. She has supported my writing from the start. I am thankful for all of her suggestions and comments, and I gratefully dedicate this book to her.[1]

Paul Copan
Oconomowoc, Wisconsin
May 1998

Contents

Introduction

Christian philosopher Alvin Plantinga recalls how his graduate school classmates at Yale University added up to a zoo of diverse philosophical animals. But all of this diversity—a happy elbow-rubbing of existentialists, pragmatists, positivists, and the like—had an unhappy side effect. Whenever the question "What is the *truth* about this matter?" came up, it was dismissed as naïve.[2]

Plantinga's experience illustrates a point the late professor Allan Bloom made central to his landmark book *The Closing of the American Mind*: "There is one thing a professor can be absolutely sure of: almost every student entering the university believes, or says he believes, that truth is relative."[3] Relativism claims that what we think is knowledge—what we think is a firm grasp of truth and reality—is really only an opinion. A fact—or a value, moral precept, or outlook on life—can be "true for you" and at the same time "not true for me." Relativists brazenly claim that objective, universal truth doesn't exist.

Relativism's rise has caught many Christians unaware, even though by 1991 the Barna Research Group found 66 percent of American adults didn't believe absolute truth exists. Specifically, they agreed that there is "no such thing as absolute truth; two people could define truth in totally conflicting ways, but both could still be correct." Even more disturbing about Barna's findings was that half of "born again" Christians—53 percent of them—and most adults associated with evangelical churches—also 53 percent—maintained this relativistic view.[4] And when polled again in 1994, a staggering 72 percent of American adults—almost three out of four—affirmed some kind of relativism.[5]

The rapid spread of relativism shouldn't surprise us. While relativism grows out of the heady freethinking of some of our culture's brightest minds, it feeds on the collapse of everyday norms. It results from the breakdown of the family brought on by divorce, illegitimacy, and the neglect of children happening in all strata of our society. The instability and insecurity our youngest generations have experienced have severely affected their ability to *love* and to *work*[6]—and, I believe—to *appreciate the existence of objective truth*. One young woman, a punk rocker, depressingly expressed this reality when she said, "I belong to the Blank Generation. I have no beliefs. I belong to no community, tradition, or anything like that. I'm lost in this vast, vast world. I belong nowhere. I have absolutely no identity."[7]

Before returning to school for further studies in philosophy, I served on the pastoral staff of a church for more than six years. I regularly dealt with the questions that arise as Christians struggle to be true to their beliefs—to take them seriously, live them faithfully, and express them verbally. All too often, I found Christians scurrying for cover when shot at by slogans such as,

- "Christianity's true for you, but not for me."
- "Everything is relative."
- "Who are *you* to judge that person?"
- "You can do whatever you want just as long as it doesn't hurt anybody."
- "Christianity is just one path among many to God."
- "Belief in Jesus as the only way to God is totally intolerant."

Too many evangelical Christians and evangelical institutions are baffled by these powerful assumptions.

True for You, But Not for Me gives Christians a concise response to our society's slide into relativism and religious pluralism. (If relativism is the belief that all "truths" are equally valid, then "religious pluralism" is the belief that all faiths lead to God or salvation.) In my own experience, the most pressing spiritual questions of Christians and non-Christians alike have to do with relativism, pluralism, the uniqueness of Christ, Christianity's claim that salvation is through Christ alone, and the fate of those who have never heard of him. The flood of books and articles challenging Christian beliefs has further convinced me that Christians need to learn to respond intelligently to the myths—by which I mean *falsehoods*—of relativism and religious pluralism. Although many of these mythical slogans tend to be conversation-stoppers, they don't have to leave Christians speechless. I offer responses to a number of these commonly parroted slogans.

I have written this book to make a case for the existence of objective truth and morality and to defend the claim that Jesus is indeed the unique and sole Savior of the world. The material is organized as a handbook. After brief background on each core issue, material is presented slogan-by-slogan, providing easy reference to specific questions. Included are some suggested responses to relativistic slogans. These aren't intended to be what cynics might call "sassy answers to stupid questions," but as hints to reopening sensitive dialogue. The footnotes add explanatory or advanced material and often cite sources helpful for further reading.

In brief, Part I looks at the *myth of relativism* by answering basic questions about truth: Is there such a thing as objective truth? Can something be "true for you" but "not true for me"? Is it arrogant to claim our belief system is true? Part II takes the discussion of relativism into the area of *morality*, especially the real existence of moral truth—the fact that right and wrong are not culturally conditioned, or mere matters of individual preference. In Part III, we look at *religious pluralism*, the assertion that all faiths lead to salvation. Part IV analyzes *the unique claims of Jesus Christ* in light of world religions. In Part V, we address the enduring question about the *unevangelized*: "What about those who have never heard of Jesus? Are they inevitably condemned?" You will find in the final section a strategic Christian response to relativism and postmodernism in both thought and lifestyle. The back of the book offers study questions for groups or individuals.

The themes of this book are closely connected to one another. Each section paves the way for the next:

(1) *Do truth and morality actually exist, or is everything an opinion?*
(2) *If there is truth, can we say that one particular religion offers a true view of the world—and shows others to be false? Are all faiths equally able to save or liberate us?*
(3) *If it is possible for one faith to be true above all others, do the unique claims of Jesus point us to the sole way of salvation?*
(4) *And if Jesus is the only way of salvation, what about those who have never heard the Gospel?*

As *True for You, But Not for Me* unfolds, you will notice one final underlying message—that many of the relativistic or pluralistic slogans we hear are, in fact, *absolute* or *exclusive*. After all, a relativist believes that absolutists are *wrong*. The religious pluralist believes that the *exclusivist* views of Christians are *wrong*. Their belief systems are no more "tolerant" or "broad-minded" than the beliefs of the Christian who claims to possess the ultimate truth about God and the meaning of life.

In reality, the relativist's disdain for truth reveals a deep-seated belief in truth. I take this fact as an encouragement. Deep in the hearts of men and women resides a knowledge that truth is a necessary bedrock for life. If we wisely use this shared need for truth as a starting point for discussing our disagreements, we have hope that someday we will win others to God's truth.

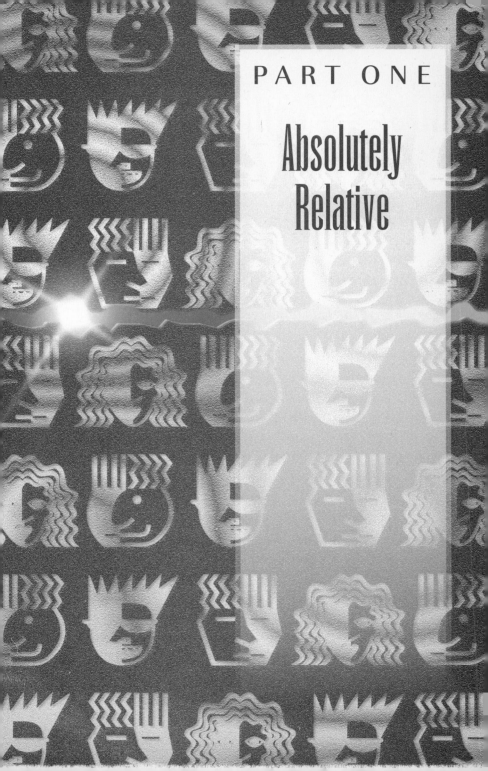

PART ONE

Absolutely Relative

IMAGINE A MULTIPLE-CAR COLLISION at a busy intersection near your home. It's an occurrence that shouldn't be hard to picture. It may, in fact, strike a little too close to home, as it did for my family and me in June of 1997.

Now stretch your imagination further. Assume we live in a less lawsuit-happy world. Instead of all parties silently exchanging license and insurance information and driving away without admitting even a sliver of blame, everyone runs into the intersection to explain his or her side of the story: "You pulled in front of me!" "But *I* had the right of way. Don't you know *red* means *stop?*" Pedestrians who witnessed the accident from the curb interject what they saw. A trucker with an elevated, commanding view of the intersection weighs in. Then perhaps the guilty party steps forward: "Well, actually, it was my fault. I was talking on my car phone. I wasn't paying attention to what I was doing. I caused the accident."

For all the post-accident debate, when a police officer arrives and begins taking notes, one truth will be clear: An accident happened. And in time, other truths will be determined. Ultimately, a description of the accident will emerge that corresponds to reality.[1]

We live our lives relying on the belief that objective truth exists—if only we can find it. We gather evidence. Weigh credibility and truthfulness. Make difficult judgments. In the end, we arrive at a close proximity to truth. We can make truthful statements that describe with reasonable accuracy how events really happened. (Or, given the right evidence, we can determine truth regarding whether the car we bought was a lemon, or how our major life decisions were right or wrong, or if God is real.) We believe that if we had a helicopter over every intersection and a video camera inside each car—to see who is on the cell phone, or shaving, or twisting up the volume—we can even discover truth about "accidents."

Truth is more than our subjective reporting of a car crash. It has objective existence. It has universal application.

Truth is true—even if no one knows it.
Truth is true—even if no one admits it.
Truth is true—even if no one agrees what it is.
Truth is true—even if no one follows it.
Truth is true—even if no one but God grasps it fully.

Although some states have given up trying to figure out whom to blame for car accidents—hence "no-fault" insurance—truth matters. And when the stakes are raised—when a child crossing the street is struck and killed, for example—finding the truth becomes essential. Serious circumstances remind us that the difficulty of finding truth is no excuse for not looking.

Enter the relativist. To the relativist, no "fact" is in all times and places true. He argues that because everyone's point of view is different, we can't ever know what really happened at the accident scene. In fact, the hard-core relativist says that given the slippery nature of what the rest of us mistakenly call "truth," we can't even settle on the fact that the accident actually happened.

As absurd as that viewpoint seems, it has arisen as a formidable opponent to the cause of truth.

Truth Wars

So deep is the struggle over truth beliefs that many see our country entrenched in a "culture war." Old divisions like Catholic versus Protestant are dissolving, with new divisions emerging on the basis of competing sources of truth. One side—dubbed the "Orthodox"—maintains that there are objective standards of truth and morality, stemming from God, the Bible, or the moral order of the universe. With regard to abortion, for example, this side claims that God's law declares the fetus is a human being whose life should not be taken. Christians aren't the only ones in the Orthodox camp. Muslims, conservatives, and traditionalists of all stripes claim to possess the truth. Whatever our other disagreements, we share the belief that a universal truth exists.

In contrast, the other side—the "progressives"—says that personal, subjective judgment defines right and wrong, truth and untruth. Choices aren't made with regard to God's existence. They defer to an "autonomous self," like the woman who assumes the absolute right to make a choice about what she does with her body, or to individually and independently decide if a fetus is a human person.

The two sides fighting the culture war are becoming increasingly polarized. There's little room left for a middle ground.[2] This deep struggle, however, isn't a war over far-off social issues. The "culture war" takes place daily at work, home, and school. It is at the heart of heated battles over right and wrong in sexual morality, business ethics, sportsmanship, and a thousand other everyday arenas.

We need to remember that the culture war isn't all that new. The belief that universal, objective truth (1) does not exist ("alethic skepticism") or (2) cannot be known ("epistemological skepticism") is certainly no newcomer to Western civilization. The sophist Protagoras (born approximately 500 B.C.) maintained that the human community is the standard of truth. Plato cited him as saying that "man is the measure of all things." Consequently, any given thing "is to me such as it appears to me, and is to you such as it appears to you"[3]—a surprisingly modern sound!

Although relativism has intermittently appeared and reappeared throughout history, its dominance of a culture is new.[4] As Christians, we are likely most aware of how a relativistic view of truth has soured society's attitude toward religion and its truth claims. Today religion is increasingly pushed aside by secularizing influences such as the university, the media, and politics. Rather than having a major voice in public life, religion has been relegated to the private and the personal. Rather than being a matter of truth, it is all just opinion. But looking beyond the religious domain, relativism implies that the pursuit of *any* truth is an exercise in futility. It clearly entails the obliteration of all knowledge, including scientific, moral, and historical truth.

The Many Faces of Relativism

Relativism is everywhere.[5] Although the list is certainly long, we'll select some of the main manifestations of relativism within our society.[6]

- *Objective relativism* is the view that the beliefs of a person or group of persons are "true" for them, but not necessarily for others. Ultimately, says this brand of relativism, no truth is universally, objectively true or false. One person's "truth," which really amounts to opinion, can conflict with another's "truth" and still be valid. Objective relativism (also known as "epistemological relativism") challenges the very existence of truth. (Epistemology is the study of knowledge—an examination of how we know what we know, our underlying assumptions, and the validity of our knowledge.[7])
- *Religious relativism* maintains that one religion can be true for one person or culture but not for another. No religion, therefore, is universally or exclusively true. Religious beliefs are simply an accident of birth: If a person grows up in America, chances are good that he might become a Christian; if in India, that he will be a Hindu; if in Saudi Arabia, that he will be a Muslim. If what one believes is the product of historical happenstance, the argument goes, no single religious belief can be universally or objectively true.
- *Moral relativism* maintains that there are no moral absolutes, no objective

ethical right and wrong. Moral values are true—or "genuine"—for some, but not for others. Since there are differing expressions of morality in the world, there is no reason to think that one is any more true and objectively binding than another. The implication is that statements of value (for example, "adultery is morally wrong") can be true for some but false for others. Something is wrong—sleeping with the boss, stealing paper clips, or leaving work early—only if you think or feel it is wrong.

- *Cultural relativism* says that what is immoral in our culture is not necessarily immoral in another culture. No one, therefore, can judge another culture's moral values. Philosopher of science Michael Ruse illustrates this view well. Ruse refers to the once widespread Indian practice of *suttee*, the burning of a widow on her husband's funeral pyre, which was later outlawed by the British: "Obviously, such a practice is totally alien to Western customs and morality. In fact, we think that widow sacrifice is totally immoral."[8] That may be what Westerners think, yet Ruse says it is wrong to judge *suttee* as a bad thing.[9] Obviously, the same principle means we shouldn't condemn slavery in America, genocide in Africa, or female infanticide in China.

- *Historical relativism* maintains that historical truth differs over periods of time. The interpretation of historical "truths" in one generation may be replaced by a subsequent one. As an example, consider Columbus Day. A generation ago students wrote reports extolling the discovery of America by Columbus. Today—if the holiday is observed at all—Columbus is cast as an evil conqueror. Historical relativists believe that researching and debating the facts of the matter would be futile.[10]

- *Scientific relativism* asserts that scientific "progress" is nothing but one theory being replaced by another. It is best exemplified by philosopher of science Thomas Kuhn, who maintains that Einstein's physics replaced Newtonian physics not because Einstein's theory was closer to correct or a truer description of reality, but merely because paradigms shuffled. In scientific relativism, there is no such thing as objective truth, even in the "hard" sciences. There is no common language between proponents of one scientific theory and those of another, and what is true or rational in one scientific perspective is not so in another.

- *Aesthetic relativism* is most easily understood as "Beauty is in the eye of the beholder." Recalling the litter of student-produced "art" scattered around the grounds of his university campus, one friend points out the remarkable ability of contemporary artists to produce works that even the artist's mother doesn't like. One person's trash might be another person's art, and one observer's standards for art are just as valid as another's. Going far beyond relativism, postmodern art abandons truth and utterly devalues human beings and the created order. Rather than being merely provocative, postmodern "art" can at times be destructive or degrading. Postmodern artists (can we call them all *artists?*) consider the emotional reaction of their audience to be part of their work of art—such as an artist's photograph of his own bowel movement or a crucifix submerged in urine.[11] Artistic standards such as technical excellence, creativity, and the capturing of universal and enduring human experience are shunned by postmodern artists.

The Implications of Relativism

In the middle of a war—whether in the broader culture or around the water cooler—no one goes on with life as normal. Society's battles over truth have far-reaching effects. Given the pervasiveness of relativism in our society, we ought to briefly consider some of its *implications*. Having noted the examples of relativism above, you have no doubt also noticed the following effects.

One implication—at least on the religious front—is that *persuasion is prohibited*. On many university campuses, evangelism—the taboo word is "proselytizing"—is viewed as "cramming your religion down someone's throat." Obviously, trying to persuade or evangelize another implies you have truth to proclaim—and that you think your listeners may well be wrong.

This brings us to a second implication: *To be exclusivistic is to be arrogant*. Given the number of different religious beliefs in the world, to claim to know something that others are ignorant of therefore *must* be wrongheaded and erroneous! Moreover, exclusive claims—especially about the uniqueness of Christ for salvation—are often confused with Western colonialism and imperialism—nothing more than bigotry and narrow-mindedness, a Western imposition of ideas upon unknowing or unwilling hearers. (To be sure, non-Christians have in some cases good reason to be critical of us. Christians invite hostility when they shout that Christianity is true and exclusive—and equally loudly proclaim that other views contain *no* truth at all. Christians can indeed appreciate much of what is true within other faiths. Since all truth is God's truth, moral truths, for instance, can be found outside the Bible—just as truths from mathematics, history, and science can be. Exactly *what* or even *whether* the Christian should *seek* to learn from or imitate ethical non-Christian religions, however, is another, more complicated, matter.[12])

A third implication is that *tolerance is the cardinal virtue*. To imply that someone is wrong is terribly intolerant, especially when tolerance is popularly but erroneously defined as being open to and accepting of all ideas. What homosexual activists call tolerance, for example, is unconditional acceptance of their lifestyle as legitimate and right. As we will see later, this attitude of open-mindedness actually turns out to be empty-headedness. It lacks discrimination and any criterion for acceptability. In the words of Allan Bloom, "Openness used to be the virtue that permitted us to seek the good by using reason. It now means accepting everything and denying reason's power."[13]

Might Makes Right

A final implication of relativism perhaps best explains how our arguments over truth can begin to feel like a war: *In the absence of the possibility of truth, power rules the day.* That is, once truth is whatever we say it is, asserting power over others is a natural next step. The German philosopher Friedrich Nietzsche (1844–1900) wrote that the obliteration of God—and therefore all objective standards for truth and morality—would usher in an age of nihilism, the rejection of all objective meaning and value.[14] All that is left is the will to power, by which only the fittest survive.

Stanley Fish at Duke University, well-known for his repudiation of objective literary or moral standards, has said, "Someone is always going to be restricted next, and it is your job to make sure that the someone is not you."[15] Many special interest groups today, though certainly not all, operate on this principle: Because they have no objective standards by which they operate—no evidence that what they advocate is good or right—they can only exert power to legitimize their views, to let their voices be heard and provoke change. Government or other social structures become weapons of power, wielded by the cultural elites and interest groups that have grabbed more influence and power than the other side.

Again, this has been observed from long ago. In another of Plato's dialogues called the *Gorgias*, a man by the name of Callicles asserts that justice is really only the rule of the powerful over the citizens of a state.[16] Whatever is best for the rulers is naturally just for Callicles. Morality is arbitrarily reduced to power.

This is the environment into which we speak—relativistic, power-conscious, hostile to truth claims, especially those that flow from faith. Though relativists claim to own the label of "tolerant," as we critique objective and moral relativism we will see how this incoherent, self-contradictory philosophy is far more dogmatic and narrow-minded than Christianity is.[17] It is strangely ironic that, despite allegations that Christians are bigoted and narrow, the Christian's absolutist position is not only true but consistent and compassionate.

CHAPTER 1

"That's True for You, But Not for Me."

ON ITS SURFACE, relativism sounds relaxed and easygoing. Only when we think through the implications of relativism and apply them rigorously to life do we see the hidden dangers of being so "accommodating." As Alister McGrath writes,

> It is utterly wrongheaded to say that something is "true for you but not for me." For example, what if I think fascism is true and you think liberal democracy is equally true? Should the fascist's repression be tolerated by the believer in liberal democracy? If not, on what grounds? Why not permit Stalinism or Satanism or Nazism? Without criteria to determine truth, this relativism fails miserably.[1]

Most of us don't want to live in that world. Relativism, however, isn't merely *emotionally* offensive. It doesn't hang together *logically*. As a worldview, it cannot be sustained.

At the beginning of his letter to Titus, the apostle Paul gives some advice to his "son in the faith" Titus, who is ministering to the people of Crete. Titus is facing a fair amount of hostile ideas. As if to say, "What did you expect?" Paul quotes Epimenides, a Cretan. He tells Titus, "Even one of their own prophets has said, 'Cretans are always liars, evil brutes, lazy gluttons.'" Most Bible readers catch the irony of the statement. If all Cretans are liars, then can Epimenides himself really be trusted?

The statement of Epimenides and relativism suffer from the same flaw. Epimenides claims to speak truth about the people of Crete. Yet he contradicts his truthfulness by calling *himself* a liar. Why believe Epimenides? Relativism claims to speak truth about at least one thing—namely, that truth can be "true for you but not for me." Yet it contradicts itself by claiming nothing is really true or false. Why believe the relativist if *he* has no truth to utter?

The claims of relativists are like saying, "I can't speak a word of English" or "All generalizations are false." Our most basic reply to the relativist is that *his statements are self-contradictory*. They self-destruct. They are self-undermining. The relativist actually *falsifies* his own system by his self-referential statements like "Everyone's beliefs are true or false only relative to himself."[2] If claims are only true to the speaker, then *his* claims are *only* true to himself. It is difficult to see why his claims should matter to us.[3]

To be consistent, the relativist must say, "Nothing is objectively true—including my own relativistic position. So you are free to accept my view or reject it." Of course, usually when the relativist says, "Everything is relative," he expects his hearers to believe his statement and adjust their lives accordingly. And he expects his statement concerns all statements *except* his own! Of course, the relativist doesn't likely believe that his relativistic position is simply true for himself. Thus, the relativist commits a second error—"the self-excepting fallacy," claiming a statement holds true for everyone but himself.[4] Oddly, the relativist is unwilling to *relativize* his relativism. And he is also unwilling to *generalize* his relativism since he makes himself an exception.

It's fair to point out to the relativist that statements like "That's true for you, but not for me" are not only self-contradictory but guilty of this self-excepting fallacy. While this statement often shuts the door on further conversation, it need not. An appropriate response to such a relativistic statement might be this: "You obviously assume the universal validity of the statement 'Something could be true for one person but not for another,' but you imply that it is applicable to *everyone's* beliefs but your own. But if you are being consistent—if your statement is only true *for you*, then I see no reason to think it applies to me."

Relativism misses on a crucial test of internal consistency. "Something can be true for one person but false for another" fails to meet its own criterion for truth. Think about it: While a worldview can be internally consistent or logical yet still be false, *no* worldview can be true if it contradicts itself.

Deflating "That's True for You, But Not for Me"

- If my belief is only true for *me*, why isn't your belief only true for *you*? Aren't you saying you want me to believe the same thing you do?
- You say no belief is true for everyone, but you want everyone to believe what you do. You're making universal claims that relativism is *true* and absolutism is *false*.

- You can't in the same breath say, "Nothing is universally true" *and* "My view is universally true." Relativism falsifies itself. It claims there is *one* position that is true—*relativism!*
- You're applying your view to everyone but yourself. You expect others to believe *your* views (the "self-excepting fallacy").

CHAPTER 2

"So Many People Disagree— Relativism *Must* Be True."[1]

T HINK BACK TO THE CAR ACCIDENT you imagined at the beginning of this section. Admittedly, in any accident everyone has a slightly different view of what happened. The relativist, however, commits a serious error when he confuses the *difficulty* of finding truth with the *possibility* of discerning truth or even affirming its existence. The diligence it takes to reconstruct an accident is no excuse for saying that truth can't be discovered or that truth doesn't exist.[1]

The elusiveness of truth in some areas of life is a major reason people believe something can be "true for you, but not for me." Looking around the world, the relativist comes to one conclusion: Too many people genuinely disagree about too many things for truth to be absolute! If people have significant, almost irreconcilable differences in vital things such as religion, morality, politics, and philosophy, doesn't it seem rash or even arrogant to say one perspective is true and all others are partly or wholly wrong? The sensible conclusion to draw, allegedly, is that relativism must be true. Somehow people move from what *is* the case (the descriptive) to what *should* be the case (the prescriptive)—from recognizing disagreement to lobbying for relativism. But concluding that relativism must be right is hardly obvious.

Now if our culture does accept anything as "objective" and indisputably "true," it clearly is the reports of people in white lab coats or of "scientific" research. But those most familiar with science recognize how difficult—if not impossible—it is to define "science."[2] Moreover, they point out how subjective elements like creativity, imagination, and intelligent guesswork play an enormous role in scientific breakthroughs.[3]

However, popular mythology holds that science is objective and its findings generally indisputable. By contrast, folks say, areas like religion, morality, art, and philosophy are plagued with disagreement and disputes, and this leads many to conclude that objective truth can't exist in such realms. (Here again we have a fact versus value, or a "provable" science versus "unprovable" faith distinction.)

But does disagreement necessarily imply relativism in any area—whether it be ethics or philosophy or religion? Not at all. Disagreement may simply indicate that some or all concerned *do not have full knowledge*, a clear grasp of the issue at hand. Until a key witness to a murder steps forward, piecing together the evidence in a criminal case may be difficult. Until then, the investigators may have inadequate knowledge, but this doesn't imply that the murderer's identity is inevitably elusive or that he doesn't exist. What we need is more evidence.

Besides lack of knowledge, *different underlying philosophical assumptions when approaching a problem* can account for disagreements. A Hindu or a New Ager, who approaches reality from a pantheistic point of view, may believe that human problems arise from ignorance—ignorance of one's own divinity or of the illusory nature of the physical world. A Christian, however, sees sin and its consequent separation from a holy God as the source of the human problem. For the former, knowledge or illumination is the solution; for the latter, it is the forgiveness of sin. Wildly differing worldviews inevitably contribute to wildly different solutions to the human problem. But this fact does not lead to an inevitable conclusion that the human problem must ultimately remain unsolved. Still less does it mean there is nothing objectively wrong about the human situation.

We can ask the relativist to show how his views are the only conclusion to be drawn from the reality of disagreement. It seems at least as obvious that disagreement stems from lack of full knowledge or from different worldviews or perspectives. We also have to be honest and admit that in some matters of life we simply don't have the resources to figure things out, either individually or collectively.

Some, like philosopher of religion John Hick, trace the root of our disagreements to the places we are born. Beliefs, he maintains, are chiefly the product of birthplace. He writes:

> For it is evident that in some 99 percent of cases the religion which an individual professes and to which he or she adheres depends upon the accidents of birth. Someone born to Buddhist parents in Thailand is very likely to be a Buddhist, someone born to Muslim parents in Saudi Arabia to be a Muslim, someone born to parents in Mexico to be a Christian, and so on.[4]

Although Hick isn't so naïve to conclude from this that all religious beliefs are therefore either saying the same thing or are equally true,[5] this conclusion is commonly drawn at a popular level—and taken as evidence that disagreements are virtually inbred in the human race and that relativism is the only workable approach to life.

That people are born into differing belief systems, however, tells us nothing about what to conclude from this fact. While birthplace may explain the *source* of belief, it says nothing about a belief's truthfulness. After all, what if a person was born in Nazi Germany or in ancient Rome? Is Nazism or a now-defunct polytheism as true as any other belief system?[6] Is Stalinism or Satanism "true for some" but not for others? When pressed, most people find such relativism hard to believe without throttling their most basic intuitions.

Deflating "So Many People Disagree—Relativism *Must* Be True."

- Disagreement doesn't necessarily mean everything is relative—or, put another way, that nothing is universally true. Disagreement can result because (a) people don't have full knowledge, or (b) people have differing underlying assumptions about reality.
- Disagreement doesn't say anything about the truth or falsehood of an argument. It simply isn't clear *what* conclusion we should draw from the fact of disagreement.
- Understanding the *source* of our differences doesn't imply our differences are meaningless. Acknowledging the roots of belief says nothing about the rightness or wrongness of different views.
- Are you really willing to say that no views are ultimately false—that Nazism or Greek polytheism is not really *wrong*? If you admit this, doesn't it imply that some views are more true than others?

CHAPTER 3

"You're Just Using Western Logic."

A LAN WATTS WAS AN ANGLICAN clergyman who later became a Buddhist. After long attempts to reconcile Christianity and Buddhism, he decided that Christianity was "incorrigibly theistic" and "invincibly self-righteous" and couldn't be harmonized with his Eastern philosophical beliefs.[1] To justify his rejection of Christianity in favor of Buddhism, Watts proposed that logic could not "bind" or govern reality. True knowledge, which can't be explained or described, is ultimately nonrational.

Watts dismissed the rationality of Christianity—such as the arguments of this book—as useless "Western logic." But there's a catch: to reject Christianity, *Watts used the very logic he denied as valid.* He knew that Christianity and Buddhism were incompatible, and he assumed that he had a yardstick to judge Christianity as being wrong. Yet as he *chose* "Eastern logic" (the absorbent "both/and" kind) rather than "Western logic" (the "either/or" kind), he had to use the "either/or" method in his selection. Put baldly, he had to *use* "Western" (or Aristotelian) logic in order to reject "Western" logic.

The notion that something is "true for you but not for me" is often applied in a broader context to argue that no system of logic is superior to another. In other words, your logic may suit you, but don't think that mine is illegitimate.

To reject basic logical laws, however, runs into real problems. We need logic in place for an everyday conversation to get off the ground. There is *the law of noncontradiction* ("A is not non-A"), which says that if something is self-contradictory—such as relativism—it can't be true. When a person claims that anything that cannot be proven scientifically cannot be true, he is taking a philosophical position that *cannot* meet his own scientific, empirical test. His view undermines itself, according to the basic law of noncontradiction.[2]

There is also *the law of excluded middle* ("either something is A or non-A"). Watt's rejection of Christianity was a living demonstration of what philosophers say of this law. He knew his two options of Christianity and Buddhism could not both be true; so he rejected one.[3] As we'll see in the chapter on religious pluralism, religious claims conflict so radically that they cannot all be true. For instance, the Christian doctrine that Jesus is God incarnate is blasphemous to the Muslim, and to accept this doctrine is to commit the sin of *shirk*—ascribing partners to Allah. Or take the historicity of Jesus' resurrection as foundational for Christianity. The Hindu would stress that it doesn't matter whether Jesus rose or not; his teachings still ring true. In these two cases, while both positions may be wrong, both cannot be right. If, as relativism maintains, both A and its opposite non-A are true, then *what is false?* Such talk negates any logic and reasoning. If someone's "truth" is the *opposite* of another's, then both simply cannot be true.

Not only do we need basic logical laws to reason clearly and communicate coherently; the truth is that we can't function without accepting some underlying beliefs.

Even the most vocal and radical opponents of truth—skeptics—believe in something. (While relativists believe that truth varies from culture to culture, skeptics believe that truth cannot be known.) Even as far back as Augustine,[4] we've known that there are certain "givens," certain undeniable truths that even skeptics utilize. For all their huffing and puffing, the skeptics really *do* hold to a set of beliefs.

So what do they believe? The rules of logic, which they use to determine whether or not something is erroneous. Admit it or not, skeptics believe that if one proposition contradicts another, both can't be true—or they wouldn't point out contradictions and flaws in reasoning. That approach in itself presupposes a belief in an objective truth worth searching for. And despite their claims to doubt, they don't doubt their own existence. There's an old story of a philosophy professor whose student asked him, "How do I know that *I* exist?" The professor looked down over his spectacles at the student and replied, "And who, may I say, is asking?" The student's questioning presupposed his own existence.

Driving home this point is crucial in our dialogue with relativists: *The idea that error exists at all presupposes that there is truth.* After all, skepticism arises because of the prevalence of human error—"To err is human," so we are told. But as philosopher Josiah Royce (1855–1913) argued, the recognition of error *assumes* that an idea does not conform to objective truth.[5] Just as disorder presupposes order, blindness presupposes sight, and evil presupposes a standard of goodness, so the notion of error presupposes the existence of truth. So when the skeptic points out errors in others, he presumes to speak and know the truth—even if he works from a negative point of view. He *truly* knows that others are wrong.

Deflating "You're Just Using Western Logic"

- To say you don't believe in basic principles of logic—that you favor the "both/and" view of Eastern logic, which denies distinctions—you have to use principles of logic. You're admitting they exist.
- You have to *use* Western logic ("either/or" logic) in order to deny its validity.
- To point out *error* in an absolutist's views, you assume that objective truth exists.
- If truth is truth, it must exclude something—falsehood. If you correct me, you assume error exists. And if you assume error exists, you assume that truth exists.

CHAPTER 4

"Who Are *You* to Judge Others?"

WHEN DAN QUAYLE SAID THAT MURPHY BROWN'S giving birth to an illegitimate child wasn't a good role model for America's youth, he was ridiculed, called "judgmental," and labeled arrogant. Who was *he* to pontificate about "family values"? Quayle wasn't hit with the criticism rightly leveled against some—that they are hypocrites. He was accused of doing what *no one* has the right to do: telling others how to live.

It's been said that the most frequently quoted Bible verse is no longer John 3:16 but Matthew 7:1: "Do not judge, or you too will be judged." We cannot glibly quote this, though, without understanding what Jesus meant. When Jesus condemned judging, he wasn't at all implying we should never make judgments about anyone. After all, a few verses later, Jesus himself calls certain people "pigs" and "dogs" (Matt. 7:6) and "wolves in sheep's clothing" (7:15)! Any act of church discipline (1 Cor. 5:5) and rebuking false prophets (1 John 4:1) requires judgment. What Jesus condemns is a critical and judgmental spirit, an unholy sense of moral superiority. Jesus commanded us to examine ourselves *first* for the problems we so easily see in others. Only then can we help remove the speck in another's eye—which, incidentally, assumes that a problem exists and must be confronted.[1]

What is interesting in these charges of arrogance and judgmentalism is this: Besides *failing to define* what is meant by "judgmentalism," the accusers often act *just as* "*arrogantly*" and "judgmentally" as the "judgmental" ones. If the Christian (or any exclusivist) is denounced for judgmentalism, he can respond that his accuser is judging him for being judgmental!

To be consistent, judgmentalism *cannot* mean "being in disagreement with someone" or "considering someone to be wrong." It is undeniable that *the relativist disagrees with the absolutist*, which makes the relativist just as "judgmental" as the absolutist. If judgmentalism is to be understood correctly (in keeping with the context of Matthew 7:1), it should be defined as *an inappropriate sense of moral superiority over another because of that person's moral failures.*[2] Judgmentalism, then, is that ugly refusal to acknowledge that "there but for the grace of God go I."

Furthermore, it is an act of theological blindness to cite the "judge not" passage while utterly ignoring Jesus' charge to make *proper* judgments: "Stop judging by mere appearances, and make a right judgment" (John 7:24).

The accusation is unwarranted that those who hold to absolute truth are absolutely arrogant. Think of Mother Teresa's speech at a Washington prayer breakfast in the winter of 1994, when she boldly spoke against abortion before the pro-abortion president and vice-president of the United States and their spouses. Although she spoke respectfully, she made powerful statements in defense of unborn human lives: "And if we accept that a mother can kill even her own child, how can we tell other people not to kill one another?" and "Any country that accepts abortion is not teaching its people to love, but to use any violence to get what they want."[3] One could hardly accuse this nun of arrogance.

There simply is no automatic contradiction between holding firmly to one's convictions and treating with dignity and respect those who disagree. Living harmoniously with people who hold radically different views is a hallmark of maturity.[4] Our society would benefit from the courageous words of qualified people who display both *firmness of conviction* and *civility* or respect,[5] which is what Ephesians 4:15 refers to—"speaking the truth in love." Martin Marty, the noted observer of religion in America, states that the problem of modernity is that the people "who are good at being civil often lack the strong convictions and the people who have strong convictions often lack civility."[6]

Christians often seem to believe that firmness of conviction entitles them to belligerence, hostility, and closed-mindedness—not to mention a lack of intellectual responsibility. To the contrary, Paul exhorts Christians, "If it is possible, as far as it depends on you, live at peace with everyone" (Rom. 12:18). They should live "peaceful and quiet lives in all godliness and holiness" (1 Tim. 2:2). On the other hand, behind the mask of an apparently sensitive and compassionate "open-mindedness," there often exists a moral gutlessness. Civility, then, is the remedy for arrogance, and conviction the corrective for spinelessness. But to achieve this uncommon balance, someone has suggested our interactions with others should concentrate on *our own sinfulness* and on *the other's humanness*—rather than the other way around.[7] Moreover, the relativist, for all his bluster about his own "tolerance" and the exclusivist's arrogance, will *still* believe things that others don't believe or agree with—namely, *he will not accept the views of the exclusivist*. If the relativist is to remain consistent, he can't legitimately criticize another's point of view. Furthermore, the relativist is guilty of the morally superior attitude that signals judgmentalism. He really thinks that *he* possesses a virtue that others don't.[8]

The Hindu philosopher Swami Vivekenanda came to Chicago in 1893 to address the World's Parliament of Religions. He told the delegates, "We [Hindus] accept all religions to be true," and "[it] is sin to call a man [a sinner]."[9]

What a problematic and self-contradictory view! The swami calls someone a sinner—because that person has called another a sinner. If the exclusivist is a sinner for calling all people sinners, then the Hindu is just as much a sinner for calling the exclusivist a sinner. Isn't the relativist being "arrogant" for disagreeing with the exclusivist?

Deflating "Who Are *You* to Judge Others?"

- When you are accused of judging, *ask* the accuser what he means by "judging."
- If the person defines judging as "thinking another person is wrong" or "disagreeing with another," you can respond, "*You* think *I'm* wrong. You're not agreeing with me."
- You're *judging* me for judging someone else.
- Before continuing, come to a consensus on what judgment means. (In the context of Matthew 7:1, it has to do with a sense of moral superiority in the face of another's failure). Remember John 7:24 ("make a right judgment").

CHAPTER 5

"Christians Are *Intolerant* of Other Viewpoints!"

I NTOLERANCE HAS BEEN COMMONLY ASSOCIATED with religion—and not without basis. For example, the passage "compel them to come in [*compelle intrare*]" in Luke 14:23 (KJV) was used by religious authorities to justify a "conquest theology" during and after the Middle Ages.[1]

The Crusades, the Inquisition, and other abuses of religion are certainly a blot on Christendom's history. However, what our society usually overlooks is both that a religious culture *can* foster genuine tolerance and that *secularism*—a "non-religious"[2] outlook on life—may pose a far greater threat to tolerance.

Closely tied to the notion of "judgment" is "tolerance." Although many accuse absolutists of intolerance, these accusers most likely have an unclear and distorted notion of what tolerance really is. They often are unaware that the concept of tolerance implies a close relationship to truth. Contrary to popular definitions, true tolerance means "putting up with error"—not "being accepting of all views." We don't tolerate what we enjoy or approve of—like chocolate or Bach's music. By definition, what we tolerate is what we disapprove of or what we believe to be false and erroneous.[3] Furthermore, tolerance presupposes an adequate grasp of what another person believes—as well as a knowledge of the strengths and weaknesses of such belief. Actually, if disagreement didn't exist, then tolerance would be unnecessary. It is because real differences exist between people that tolerance becomes necessary and virtuous.

The contemporary definition of tolerance as acceptance is simply wrongheaded. It lands a person in massive inconsistencies. Take the matter of "comparative religions." The leveling approach of comparative religions ("when we talk with people from other religious groups, we should consider all religions equal") arbitrarily asserts without qualification the equal validity or relative nature of all religions. Dialogue, however, shouldn't begin by assuming the *equality of all religions or truth claims* (the erroneous definition of tolerance), but with regard for the *equality of persons*. Dialogue implies respect, not agreement.

A Christian can interact with and respect a Buddhist while still believing on rational grounds that he is mistaken. In fact, the belief that both views cannot be right is an *impetus* to engage in meaningful dialogue. Dialogue thus becomes an opportunity for *both* sides to reexamine their presuppositions and clarify their positions.[4] True tolerance grants people the right to dissent.

It is *very* important that a Christian criticized for intolerance asks his accuser what he *means* by "intolerance." The accuser will probably say something like "not being accepting of another's beliefs." To this the Christian can gently respond, "But *you* are not being accepting of *my* position. You think *I* am wrong." The relativist simply cannot be accepting of all positions as true without falling into severe contradictions.

One of the ironies of relativism is that it exalts tolerance to the status of an absolute. A belief is "true for you" *as long as* it doesn't interfere with the belief that's "true for me." The relativist often says something like this: "You can legitimately hold your belief, *but* you should be tolerant of other views." To be a bit more consistent, the relativist should say, "It doesn't matter what you believe"—period. Yet popular relativism slips absolutes in through the back door: ". . . just don't be judgmental" or ". . . but be tolerant" or even ". . . just as long as you don't interfere with another's freedom/happiness." So, besides relativism's being intrinsically absolutist (because it says "*everything* is relative" or "there are *no* absolutes"), it holds to yet another absolute—the hallowed standard of tolerance. In other words, relativism is *packed full of* absolutes.

The reality of God actually makes tolerance intelligible, because God is the source of truth and because God has made human beings in his likeness. Naturalistic secularism has no such foundation for tolerance. If tolerance is a value, it isn't obvious from nature; so if there is no God and we are just hulks of protoplasmic guck, how could tolerance be an objective value at all? Instead, if objective truth exists, as religion maintains, then we musk seek and seriously discuss it despite our differing worldviews. But if objective truth doesn't exist, as secularism generally maintains, then relativism obliterates genuine differences of perspective.

The man who pretends a lofty neutrality above the mass of men is more vulnerable to human sins than the person who admits his perspective and respects the viewpoints of others. The new citizen, friendly to all convictions, but attached to none, is a menace. The trend can only issue in the destruction of all values.[5]

Lacking a real standard of truth, relativism makes personal power-grabbing an end in itself: "In the absence of truth, power is the only game in town."[6] Why respect another person's freedom if objective truth doesn't exist? There is simply no way to define or constrain the *proper use* of power without truth. If *no universally binding standards* exist to which opposing parties can appeal, "a struggle to the death is as likely a result as is tolerance."[7]

Deflating "Christians Are *Intolerant* of Other Viewpoints!"

- Again, ask what your relativist friend means by "(in)tolerant." (Perhaps you can ask him if he "tolerates" chocolate or gourmet ice cream!)
- If by "tolerance" the person means "accepting all views as true," then you can say, "You don't accept *my* view as true. Are you being intolerant?"
- Point out that the *historical* definition of "tolerance"—putting up with error—will be the consistent one. "Acceptance of all views" doesn't work because *tolerance is closely linked to truth*.
- Real discussion doesn't begin with the acceptance of all truth claims as equal; it begins with the equality of *persons*.
- Ask about the set of absolutes that relativists typically maintain:
  (a) "You can't judge" (or "judging is wrong").
  (b) "You can't be intolerant" (or "intolerance is wrong").
  (c) "You can't hurt others" (or "hurting others is wrong").
- It seems that being we are made in the image of God—and thus have intrinsic value—is a better basis for true tolerance and treating people with equality than is believing we live in a materialistic universe in which humans ultimately have no value.

CHAPTER 6

"What Right Do *You* Have to Convert Others to Your Views?"

A WOMAN WHO WORKED WITH A FRIEND of mine was known for telling her co-workers how arrogant and narrow-minded one "born-again Christian" was for telling people about his faith in order to "convert" them to his point of view. My friend spotted and wisely pointed out her inconsistency: "You're accusing this Christian," Tom said, "of trying to change people's minds about what they believe. You're doing the *same* thing by trying to persuade others to believe *you* instead of this Christian." Tom's co-worker was being a *crypto-evangelist* for her own relativistic position. *Trying to persuade others not to persuade* is typical of relativists. But it is very absolutist!

Anything that smacks of "proselytizing," "conversion," and "evangelism" is usually condemned as immensely arrogant. Of course, this presupposes that truth is relative. And it assumes that all Christians act like Crusaders, who at least on a popular level are known only for "cramming" their beliefs "down another's throat." God calls us, rather, to communicate and defend our faith with *gentleness and respect* (1 Pet. 3:16), being careful of the *manner* or *method* of persuasion—and overflowing with tact, grace, and personal warmth.

After all, *persuading* someone else by offering good reasons to change beliefs—as we often see the apostle Paul doing in the book of Acts—is hardly arrogant or intolerant. Done well, it's just the opposite. It expresses *concern* for people interested in pursuing truth (2 Tim. 2:23–26), and it respects them as *thinking* beings. If we are eager to get recommendations on good (and inexpensive!) ethnic food or to ask for leads on shopping bargains, why not when it comes to discovering a life-changing message?

When Christians hear that they are arrogant for evangelizing, they should ask, "Isn't your telling me to stop evangelizing implying that truth is relative? Yet don't you believe that *your* viewpoint rather than mine is true and ought to be followed? Then on what basis do you think I should stop telling others about Christianity?" Simply proclaiming what we believe to be true to anyone willing to listen is more than appropriate.[1] This is far different from "forcing" another to believe.

Nonbelievers often assume they are exempt from being pushy or using obnoxious persuasion techniques. The atheist Michael Martin wrote in *The Case Against Christianity* that "a person full of religious zeal may see what he or she wants to see, not what is really there."[2] Martin naïvely believes that as an atheist he is free from any religious zeal about his views, yet atheists can be as "religiously zealous" as anyone. The sword cuts both ways. Secularism can be ruthlessly militant and fanatical—as it obviously was in the Enlightenment. One man from this era wrote in his last will and testament: "I should like to see, and this will be the last and most ardent of my desires, I should like to see the last king strangled with the guts of the last priest."[3] This sounds like "religious zeal" in no uncertain terms.

Those who say, "Everything is relative" or "Your Christian beliefs are true for you, but not for me" are not simply neutral, disinterested, or objective. Instead, they often seek to persuade others with as much zeal as those who say, "Jesus is Lord."

Deflating "What Right Do *You* Have to Convert Others to Your Views?"

- Ask the relativist if there is any difference between *persuading* and *converting*. ("Convert" is often a loaded term.) Is *persuasion* ever legitimate?
- Those who try to discourage or prevent others from evangelizing are themselves "evangelists" for their viewpoint. Talk about the tactics of the "crypto-evangelist."

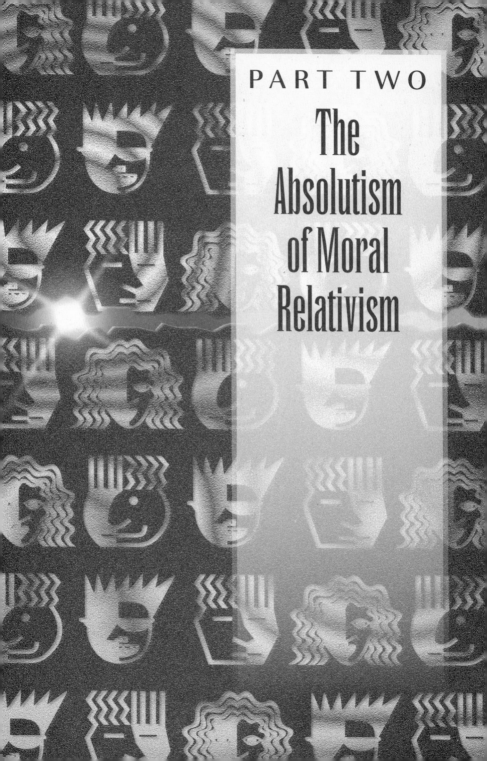

PART TWO

The Absolutism of Moral Relativism

A FEW YEARS AGO at the American Academy of Religion/Society of Biblical Literature conference, an annual gathering that tends to be more politically correct than religious or biblical,[1] there was a session entitled "Biblical Authority and Homosexuality." All five of the speakers on the panel (as well as the moderator) were predictably pro-homosexual. No defender of the traditional biblical perspective on homosexuality had been asked to participate. So much for diversity!

The audience was told that scriptural prohibitions against homosexuality were purely cultural. "Scripture," one of the panelists stated, "contains no timeless, normative, moral truths." After some meandering discussion of moral relativism, a member of the audience stood up. "Wait a minute," he told the panelists. "I'm rather confused. I'm a pastor, and people constantly come to me, asking if something they have done is wrong and if they need forgiveness. For example, isn't it always wrong to abuse a child?" A female panelist issued this shocking response: "What counts as abuse differs from society to society; so we can't really use the word 'abuse' without tying it to a historical context."[2] To the relativist, what we think of as philosophical truth isn't the only brand of truth that is relative and culture-bound. Moral truth also varies from place to place—and so it too is relative. In other words, there are no all-encompassing, objective moral laws to which we must all submit.

According to moral relativism, "morality arises when a group of people reach an implicit agreement or come to a tacit understanding about their relations to one another."[3] Morality is relative to our culture or the particular chunk of history we occupy, and two people can believe contradictory ethical views and both still be correct. One culture's taboos and customs are as true as another's.

One inescapable sign of our postmodern society's flight from belief in moral absolutes is its dressing up evil in psychobabble and victimology. Take, for example, the Liverpudlian youths who kidnapped and murdered a two-year-old boy; or street gangs involved in senseless drive-by shootings; or the eight youths who rampaged through Central Park, beating, raping, and killing a woman jogger. Sophisticated elites tend to blame such crimes on poverty, stress, boredom, or rage. But what about *evil*? Too "simplistic" and "altogether outmoded," we're told. And because we take evil lightly, we take its punishment lightly as well. As columnist George Will notes, "A society that flinches from the fact of evil will flinch from the act of punishment. It should not wonder why it does not feel safe."[4]

Tolerance purports to show the ultimate respect for human beings, offering sympathetic support for whatever people choose to believe. But when we abdicate making moral judgments about their actions, we actually *diminish* our view of them. We reveal a cheapened view of persons when we turn them into victims rather than responsible moral agents:

> . . . the elimination of the possibility of judgment, the evacuation of the very capacity of judging, would spell the end of the human subject as a self-respecting, accountable being. Judging is a sign, a mark, of our respect for the dignity of others and ourselves.[5]

When we make moral judgments, we start by recognizing our *own* capacity for sin. We acknowledge that apart from God's grace *we* are potential Hitlers or Stalins. So when we forego our responsibility to make moral judgments, we slight our own humanity and contribute to social decay. This is the tragedy of moral relativism.

Understanding the Terms

Before we look at the contrast between relativism and objective morality, we need to make a few qualifications. First, in this context, what does "objective" *mean*? By *objective*, I refer to the fact that moral principles are true invariably and universally—that they always have and always will normatively apply to all rational beings. In other words, morality is objective in that it isn't a function of individual or cultural preferences, opinions, or responses. Morality is objective in that it is *recognized* and *discovered* rather than *invented* by humans. If moral norms are universally true, all human beings are obligated to carry out their moral, universally binding duties.

Second, objective morality also includes the notion of *obligation*, a duty to comply with what we *ought* to do (the good) and to avoid what is forbidden (the bad). So objective morality relates to rightness and wrongness. It has to do with what obligates us, with what our duty is. To do what is right is morally praiseworthy, and to act wrongly is morally blameworthy. Some argue that genuine morality or virtue refers *only* to "personal excellence" and character development—"virtue ethics."[6] But any view of morality that eliminates obligation (or the *deontic*) as a major component is highly restrictive.[7] Besides virtue ethics, morality also deals with right and wrong and with one's *obli-*

gations to do right and avoid wrong. We address this "must-do" element of morality when we ask the question, "Why *should* we act in certain ways and not in others?"

Third, *we can't confuse lack of belief in God with lack of morality.* A common misperception among Christians is that atheists automatically have no moral backbone. But atheists or non-theists are often highly moral in character or uphold moral systems that compare favorably to those of theists. Confucianism and some forms of Buddhism (such as the Theravada school) uphold moral beliefs without affirming the existence of God. *Belief* in God isn't a requirement for being moral, although, as we will see, the *existence* of a personal God is crucial for a coherent understanding of objective morality.[8] That is, *one can't be a moral being unless God exists*—whether or not one *believes* God exists.

Fourth, *there is a difference between moral* principles *and* expressions *(or practices) of morality.* Anthropologists regularly remind us of the vast array of customs throughout the world. In some cultures, men don't wear pants and women don't wear shirts. What counts for showing honor to parents in a Chinese culture is certainly different from how we show honor in the West. Do these differences mean that moral *norms* are necessarily in conflict? Not at all. Cultures throughout the world possess *general principles* of behavior: People shouldn't steal or inflict unnecessary pain on others; people should keep commitments and show kindness to needy people; people shouldn't take human life unjustifiably. But these universal principles are to be distinguished from various cultural *expressions, customs,* or *applications* of morality that hinge on the particular ideals of a society or on differing circumstances.

This isn't to say that there is no *genuine* conflict of moral behavior between certain cultures. When the Spanish conquistadors confronted the human sacrifices of the Aztecs, there was a genuine clash of moral points of view—not merely expressions of morality or social customs particular to one culture. However, what some take as conflicting moralities are actually various ways of applying broad, universally accepted moral principles such as modesty, honor, or loyalty to one's family or clan.[9] So while diversity of actions exists, this does not tell the whole story.

This leads us to a fifth point: *Moral conflict can result from the simple fact that some persons are more experienced moral judges than others.*[10] Though it strikes the relativist as politically *in*correct, we will see that some people or even cultures in some areas may be less developed morally than others. A person with a cultivated character and extraordinary moral sensitivity will see and act on moral insights that escape the moral novice.

With those terms and assumptions in mind, we will next answer several slogans that expose the agenda of the moral relativist.

CHAPTER 7

"Your Values Are Right for You, But Not for Me."

PHILOSOPHER OF SCIENCE MICHAEL RUSE claims that morality is just like hands, feet, and teeth—the "ephemeral product of the evolutionary process."[1] Morality, according to Ruse, isn't objective: "Morality is just an aid to survival and reproduction, and has no being beyond this."[2] Ruse brings up the once-acceptable Indian practice of *suttee*—widows being burned alive on the funeral pyre of their deceased husbands. From *our* perspective, this is wrong: "Obviously, such a practice is totally alien to Western customs and morality. In fact, we think that widow sacrifice is totally immoral."[3] Ruse's evolutionary naturalism leads to the belief that one culture's virtue is another culture's vice. But he finds no *objective* grounds to condemn a "vice" like widow-burning.

Is morality relative, as Ruse seems to think? Is it nothing more than the by-product of evolutionary and social development? Is one culture's virtue really another culture's vice? While morality is considered relative by many in our culture, this view *cannot* be sustained—not only because it is illogical but also because it is simply unlivable.

When someone told the great British essayist Dr. Samuel Johnson that one of his dinner guests believed that morality was a sham, Dr. Johnson replied, "Why, sir, if he really believes there is no distinction between virtue and vice, let us count our spoons before he leaves." In other words, how can the moral relativist really be trusted? Moral relativism leads to an inevitable breakdown of relationships and of society. It is *existentially* (or practically) unworkable.

We have seen, however, that many people who *claim* to be relativists at heart are *not*. We simply can't live without a belief—explicit or assumed—that moral standards exist. One Christian philosophy professor, for example, had an outspoken moral relativist in his ethics class. All semester the student contested the professor's absolutist views about ethics. When the time came for the course final, the student, who had prepared well, took the exam and assumed that he had passed without a problem. He was shocked and infuriated to find an F instead of an A at the top of his paper—and without any explanation. The relativist stormed into the professor's office demanding an explanation at this unfairness. The professor asked, "Did you say 'unfairness'? So you *do* believe in moral absolutes after all!" With that, the professor took the exam out of the student's hand, crossed out the F and put an A at the top of it. The student silently walked out of the office, realizing his inconsistency.[4]

The person who is, say, the victim of torture, slave labor, child abuse, rape, or apartheid intuitively knows that justice is being violated. Are we really willing to concede that there is ultimately no significant moral difference between Hitler and Mother Teresa? Are we really willing to believe that genocide, rape, and murder are just "cultural" behaviors? The person who embraces moral relativism needs to be pressed: What if he were arrested and tortured for no reason? Why should he protest if you took a sledgehammer to his BMW? If he were a Jew in Nazi Germany, where the culture was horrifyingly anti-Semitic, why should his disagreement with the standards of the surrounding culture carry any weight at all? Why should his wishes be respected? After all, for someone who says, "Your values are true for you, but not for me," there can be no objectively morally degrading actions. Moral relativism is utterly unlivable.[5]

As you talk with moral relativists, remember these things:

(a) Morality has, in large part, to do with *obligation*.

(b) People *can* be moral or create moral systems without believing in God.

(c) There is a difference between moral *principles* and *expressions* of morality.

Deflating "Your Values Are Right for You, But Not for Me."

- Moral relativism is unlivable. If we were arbitrarily failed in school or imprisoned without cause, what grounds would we have for protest?
- Is there *really* no difference between Mother Teresa and Adolf Hitler?

CHAPTER 8

"Who Are *You* to Say Another Culture's Values Are Wrong?"

WHEN I VISITED CITIES IN INDIA such as Calcutta, Bombay, or Madras, I was struck by all the beggars lining the streets, some of whom were seriously malformed and crippled. I later discovered that many of these abnormalities weren't genetic defects. They were inflicted by parents on their infant children. Limbs were deliberately broken and twisted so that children would grow up to make better beggars to support their families. This raises serious problems for the moral relativist: How could the relativist justifiably bring reform in such a situation?

What are the logical implications if we assume that moral relativism is true? It seems clear that there is no basis for opposing or rooting out things like ethnic cleansing, slavery, terrorism, genocide, racism, and the like. To speak out against such atrocities implies the existence of a moral standard to which all should conform. The speaker who claimed we can't tell what constitutes child abuse apart from a historical context implies that an individual or culture shouldn't try to define or reform immoral practices.

Anthropologists tend to look down on missionaries because they supposedly "impose" their values on tribal cultures. Anthropologists, however, almost always approach their discipline with the assumption of moral relativism and with a relativistic "respect" for these cultures. What this attitude ends up doing, however, is precluding any attempt to influence other societies for good.[1] Wasn't the eradication of slavery in the West a moral victory? Wasn't the granting of equal rights to blacks in America a significant moral gain? A band of moral relativists could never have achieved such milestones in the

West. In fact, for a relativist there is no such thing as a "reformer." No relativist could rise to the stature of a Martin Luther King Jr. or a Mahatma Gandhi. There is no reformation, only a change of the status quo.

Besides suffering from the "reformer's dilemma," moral relativism *cannot adjudicate between conflicting moral beliefs*. For example, simply condemning Western culture in favor of another one—like the Stanford University students who chanted, "Hey, hey! Ho, ho! Western culture's got to go!"—ends up being arbitrary. Although "dead white males" like Plato, Shakespeare, and Milton have written penetratingly and have pointed our civilization toward truth and virtue, the Stanford students associated these dead white males with slavery, colonialism, and the oppression of women (all except Karl Marx, of course!). Rather than study the works of these highly significant thinkers, the students wanted a multicultural curriculum. So in 1989, the administration caved in to the students' protests by replacing this Western curriculum with the "CIV" curriculum—"Cultures, Ideas, and Values."

While I am not opposed to including minority voices within a "cultural canon," it is highly ironic that the students who have protested against the alleged oppressiveness of Western civilization fail to realize that non-Western cultures have, in general, not developed a tradition of racial equality to the extent of the West. They seem unaware of the fact that despite the history of slavery in antebellum America, it was African tribal chiefs who sold their *own* people into slavery in exchange for Western goods. They seem blind to the fact that non-Western cultures have often oppressed women through female circumcision, widow-burning, or the burdensome dowry system. These "tolerant" relativistic Stanford students willy-nilly embraced the non-West over the West and merely swapped one authoritative cultural canon for another.[2] They opted for an Afrocentric canon over a Eurocentric one.

Despite campus outcries against the evils of Western civilization, however, those who advocate the multicultural curriculum really have no grounds for condemning the West if morality is ultimately relative. How can morally relativistic feminists condemn abortions based on sex selection in countries like India and China, where girls are killed in favor of boys? By what standard should Auschwitzes or gulags be opposed? Why should Pol Pot's extermination of millions of Cambodians be condemned? Should the Ku Klux Klan's racial hatred really be condemned as wrong? Moral relativism is intellectually bankrupt in the face of these questions.

"Who are *you* to impose *your* moral values on someone else?" is one of the lines we hear most frequently parroted in a discussion of moral absolutes. Too often this question needlessly halts conversation. It need not. In all likelihood, the slogan has little reflection behind it. In the first place, the relativist who talks about "imposing values" can be asked, "Do *you* think there is *no* moral distinction between a Mother Teresa and an Adolf Hitler? Do you believe that trying to rescue a drowning child and murdering that child are morally neutral?" We should find out early in any discussion if our questioners are aware of the implications of what they say.

Second, we can ask the relativist, "So you think it is *morally wrong* to impose your values on someone else—that this *shouldn't* be done? But then who are *you* to impose *your* morality on those who want to impose their morality on others?" The moral relativist thinks that something ought not to be done, that any "imposition" is somehow "wrong." That thinking betrays that he or she believes in an implicit moral standard.

Third, we can respond to moral relativists' questions by asking other questions:

- Do you think it was wrong for the Allied forces to "impose" their morality on Hitler, who invaded many militarily weaker countries and exterminated six million Jews?
- Aren't you glad our government "imposes its morality" on rapists, murderers, thieves, and child molesters? Shouldn't we have a police force to help deter crime and protect citizens—most of whom think it is wrong to murder or rob—from those who don't care about morality?
- Do you think the South should still be enslaving blacks and that Abraham Lincoln and the North were wrong to impose their ideals of freedom upon others?
- If your sister or mother were being raped, would you stand by because you wouldn't want to impose your morality on the rapist? (We could throw in a Stalin or Mao—who obliterated millions more than Hitler—or a Pol Pot, and ask if another's morality should have been imposed on them.)

When given more serious reflection, moral relativism's illogic and bankruptcy are exposed.

Fourth, when we are challenged about *whose* morality we should all follow, we can clarify our own position and clear it from charges of arbitrariness: "The kinds of moral views I favor aren't idiosyncratic preferences; they tend, rather, to be generally agreed-upon ideals and traditions that span history and cultures and world religions (they reflect a 'natural law,' to which Romans 2:14–15 refers). Why not take this general consensus of what is virtuous (love, kindness) and obligatory (not murdering, stealing, or committing adultery) as starting points for discussing the content of morality? Or do *you* think it is morally permissible to murder or steal or commit adultery?"

We should notice, furthermore, that the question "Who are *you* to judge others?" implies—even if it isn't intended—an invitation to rational debate about moral issues, using rationally objective criteria. So when you hear this slogan, welcome it as an opportunity to talk about objective moral standards and their origin. In fact, the very *question* presupposes a certain objectivity! And since many people have never thought about these issues, you can respond by asserting your credentials: (1) "I haven't abandoned the quest for moral truth"; (2) "I've reflected long and hard on these issues"; and (3) "I have tried hard to cultivate moral character and conscience."[3]

Deflating "Who Are *You* to Say Another Culture's Values Are Wrong?"

- If moral relativism is true, there is no basis for opposing genocide, racism, terrorism, torture, and the like.
- Moral relativism could never bring about the abolition of slavery or the equal rights of women, but most of us intuitively recognize these as moral milestones.
- Should we "respect" the "right" of a Nazi Germany to invade relatively powerless nations?
- Moral relativism cannot judge between conflicting moral beliefs and practices. What should cultures that do not practice, say, cannibalism or human sacrifice think of those that do?
- Those who oppose "Western" culture's values tend to replace them with another set of values, an arbitrary move if there is no objective morality. Why think "Western culture's got to go" if everything is relative?
- "Who are you to impose your values?" can be countered by another question: "*Should* no values be imposed?" The moral relativist seems to be saying that such an "imposition" *ought not* be done, which implies moral absolutes. If the moral relativist thinks this *ought not* be done, then gently ask, "Who are *you* to impose your values on those who want to impose their values on others?"
- Should governments not "impose" their morality on rapists, murderers, thieves, and child molesters?
- Many cultures and religious traditions affirm the same kinds of values. So "imposing values" need not be viewed as arbitrary.

CHAPTER 9

"You Have the Right to Choose Your Own Values."

NOT LONG AGO I came across a booklet entitled *The Quest for Excellence*, which is an adolescent's guide to sex, AIDS, "self-esteem," and other such topics. One paragraph reads,

> Early on in life, you will be exposed to different value systems from your family, church or synagogue, and friends. You may accept some of these values without questioning whether or not they are the right values for you. But you may eventually realize that some of these values conflict with each other. It is up to you to decide upon your own value system to build your own ethical code. . . . You will have to learn what is right for yourself through experience.[1]

This booklet offers a smorgasbord morality where a person is supposed to choose what moral values are "right for him."

As with objective (or "epistemological") relativism, moral relativism arises in the context of differing moral beliefs or practices. The typical conclusion people draw from diversity is that every belief or value claim is equally true. So *The Quest for Excellence*, after noting our human differences ("The range of human diversity is limitless"), goes on to make the pronouncement: "Your sexual identity can be defined in any way you choose. . . . Only you can decide what is right and comfortable for you."[2] (One wonders *who* decided this!)

But do the differences in expressing moral values necessarily imply that morality is relative rather than objectively real? This simply doesn't follow.

First, we noted above that different cultures express the same underlying moral principles differently.

Second, even if certain moral values actually vary from culture to culture (cannibalism, slavery) or individual to individual, there *still* may be objective moral norms and obligations that are universally binding on all—whether or not they are believed or even known by anyone at all. As already observed, diversity of moral perspectives doesn't necessarily lead to the conclusion that there are no objective moral values whatsoever. If morality is strictly *naturalistic* (e.g., biologically or socially based), no *ought* is possible—as we will see in the next chapter. *Ought* doesn't come from strictly natural properties. Strikingly, however, our moral intuitions *give evidence* that transcendent moral duties exist.

Third, people who observe conflicting moralities between individuals or cultures don't have to conclude that morality is relative. It's possible that *some moral beliefs are inferior to others*. At the beginning of this century, Emile Durkheim made the anthropologist's mistake when he wrote,

> It can no longer be maintained nowadays that there is one, single morality which is valid for all men at all times in all places. We know full well that morality has varied. . . . The moral system of the Romans and Hebrews was not our own, nor could it have been so. For if the Romans had practiced morality with its characteristic individualism, the city of Rome would never have been, nor consequently would the Roman civilization, which was the necessary antecedent and condition of our present civilization. The purpose of morality practiced by a people is to enable it to live; hence morality changes with societies. There is not just one morality, but several, and as many as there are social types. And as our societies change, so will our morality. It will no longer be in the future what it is today.[3]

Another conclusion can be drawn from morally diverse cultures. When Spanish explorers came to Mexico, for example, they were horrified by the practice of ritualistic human sacrifice there—and rightly so. The sacrifice of infants to the Ammonite god Molech or the infanticide practiced in antiquity—or even the practice of abortions of convenience so common today—is simply not a "different morality." It is rather a *defective* and *inferior* morality. The same applies to cannibalism, torture, racism, and a host of other evils, which are not just "customary for some peoples but not others." One philosopher rightly comments: "If [members of a particular tribe] think that it is acceptable to engage in practices like the sacrifice of firstborn children, then their grasp on the conception of morality is somewhere between inadequate and nonexistent."[4] When people have fallen that far in their moral understanding, it is very difficult to discuss the nature of morality with them. They simply have deep, internal problems.

Fourth, despite his alleged value-neutrality, the culturally and morally relativistic anthropologist isn't merely being *descriptive* in his approach to other cultures. He is acting *prescriptively*. That is, he makes moral judgments and pronouncements himself—especially about his nemesis, the missionary! The anthropologist makes his own moral recommendations—that one *ought* to respect the moral claims of other cultures as being true for them. (And we could rightly ask, "*Why* should I be tolerant?") When any moral critique is leveled against another culture, the anthropologist condemns this as the "sin" of ethnocentrism. In fact, the anthropologist—the exemplar of moral relativism—has in his arsenal an array of morally loaded epithets to hurl at the missionary and his methods: "ethnocentrist," "colonialist," "exploiter," "ideologue," and the like.[5] So despite their claim to do only objective and descriptive cultural analysis, anthropologists have moral biases they hold dear. And they expect us to embrace their views!

One final problem with moral relativism is that *it removes the incentive to live ethically and to cultivate character*. Historically, it has been understood that upright ethical living and good character require *effort* to cultivate. Parents have known that the immensely important task of rearing children requires self-sacrifice and surrender of convenience. Relationships take work, or they don't survive. Integrity has been seen as a noble and honorable trait that is not to be cheapened or eradicated through compromise. But moral relativism negates all such efforts. There is simply no good reason, given moral relativism, to rise above moral mediocrity—which may be part of its appeal. To make an attempt at moral excellence would elevate an ideal to strive toward. The moral relativist denies this. But why not cheat on income tax forms if we can get away with it? Why take the narrow, difficult moral road when the broad one requires no resistance? Enthusiastically embracing moral relativism contributes to the corruption of character. The "quest for excellence" turns out to be nothing more than doing what one wants to do.

Deflating "You Have the Right to Choose Your Own Values."

- Moral relativism doesn't follow from morally differing beliefs. Objective moral values can still exist even if no one recognizes them.
- The conflict of moral beliefs might be due to the fact that some are *inferior* to or *defective* in comparison to others.
- When people *really* deny the rightness of kindness or the wrongness of murder or torturing babies, it is appropriate, as a last resort, to question their psychological health.
- The "descriptive" anthropologist actually makes *moral* pronouncements

about missionaries (by implying that one *ought* to leave other cultures alone).

- Moral relativism removes any reason to live morally and cultivate character.

CHAPTER 10

"We Act Morally Because of Biological Evolution or Social Conditioning."

I F GOD DOESN'T EXIST, EVERYTHING GOES. Without God, morality is arbitrary.

One need not be a believer in God to recognize this.

Arthur Allen Leff was a non-Christian lawyer who described with great honesty how ethics and justice inevitably turn out when God is excluded. Leff desperately wanted to believe two things: that humans could uncover authoritative rules for life *and* that humans are wholly free. Lacking God, Leff believed, human beings don't have access to authoritative rules. And, he admitted, we are left with complete *arbitrariness*. To any human moral pronouncement, we can respond, *"Sez who?"*

Leff concluded one lecture by recounting quite openly the arbitrariness of morality without God:

> . . . it looks as if we are all we have. Given what we know about ourselves and each other, this is an extraordinarily unappetizing prospect; looking around us, it [sic] appears that if all men are brothers, the ruling model is Cain and Abel. Neither reason, nor love, nor even terror, seems to have worked to make us "good," and worse than that, there is no reason why anything should. Only if ethics were something unspeakable by us, could law be unnatural, and therefore unchallengeable. As things now stand, everything is up for grabs.
> Nevertheless:
> Napalming babies is bad.
> Starving the poor is wicked.
> Buying and selling each other is depraved.

Those who stood up to and died resisting Hitler, Stalin, Amin, and Pol Pot—and General Custer, too—have earned salvation.
Those who acquiesced deserve to be damned.
There is in the world such a thing as evil.
[All together now:] Sez who?
God help us.[1]

Was Leff correct? Can a worldview without God explain objective morality and obligation at all? Why should a person be moral if a naturalistic understanding of the universe is true—in other words, if the world is wholly without God and nothing exists beyond what we can see? Some thinkers strongly disagree with Leff. They believe that a naturalistic or nontheistic basis for ethics does exist. Let us briefly look at a range of explanations they have suggested.

One commonly proposed naturalistic basis for ethics is *evolutionary development or biological adaptations*. As we noted above, Michael Ruse maintains that morality is merely a biological adaptation like hands, feet, and teeth: "Our sense of morality is an adaptation. . . . This is not in any way to say that that which has evolved is morally good."[2]

Ruse believes that the command "Love thy neighbor" is just an aid to survival. Whatever helps us survive is "good," Ruse would have us believe.

Unfortunately for him, the view that ethical standards are ingrained into us by the drive to survive is an inadequate basis for morality for the simple reason that there is no good reason to think these moral beliefs are *true*. They just *are*. We could have developed, for example, a moral instinct favoring rape—which *could* be an aid to survival. Rape, then, would be "good" because it helps us survive. But we sense that rape is immoral even if it may be biologically advantageous and could help us survive. While we may acquire certain moral beliefs through biological adaptation in the struggle for survival, this is a different issue from how moral principles could *exist* in the first place or what it is that *grounds* them as morally binding. There would be nothing *inherently* wrong with rape or theft—even if it goes against one's ingrained moral sense.

In a humorous but illuminating illustration, John Hick writes about atheist Bertrand Russell's view that each individual naturally seeks his own good. Hick asks us to imagine an ant, whose function is to live for the sake of the ant heap. If the anthill is in danger, he instinctively sacrifices his life for the entire ant colony. He does not act voluntarily, on the basis of choice, but by instinct. But let's turn the tables:

> Imagine for a moment an ant suddenly endowed with the knowledge contained in Russell's book and with the freedom to make his own personal decisions. Suppose him to be called upon to immolate himself for

the sake of the ant hill. He feels the powerful pressure of instinct pushing him toward self-destruction. But he asks himself why he should voluntarily embrace this fact. There is a cause that may lead him to do so, namely the force of instinct. But is there any *reason* why, having the freedom to choose, he should deliberately carry out the suicidal program to which instinct prompts him? Why should he regard the future existence of a million other ants as more important to him than his own continued existence? After all, they are all ants, all but fleeting moments of animation produced and then annihilated by mindless and meaningless forces—for that an ant [using Russell's words about the human being] "is the product of causes which had no prevision of the end they were achieving; that his origin, his growth, his hopes and fears, are but the outcome of accidental collocations of atoms. . ." is so nearly certain that it would be irrational to act on any other assumption. Since all that he is and has or ever can have is his own present existence, surely insofar as he is free from the domination of blind force of instinct, he will opt for life—his own life.[3]

On Ruse's account of ethics, there is simply no good reason why someone should give up his own brief life for the sake of others.

Another naturalistic attempt to ground morality is *the social-contract view*, in which human beings form a society and formulate mutually agreeable rules to make life orderly and civil. The U.S. Constitution would be one such "contract." But this view, too, is problematic for at least four reasons.

First, social-contract morality isn't binding for the person who refuses to go along with it.

Second, the fact that an institution or a contract says something is right doesn't thereby render something good: "The social imposition of duties does not *ipso facto* make them morally right."[4] A would-be member of a gang or the Mafia, for instance, might be required to murder someone before he can become a member of the group, but this is clearly immoral.

Third, if someone can escape the consequences of violating a social contract, why then should a behavior be considered objectively immoral? If one can get away with breaking a social taboo, why not do it?

Fourth, we instinctively know that certain things are objectively wrong—a gut-level knowledge that a social contract cannot explain. Hitler's extermination of six million Jews or Stalin's purges were wrong not because they violated some social contract. If someone brutally raped and murdered a man's sister or wife, the response of the offended would not merely be that a social contract had been violated. He intuitively knows that such a horrific crime is wrong.

Another naturalistic basis for morality is that of *self-interest*, popularized by Ayn Rand.[5] This morality of "egoism" revises the Golden Rule, advocating that we "do unto others since they will eventually (hopefully) do the same unto us." If we scratch a back or two, eventually our own backs get scratched. The self-interest basis for morality, however, is problematic. Self-interest can't justify one particular action we take to be right and noble—namely, *giving one's life for another*. Why should a mother give up her brief existence when her child is about to be struck by a car? There seems to be no rational reason to surrender life so others may survive. Furthermore, if self-interest as a moral position is universalized, how then do we resolve the conflict of competing interests? And why even think that my own interest is the *only* good there is?

A fourth suggestion for how a naturalistic worldview can provide a basis for morality is *the "survival of the fittest" mentality*. The Darwinian struggle for survival becomes the name of the game. And how well would *that* work? This is a view that would permit the eradication of the helpless and elderly—both a "drain on society's resources." It merely promotes a "might makes right" society. When power becomes the absolute, the value of people becomes subordinate to this power. This perspective is, of course, arbitrary and counterintuitive. We know instinctively that if we are in the position of the powerless, it is wrong to be exploited by the powerful. This naturalistic view of ethics appeals to the powerful—until *they* are somehow incapacitated and become victims of their own philosophy.

Another naturalistic view of ethics is that *moral beliefs are based on cultural conditioning*. Where do our moral values come from? We assimilate them from our society, our environment. We are brought up to believe certain things are right and others wrong. But if we grew up in another culture, we could have held the *opposite* moral beliefs.

Through a friend, I came into cyber-contact with an atheist, who e-mailed me concerning the origin of morality. When I mentioned my belief in objective morality, he confidently wrote, "That's another one I've heard before and can refute." This is what his "refutation" amounted to:

> . . . how different would your "absolute and objective" morals be if the Third Reich ruled the world and taught you morality from childhood? Would you believe that the Aryan race has "absolute moral authority"? If you were born 700 years ago, would you believe in the absolute moral authority of a monarch? I think you would, and I think you would be just as convinced of the "absolute objectivity" of your moral system as you now are convinced of the "absolute objectivity" of the moral value of not eating your children.

The chief problem with my atheistic acquaintance's beliefs about morality is that these beliefs are *themselves* the product of his culture and are therefore no more objective than the next person's. So his argument against objective morality is just as irrelevant as another's, and there is no reason to embrace it! In other words, *Why should I believe this atheist is right if his views have been shaped by culture just as mine have been?* Moreover, this view again rubs against the grain of what we know to be true by eliminating any basis for moral reform. Yet evils like apartheid, genocide, kidnapping, slavery, or torture should be opposed precisely *because* objective morality exists and some cultures are less morally developed than others.

Some say that morality is based on *the intrinsic worth and dignity of the human being.* For instance, the United Nations Universal Declaration of Human Rights of 1948 declares, "All human beings are born free and equal in dignity and rights. They are endowed with reason and conscience and should act toward one another in a spirit of brotherhood." Unlike the Declaration of Independence, which roots human dignity in being created by God ("that all men are created equal, that they are endowed by their Creator with certain unalienable rights"), the United Nations document simply *assumes* the intrinsic worth of human beings. But if naturalism is true, it is extremely difficult to see why humans have intrinsic dignity.[6]

So why are humans more valuable than roaches, rats, or monkeys, if we are nothing more than matter? Should a person be tried for murder when he kills an insect? Or why should we object if a more evolutionarily advanced alien race invaded our planet and attempted to eat humans just as humans eat cattle? What gives *any* of us value in the first place? Why, then, should we be concerned about endangered species? Naturalism, it seems, fails to offer a sufficient response for human worth.

A final nontheistic (although *not* relativistic) explanation for morality is that *moral principles are simply given and intrinsic to the universe*—a "Neoplatonic" idea.[7] Like laws of logic, morality is part of the furniture of the universe—mere brute facts, and we intuitively know that there are intrinsically valuable states of affairs that are to be preferred above others. It is clearly better to be hard-working, honest, and selfless rather than indolent, mendacious, and narcissistic.

This Neoplatonist view, though, fails for at least four reasons—for which we lack the space to detail here. First, it is insufficient in that it cannot explain *why* we should feel guilt toward mere principles when we do wrong. People, not principles or rules, prompt guilt and shame in us. Second, from our experience it seems that moral obligation is bound up with persons rather than abstract principles. W. R. Sorley captured this nicely when he wrote, "Goodness—when we distinguish it from beauty and truth—does not belong to material things, but to persons only."[8] Third, how could these impersonal and abstract moral principles bring about a world with moral human beings in the first place? These abstract principles are purely "passive."[9]

The fourth point is that it seems odd to assert this nontheistic view because it implies that moral values somehow *anticipate* in some purposive way the existence of human beings who can appreciate and appropriate these moral principles. Yet if God does not exist, we have to wonder why morality should even apply to human beings, who are just advanced animals. Moreover, these moral laws imply the intrinsic value of human beings who are capable of making moral choices. But again, if God does not exist, it seems difficult to make any distinction between human beings and their evolutionary predecessors since we are all made out of the same stuff and by the same processes. It's easier to accept the belief that a personal Being is responsible for the origin of the moral principles in the universe.[10]

While we can't examine other naturalistic theories of ethics, it seems that they are all vulnerable to the same criticisms: Why should we assume that human beings have *intrinsic value* or dignity? Why should we think that the moral instincts we have inherited are *right*? How do we know whether we should *comply with* our moral instincts or *resist* them? Why should we act morally when it seriously conflicts with our self-interest? How do we mediate between conflicting moral beliefs in a pluralistic society? If God doesn't exist, then why should we sacrifice our lives for others? Why should powerful despots like Saddam Hussein behave morally if they can get away with oppressing or murdering others? It seems that naturalism has serious difficulties dealing with such questions.

The atheist Kai Nielsen has admitted that naturalism can give no answer to the question, "Why be moral?"

> We have not been able to show that reason requires the moral point of view or that all really rational persons, unhoodwinked by myth or ideology, not be individual egoists or classic amoralists. Reason doesn't decide here.
> The picture I have painted for you is not a pleasant one. Reflection on it depresses me. . . . The point is this: Pure, practical reason, even with a good knowledge of the facts, will not take you to morality.[11]

Deflating "We Act Morally Because of Biological Evolution or Social Conditioning."

"Ethics is based on evolutionary development or biological adaptations."

- These moral beliefs aren't *true*; they just *are*. We could have developed the belief that rape is biologically advantageous.
- Why should a mother give her life for her child and surrender her brief existence?

"Ethics is based on a social contract."

- Such morality isn't binding upon the person who does not want to go along with it.

- Even if people agree to a social contract, this doesn't mean that their actions are right. To become part of a gang, for example, a person might be required to commit murder.
- Why should an act be deemed wrong if we can escape the consequences of violating the social contract?
- We instinctively know that certain actions are right (helping the disadvantaged) or wrong (Hitler's extermination of six million Jews)—without appealing to a social contract.

"Ethics is based on self-interest."

- How do we resolve conflicts of self-interest?
- We take for granted that laying down one's life for another is noble and right.
- Why assume that self-interest is the *only* good?

"Ethics is based on the survival of the fittest."

- Should we exterminate those who can't care for themselves?
- What if we find ourselves in the position of powerlessness? Would we still agree with such an ethical view?

"Ethical values come from cultural influences."

- The relativist who makes this claim has been influenced by his culture just like the absolutist. So why should the relativist's view be preferred?

"Ethics is based on the intrinsic worth and dignity of human beings."

- Why should we *assume* that human beings have intrinsic dignity if we are the results of materialistic processes?
- Why would humans be considered more valuable than fleas or rats? (Or should people be tried for murder if they kill insects?)

"Moral principles are basic givens and are part of the furniture of the universe."

- Why should we feel guilt toward abstract moral principles? We typically think of moral obligation and guilt in relation to *persons*.
- Why should we think that these objective moral principles have anything to do with human beings? If human beings evolved, it seems strange that these moral principles would somehow *anticipate* moral beings (humans).
- Why should we assume that human beings have intrinsic worth as distinct from other animals?

CHAPTER 11

"To Be Good, We Don't Need God."

F OR MANY CHRISTIANS, one of the greatest difficulties of telling others the Gospel—or just getting along in this world—is facing up to the admirable morality of the nonbelievers next door. As one friend says, "Work *that* into your theology."

The typical naturalistic attempts to supply a *why* and *how* for morality, we've seen, come up short. But that doesn't necessarily convince the people we talk with that God's existence is the only satisfying explanation for objective morality. Atheists *can* be morally upright. People *do* construct fine ethical systems without God. Even so, we can point out, questions linger: "Why *ought* I to be moral at all?" "Why *should* I do the right thing if it doesn't pay off?" "How did I get to be a moral being?" "Why do human beings have dignity and value?" At this point, we can argue that the God of theism offers solid grounding for moral obligation, accounting for a number of facts that naturalism can't explain.

We start by saying, *There is no good reason to deny the general reliability of our most basic moral instincts.*[1] Humans intuitively know that certain objective moral values exist. For example, we know that kindness is a virtue and not a vice, that torturing babies is immoral, that child abuse is wrong, that a person like Hitler or Stalin is morally repugnant. We know these things virtually without reflection, without thinking them through.[2] While reason *confirms* the basic rightness of these intuitions, we don't seem to know this *by means of* reason.[3] And we regularly rely on these intuitions to make practical, everyday moral judgments.[4] To deny such beliefs flies in the face of basic human knowledge and instincts.

If someone doubts these moral basics—someone, for example, who sees no ultimate distinction between a Hitler and a Mother Teresa—we can't really carry on a decent conversation about morality. Instead of trying to prove the evilness of evildoers, we should call into question that person's mental health. Denying the objectivity of our moral intuitions is denying a deep part of our humanity. We can press the moral skeptic by making our point another way. We could say, "Most people would find themselves in confident *disagreement* with your attitude. Now, why is this? How would you explain it?"[5]

Second, *God's character explains the objective moral values that logically precede our having a moral sense.* Although the nontheist may believe that objective moral values *exist* without reference to God, there is an ultimate question: What *underlies* those objective moral values?

Let's hear the opposing point made by atheist Kai Nielsen. He admits that objective moral obligation exists. Though he maintains that naturalism can't account for this, he won't concede that theism offers a better solution to the problem. He presents the following interesting argument.[6] Suppose a parent who believes in God "abandons" or "loses" his faith in God. Is that parent going to love his child less—or not at all—because his supposed "basis for objective morality" is apparently lost? Of course not, Nielsen asserts. A parent would still maintain that it is objectively right to love his child even if God doesn't exist.

Nielsen offers other evidence to deny that God is necessary to explain the existence of objective morality. He says that when Christians, for example, make moral judgments about God's acts and commands or about the superb ethic of Jesus Christ's Sermon on the Mount, that implies a standard of good-ness *independent* of whether God exists. To make moral assessments about God's actions or Jesus' teachings *presupposes* the existence of an objective mo-rality.

This apparently persuasive argument, however, is flawed. It rests on a confusion of *being* and *knowing.* The normal sane person certainly *knows*— or at least acts as though he knows—that objective morality exists. But here is the crucial question: How did we get to *be* that way—moral beings who recognize right and wrong? We have to *be* moral beings before we can *know* what is moral. An atheist might suggest that if all humans—both those who believe in God and those who don't—have correct, objective moral sensibil-ities, that fact implies moral intuition isn't somehow rooted in God.

Nielsen, as an atheist and materialist, seems hard-pressed to show how randomness and chance can make sense out of moral obligation or human dig-nity. Getting back to the parent-child relationship, we have to ask how we could show love and sacrifice when it conflicts with our natural self-interest. Why resist selfish interests for the sake of the children? As the philosopher

George Mavrodes has argued, a solely materialistic universe *might* produce in us *feelings* and *beliefs* of obligation—like the protection of our children or the survival of our species or subculture—but that's a different matter from actually *having* such obligations we *ought* to carry out. It truly seems odd that objective moral obligation could arise in such a world.[7]

In the third place, *the connection between objective moral values and God has to do with God's personhood and ours.* Christians see an unbreakable connection between objective morality and God.

If objective moral values exist, as even atheists like Kai Nielsen believe, it seems plausible to argue that a personal, transcendent, perfect God is the source of and ground for morality. We resemble God—created as valuable persons by a personal Being, divinely endowed with conscience, with a capacity for morally significant relationships, and with certain objectively correct moral intuitions. We are moral beings because we have been created in the image of a moral God. Even those who don't believe in God possess an ingrained moral sense that corresponds in some measure to God's moral sense.

This explains how an atheist can *know* the content of morality *without* acknowledging God's existence. For instance, we read in Amos 1 and 2 that God threatens judgment upon the neighbors of Judah and Israel. Why? Because they have flagrantly violated an objective moral law that they knew and should have obeyed. Syria treated its enemies barbarously (1:3); Philistia, with utter inhumanity, sold whole communities into slavery (1:6); Tyre broke a pact and treated Edom treacherously (1:9). The citizens of such nations should have known better.

In Romans 2:14–15, we read,

> Indeed, when Gentiles, who do not have the law [of Moses], do by nature things required by the law, they are a law for themselves, even though they do not have the law, since they show that the requirements of the law are written on their hearts, their consciences also bearing witness, and their thoughts now accusing, now even defending them.

Scripture assumes that God has written this binding law on the hearts of people. Although the awareness of these objective standards is clouded by the Fall, a seared conscience, and social decline, this doesn't mean people can't form moral beliefs or act virtuously through God's common grace to all.[8]

Another indication that God is the basis for morality is *the problem of evil.* One of the most common objections to a nontheist's belief in God is that evil exists—and that it exists in such vast measure. Why does God allow Bangladesh to get hit again and again with disastrous tropical storms? Why does he let child molesters carry on their vile activities? Why would he permit large-scale inhumanities to take place in an Auschwitz—or through the brutality of

Soviet communism?[9] Although those who raise this objection seldom realize it, the existence of evil and our grasp of the awfulness of evil cries out for an explanation. Even in a relativistic world, people are *still* struck with horror at human atrocities like genocide or gang rape. They get the distinct impression that evil *really* exists. Although the problems raised by evil are frequently marshaled *against* belief in God, an often-overlooked presupposition in the discussion of evil is *God's very existence*.

What is evil? It isn't simply chaos or pain or feeling bad. Real, objective evil is the lack or absence of goodness. That is, the presence of evil *presupposes* the existence of an objective moral standard that is being violated. If real evil exists, then an objective standard of *goodness* by which something is deemed evil must also exist. It is hard to see, given a naturalistic view of things, where this standard of goodness could come from if we are simply cosmic accidents produced by purely physical forces.

Theism answers questions that are problems for the naturalist: Why should we deem human beings to be intrinsically valuable? Why should I sacrifice my brief life for another human being? Why should we take the moral point of view when it seriously conflicts with our own self-interest or does not satisfy us? Appealing to a social contract or pragmatic basis for acting morally doesn't work. It tells us only that doing the right thing is, practically speaking, *a good idea*, but this hardly shows why we're dutifully *obligated* to be moral.[10] Rather, we act morally for *moral reasons*, because it is morally right to do so—just as we should believe the true thing because it is true. No further reason is needed. Nontheists can agree about such basic moral truths, but what are the *grounds* for these truths and human dignity?

Theism provides adequate answers to the questions just raised. We ought to be moral because we have been *made as moral beings in the likeness of God*, to whom we are also personally responsible as his creatures. Furthermore, knowing this God personally is the highest end of humans. When we are in right relationship with God, all other goods—which have also been created by God—find their proper place.[11]

When we carry out our moral duties we approximate the character of the Creator, the ultimate Good, and function *according to God's design for us*. We carry out the purposes for which we were made. We find self-sacrifice praiseworthy because it fits these purposes and assumes the intrinsic dignity of others. We experience guilt not simply because we have violated laws of society or of the universe but because we have violated the ultimate Source of moral values—a personal God. And just as human relationships serve as a motivation and basis for loyalty and obligation, so our having been created by God—and our relationship with him—serves as the source of ultimate obligation and the one real basis for a moral understanding of human relationships.[12]

Deflating "To Be Good, We Don't Need God."

- We should not confuse our *knowledge* of ethical values (epistemology) with the *basis* for ethics (ontology). While atheists may believe in objective moral values, at issue is the fact that we are moral beings. The fact that we are made in God's image furnishes us with the basis for believing in objective morality and human value—even if we reject God's existence.
- Our moral intuitions generally reflect an objective moral order.
- Most people believe in the intrinsic worth of human beings. Is the more plausible explanation that we are nothing more than matter, or that we are made in God's likeness?
- If people object to God's existence on the basis of evil, they are assuming that objective moral values exist. Evil presupposes a standard of goodness.
- We can ask, "What kind of universe makes the best sense out of our moral intuitions, our sense of guilt, and our belief in the intrinsic value of persons—naturalism or theism?"

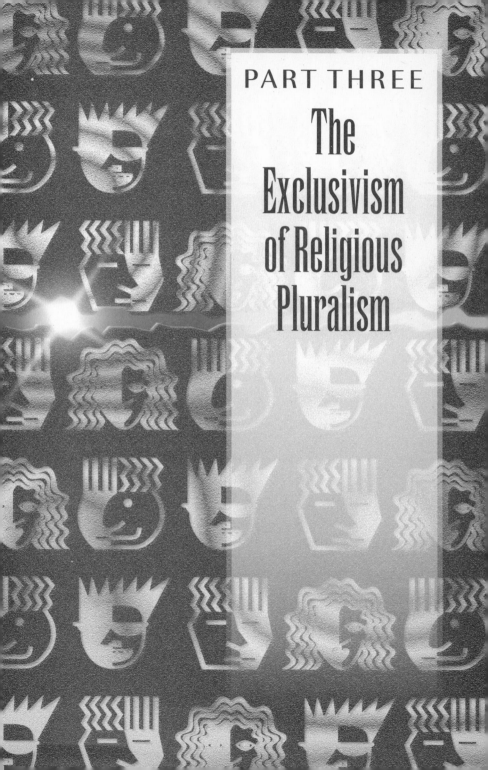

PART THREE

The Exclusivism of Religious Pluralism

IMAGINE THAT A TIME MACHINE enables a group of scientists to gather together for a symposium on physics and astronomy. Some are from medieval Europe. Others are from ancient Greece and Egypt. Some Hindu philosophers happen to come along, and Galileo, Copernicus, Newton, and Einstein join the group as well. Now, if relativism were true, some obvious nonsense would emerge from this symposium—that even though each person disagrees with everyone else present, all are correct. It would be true that the earth is *both* flat *and* spherical, that the earth is *both* the center of the universe *and* that it is not, that the universe is *both* stationary *and* is expanding at a terrific speed, that the physical world is *both* illusory (as Advaita Hindus claim) *and* real.

What is clear is that not everyone could be right. The nature of the universe simply *is* as it is—regardless of what we believe. Someone can be a sincere "flat-earther," but this doesn't alter the fact that that person is wrong. Beliefs are simply not to be *equated* with truth or reality; rather, they are to *conform* to truth.

This symposium example undoubtedly goes further than the average American relativist takes his relativism. Relativism generally doesn't come up when talking about astronomy, the weather, or the stock exchange. It usually arises only when discussions turn to God, to truth and falsehood, moral right and wrong, or to aesthetic standards—all of which allegedly pertain to "values," not scientific "facts."[1] But reality is what it is whether all agree on it or not. Let's now apply this to religious belief.

At its most popular level, religious pluralism goes so far as to say that not only are all religions equally true but that they all say roughly the same thing. Many of Christianity's critics, however, are more sophisticated than that. And, sadly, many have been exposed to Christianity long enough to feel that they have seen its sights and explored its back alleys. John Harwood Hick was born in Yorkshire, England, in 1922. He grew up in the Anglican tradition.[2] The church services, although infinitely boring, furnished Hick with a strong sense of God's reality and love. At age nineteen, he became involved in an Inter-

Varsity Fellowship group at University College, Hull. His study of the New Testament and spiritual discussions brought him to the point of conversion to Christianity. While on the top of a double-decker bus, he experienced something quite profound:

> . . . all descriptions are inadequate. But it was as though the skies opened up and light poured down and filled me with a sense of overflowing joy in response to an immense transcendent goodness and love. I remember that I couldn't help smiling broadly—smiling back, as it were, at God—though if any of the other passengers were looking they must have thought that I was a lunatic, grinning at nothing.

Hick embraced "the entire evangelical package of Christianity." When he went to study philosophy in Edinburgh, he joined the Presbyterian Church of England and become heavily involved in Bible studies and evangelistic activities.

During his studies at Edinburgh under the Kant scholar Norman Kemp Smith, his thinking about evangelical Christianity began to change. He became increasingly distressed at the "narrowness and lack of sympathy with questioning thought" among his fellow evangelical students. Moreover, seeds of skepticism were sown in his mind, due to the belief that the structure of human minds shapes our perceptions of reality.

From this point on, he moved further away from Christian orthodoxy. He later rejected the Incarnation of Christ and the historicity of the Resurrection. By 1967, when he became professor of theology at the University of Birmingham and was exposed to a religiously diverse environment, his identification with orthodox Christianity came to an end. While attending worship in mosques, synagogues, and temples, it became evident to him that "the same kind of thinking [was] taking place in them as in a Christian church—namely, human beings opening their minds to a higher divine Reality."

Hick found this discovery of "God's universal saving activity" incompatible with the belief that there could be only one true religion. He became convinced that no religion has a monopoly on truth and that all religions are a human attempt to understand the Ultimate Reality. Over the years, Hick has established himself as an outspoken, highly respected proponent of religious pluralism—a view that is gaining a following in the Western world.[3]

John Stott points out that new global consciousness, a new appreciation for other religions (due, for example, to television and travel), and a new post-colonial modesty[4] have made pluralism quite attractive for many people.[5] So today's Christian student in the university is inevitably told, "Your religion is okay for you and brings you satisfaction, and that's fine. But what about other religions and holy books? You're not going to tell me that they're wrong and you're right, are you?" The increasing trend toward religious pluralism should prompt us to very seriously and skillfully respond to it, and to graciously defend the uniqueness of God's revelation through Jesus Christ.[6] We'll argue below that religious pluralism is another postmodern myth.

Elephants, Rings, and Religions: A Naïve Version of Religious Pluralism

To criticize religious pluralism fairly, we need first to know what it is, lest we knock down a mere straw man. To understand religious pluralism, we will first examine a relatively naïve view of pluralism before moving on to its more sophisticated version.

Orthodox Christianity has historically been viewed as *particularistic* or—to use a term with often negative connotations—*exclusivistic*. That is, Christianity claims to be true, and if another religion contradicts what its Scriptures teach, then that religion errs. At the other end of the spectrum is religious *pluralism*, which maintains that no religion can be considered superior to another. To make an exclusivistic claim is deemed "intolerant" or "arrogant" by the pluralist.

Religious pluralism is not a new wave of thought, however. The early church was surrounded by religious pluralism and syncretism. Origen (*ca.* A.D. 185-*ca.* A.D. 254) criticized a man named Celsus, a pagan who attacked Christianity. Celsus wrote, "It makes no difference if one invokes the highest God or Zeus or Adonai or Sabaoth or Amoun, as the Egyptians do, or Papaios, as the Scythians do."[7] Today, Christians who uphold Christ's uniqueness also encounter such assertions. Many are familiar with the parable of the blind men before the king of Benares, India, who touched different parts of the elephant. Since none of them can see, each gives a different perspective of what he believes the elephant to be—a rope, a tree, a large wall, a snake. In their ignorance, they argue about what an elephant is. Each one is partly right, but "all were in the wrong," in the words of John G. Saxe's poem:

> So, oft in theologic wars,
> The disputants, I ween,
> Rail on in utter ignorance
> Of what each other mean,
> And prate about an elephant
> Not one of them has seen!

A kinder image pictures religion as a mosaic or a kaleidoscope in which a number of differing beliefs make up an entire pattern about the nature of God/Ultimate Reality.[8] Or like one of many roads going up a mountain, each religion is thought to lead a person to this Reality, and there is no need to resolve or argue over conflicting truth claims among religions. As the god

Krishna says in the *Bhagavad Gita*, "In any way that men love me, in that same way they find my love: for many are the paths of men, but they all in the end come to me" (4:11).

During the Enlightenment, the biblical critic Gotthold Lessing (1729–1781) wrote the story *Nathan the Wise* in support of religious pluralism. In this story, Nathan, the wise man, describes a father "in a far Eastern clime" who had a priceless magic ring. He had three sons whom he loved alike and to whom he desired to give the ring before he died, and, having foolishly promised it to each, could only give it to one. In order not to appear as though he was showing favoritism to one, he had two replicas made of the authentic ring. He separately called his sons into his presence, gave them each a ring and his blessing, and then he died. Each son left his presence thinking that he had the magic ring and that the others had the imitations. Each one claimed to be "True prince o' the house." Nathan, who parroted the religious views of Lessing, said,

> . . . Vainly they search, strive, argue.
> The true ring was not proved or provable—
> Almost as hard to prove as to us now
> What the true creed is.[9]

These sons went before the judge, who told them,

> . . . let each strive most zealously
> To show a love untainted by self-care,
> Each with his might view with the rest to bring
> Into the day the virtue of the jewel
> His finger wears, and help this virtue forth
> By gentleness, by spirit tractable,
> By kind deeds and true piety toward God.

By way of application, history can tell us nothing about the objective truth of one faith over another, Lessing would have us believe, since we are simply the religious products of our upbringing.[10]

A More Sophisticated Version of Religious Pluralism

Thinking about religious pluralism has become more refined since Lessing's day, however. John Hick has become a chief defender of pluralism today. (For the sake of convenience, note that when I refer to "pluralism," I mean *religious* pluralism.) Let's examine his view of pluralism at this point.

1. *Pluralism recognizes that there are serious conflicts regarding the truth claims and doctrinal content of the world's religions:* One can't simply say that all religions are essentially the same, as the pop version of religious pluralism

often does. To illustrate, the various world religions view the *human problem* differently—whether it stems from desire (Buddhism), ignorance (Hinduism), or sin and rebellion against a holy God (Christianity). Different views of the human problem will affect *the path of "salvation" or "liberation"* to be sought. Most religions tend to see salvation as achieved through human efforts—whether through asceticism, mysticism, illumination, or good deeds. Christianity, on the other hand, asserts that salvation isn't the result of human achievement[11] and human endeavor but through the initiating kindness of God's grace in Jesus Christ. Moreover, theistic religions have a different understanding about the *Ultimate Reality*—a personal God—than do most Eastern religions—an impersonal Reality. And even among the theistic religions there is significant disagreement: Christianity has a Trinitarian conception of God, whereas Judaism and Islam share a unitarian view.

There are indeed genuine differences that cannot be papered over, and careful religious pluralists recognize this. To say that all religions are essentially saying the same thing is "absurdly simplistic."[12] Rather, as we shall soon see, pluralists like Hick deal with these differences in a more refined fashion.

2. *All religions speak of an ultimate transcendent Reality:* The poet Alexander Pope wrote in his "Universal Prayer":

Father of all, in every age
In every clime, adored
By saint, by savage, or by sage,
Jehovah, Jove, or Lord.

Whether one worships *Adonai* in an Israeli synagogue, the Trinity in a church service in Seoul, *Allah* in a Kashmiri mosque, or Krishna in a South Indian village, this worship—the pluralist argues—is directed at the same Ultimate Reality, the perceptions and intentions of the worshipers notwithstanding.

The Real, Hick and others contend, is "experienced and thought by different human mentalities" through the various deities and absolutes. These manifestations of the Ultimate "are not illusory." They are experientially real and "authentic manifestations of the Real."[13] Hick claims to take the wide range of religious experiences seriously and realistically. Whatever varying conceptions world religions have about the Ultimate, they are *genuine* displays of the divine.

In 1972 Hick called for a "Copernican revolution in theology."[14] This meant that Christians should no longer be "Ptolemaic" in their view of other religions, holding as absolute truth that "salvation is through Christ alone." Rather, the Copernican view would require a shift to recognize that the religions are like planets that circle round the one absolute truth. So even though each of these religions cannot be considered to have an accurate understanding of Ultimate Reality, each points to it and "strives toward" it.

3. *Religions and theology are limited human creations, which reflect cultural assumptions and biases about the Ultimate:* John Hick asserts that the world religions are "different culturally conditioned responses to the ultimately Real."[15] All religions are different human—and thus, inadequate—attempts to know the Ultimate Reality. Hick prefers the term "the Real" rather than "God," when speaking of transcendent Reality. This is because "the Real" is more tradition-neutral than "God" and extends beyond the gods and the absolutes of Western and Eastern religious traditions.[16]

When it comes to religion—from an observational perspective—the deities and ultimates as humans experience them in various world religions differ significantly.[17] Moreover, they are not identical with the Ultimate Reality as it exists in itself, which transcends human experience.[18] Religions, as human manifestations of an attempt to grasp the Real, cannot grasp the Real as it really is.[19]

Hick claims to begin his study of religion inductively—"from below." That is, Hick starts by observing the broad range of human religious experiences. He notices that the world religions perceive the Ultimate Reality differently and thus respond differently to it from within their various cultures. In starting "from below," Hick believes he is doing justice both to the differences between the world's great religions and to their commonality in responding to the Ultimate Reality.[20] The world religions, then, are true in one sense and false in another. They are *true* in that they produce moral virtue, social concern, selflessness, and compassion in their adherents. They are *false*, however, in their claim to ultimacy, superiority, or finality.[21]

4. *Religious pluralism says that all religions are equally capable of bringing salvation and producing morally upright people.* Many people point to Tibet's Dalai Lama or Mahatma Gandhi as "saints" from a non-Christian religious tradition. They display the same type of virtues that are commended by Christianity. Saintly Christians, many feel, do not seem to be morally superior in any way to "saints" from other religious traditions. It appears that non-Christians can equally well display the fruit of the Spirit—"love, joy, peace, patience, kindness, goodness, faithfulness, gentleness, and self-control" (Gal. 5:22–23). And since the saving power of any religious tradition can really only be judged by the moral uprightness of persons within those traditions, all great religions must be equal in their capacity to save or liberate.[22] Pluralists maintain that within all religions, "the same salvific process is taking place; namely, the transformation of human existence from self-centeredness to Reality-centeredness."[23]

To sum up, religious pluralists believe that all religions have essentially the same capacity to transform human beings from being self-centered to Reality-centered. These distinctive religious paths still lead to roughly the same kinds of moral virtue in many of their adherents. So all religions, according to pluralists like Hick, are varied human attempts to know the Real. Though each religion is inadequate, each is equally legitimate as a means of achieving "salvation," defined as the moving away from *self*-centeredness and toward *Reality*-centeredness.

Before offering a Christian response to pluralism, we must understand something about religious exclusivism—and how it applies to Christianity in particular. When we assert that Christian revelation is true, we aren't saying that all non-Christian religions are *wholly* false. This is the impression that Christians often give, and pluralist arguments wrongly imply this as well (when, for example, they deny that any religion has "a *monopoly* on the truth"). The Christian doesn't claim exclusive possession of truth, because *all* truth is God's truth. As the Scottish writer and pastor George MacDonald rightly remarked, "Truth is truth, whether from the lips of Jesus or Balaam."[24] The Christian is to affirm truth and virtue wherever they are found. But the Christian maintains that God's revelation in Jesus is true and that other religious systems are wrong where they *contradict* Christian revelation.

So Christians can cooperate with those of different faiths in various social and moral causes—opposing abortion-on-demand and speaking out for religious liberty, for instance—without denying their commitment to Christ's uniqueness. Familiarity with the world's religions helps Christians discover the positive elements of other faiths, a bridge not only to relationships and interreligious understanding but also to effectively communicating God's love in Christ.[25]

CHAPTER 12

"Christianity Is Arrogant and Imperialistic."

T ODAY'S ULTIMATE VICE IS MAKING an exclusivistic claim. Whether at the water cooler or in the student union, it appears that the only heresy around is orthodox Christianity—because it makes just such claims. What we need to understand is that those who criticize Christianity are equally as exclusivistic in their "tolerance."

We should know, first of all, that religious pluralism doesn't exist. *It is a myth.* Religious pluralism is just as exclusivistic as a religion like Christianity, logically no different than the exclusivist position. How so? The exclusivist affirms that if a particular claim or proposition is true (such as "Jesus died for the sins of the world"), then a religion that rejects this is in error. But the pluralist believes that *his* claim is true and that the exclusivist is wrong. So there is no pluralist on one end of the spectrum and an exclusivist on the other. The pluralist is actually one brand of exclusivist.[1] So those like Hick and Paul Knitter, who consider themselves pluralists, are actually crypto-exclusivists. Logically speaking, "the pluralist is, in fact, no different from the exclusivist, except in the criteria employed for what counts as truth."[2]

Despite this similarity between Christianity and pluralism, Christianity is ironically condemned on university campuses or in the media as imperialistic, oppressive, arrogant, or chauvinistic. Pluralist Rosemary Radford Ruether makes this very assertion: "The idea that Christianity, or even the biblical faiths, have a monopoly on religious truth is an outrageous and absurd religious chauvinism."[3] But *if* Christianity is imperialistic, oppressive, and arrogant, then so is pluralism, since it deems exclusive religions like Christianity to be in error and its own outlook as the preferable religious view. If Christianity is exclusive, it is no more so than religious pluralism. If exclusivists are vulnerable to criticism, so are pluralists, who believe they possess a virtue that a traditional Christian or Muslim does not.[4] So by the pluralist's own criterion, the idea that the *pluralist* has a monopoly on religious truth is "an outrageous and absurd religious chauvinism"! It turns out that the pluralist is just as "intolerant" toward the claims of the Christian and Muslim exclusivists as he thinks they are toward him.

The same inconsistency applies to Paul Knitter, a popular writer who takes a more pragmatic approach to religions. Religions are judged to be true on the basis of their *bringing liberation from oppressive societal, psychological, and spiritual structures.* If religions do not in general further the cause of, say, women's rights, the poor, justice, or peace, then they are judged to be *false*.[5] But these ethical criteria, far from being pragmatic, embody a particular perspective about certain social actions and sustaining beliefs and commitments that *exclude* other types of social action and their sustaining beliefs as wrong.[6] For example, in defending women's rights, should we permit the right to abortion, or should we deny it in the interests of the life of the unborn child? And what about unborn female children in India or China, who are routinely aborted? How far do women's rights extend in this situation? For *whose* rights should a pluralist like Knitter plead?

In the end, the pluralist hasn't shown that an adherent to a particularistic religion is wrong simply because there are other religious options. Rather, the pluralist's position is nothing more than exclusivism dressed up in a costume of "tolerance."

Second, *religious pluralists end up distorting and even relativizing the claims of the world religions by imposing their own framework upon them*: What Hick and others tend to do in their analysis of religions is to stand in judgment of them. They do not let other religions simply be themselves.[7] Evangelical theologian Alister McGrath rightly points out that this crude homogenizing of religions implies that only the Western liberal academic can *really* understand the world's religions. Even though the adherents to the various religions—poor goons that they are!—think they hold to beliefs that are true, it is only Western liberal academics who have such privileged access.[8]

For instance, Hick edited the book *The Myth of God Incarnate*, in which he asserts that to speak of the Christ of Christianity, the second person of the Trinity who became a man, is a "mythological and poetic way of expressing his significance to us."[9] Hick tells us that Jesus was *not* the two-natured God and man. He was "wholly human." In fact, whenever self-sacrificial love is lived out in response to God's love, to that extent "divine love has become incarnate on earth."[10] Hick even (wrongly) compares the ascription of deity to Jesus with the process of Buddha's divinization. So we can thank Hick for telling Christians what they should *really* believe (or Buddhists or Muslims, for that matter) as opposed to what they *thought* they believed![11] Hick doesn't let Christianity stand on its own claims but has to deny certain key tenets in order to live more comfortably with it. Mythologizing Christianity's central tenets about the deity and resurrection of Christ takes away the sharp edge of its exclusivity.

We could look at another example from Zen Buddhism,[12] which causes real problems for Hick. The Zen belief of *satori* refers to the *direct and immediate apprehension of Ultimate Reality*, which is absolutely unique and unrivaled among religious experiences. Although Hick attributes this perception to the product of the Zen Buddhist's culture, he ends up (as he does with crucial Christian doctrines) *reinterpreting* the Buddhist doctrine of *satori* to fit his own pluralistic outlook.

This pluralist strategy is indeed ironic in light of the fact that a number of conflicting religious ideas were *fundamental tenets* expounded by the founders and spokesmen of the great religions.[13] For example, in the sixth century B.C., Gautama Buddha rejected the notion of *atman*, the eternal soul, which was commonly accepted in India in his day. The Hebrew prophets rejected Baal and other forms of idol worship. Jesus denounced the legalism and formalism in the Judaism he observed. Muhammad denounced polytheism. These were no mere superficial trappings, but central to matters of "salvation" for these religions.

Pluralists like Hick make the sweeping claim that the differing and conflicting truth claims aren't of great religious importance; what matters, they say, is that despite their differences, all the great religions are capable of bringing salvation or liberation. Doctrines are merely secondary in terms of saving a person.[14] But although Hick denies that his pluralism is a view from "on high,"[15] he certainly appears to claim the vantage point of the king of Benares, telling us poor blind men that we, unlike him, are seeing only part of the picture.

One Christian philosopher aptly writes that the religious exclusivist doesn't necessarily need a religious outsider to give clarity about the status of his religion:

> Perhaps an observer who stood outside the whole religious enterprise and who had no religious experience of her or his own would be unable to decide among these competing [religious truth] claims. But I don't know why such a person should be thought to be in any specially favorable epistemic position with respect to this question. Nor is it clear why anyone within one or another of the religious traditions should feel obliged to defer to this outside judgment.[16]

As it turns out, it is the *pluralist* who acts in an arrogant manner, not the exclusivist. As another philosopher puts it, "Despite the fact that I reserve the right to believe things that are not believed by Muslims, *I leave it to the Muslims to decide what is and what is not essential to Islam.*"[17] But the religious pluralist won't allow them this prerogative. The Christian's religious views are inconsistent with those of Islam, but *so are the pluralist's!* In the end, pluralism is just another example of exclusivism.[18]

Deflating "Christianity Is Arrogant and Imperialistic."

- Religious pluralism is *just as exclusivistic as Christianity.* The pluralist believes that the exclusivist is *wrong* and that his position is *false.*
- The pluralist tends to be "intolerant" of exclusivistic religions and must water down or relativize their beliefs (for example, Jesus as the "Son of God" is just a metaphor for his being "God-conscious"). The pluralist tends to assert what is essential and not essential for the exclusivist to believe.
- The pluralist seems to overlook the fact that the major religions were founded on fundamental, often conflicting, beliefs that affect the salvation of one's soul.
- Just because the pluralist appears to stand "outside" a religious tradition, this doesn't necessarily make him more objective than the religious exclusivist.

CHAPTER 13

"If You Grew Up in India, You'd Be a Hindu."

I F YOU HAD BEEN BORN IN ANOTHER COUNTRY, is it at all likely that you would be a Christian?

Eric looks back at his family—devoutly Christian for four generations in Europe and America, twelve pastors among his relatives, an inner-city school-teacher and Christian writer for parents—and readily acknowledges that his environment made it easy for him to become a Christian. Still, his faith was exposed to severe challenges as he rose to the top of his university class and as he lived in Asia as a college student. And he knows it took a conscious series of wrenching decisions in his teens and early adult years for him to choose to remain a Christian. Oddly, one of the biggest influences on his faith came from outside his culture through Chinese Christian friends.

John Hick has asserted that in the vast majority of cases, an individual's religious beliefs will be the conditioned result of his geographical circumstances.[1] Statistically speaking, Hick is correct. But what follows from that scenario? We saw in an earlier chapter that the bare fact that individuals hold different views about a thing doesn't make relativism the inevitable conclusion. Similarly, *the phenomenon of varying religious beliefs hardly entails religious pluralism.* Before becoming a religious pluralist, an exclusivist has a few equally reasonable options:

- One could continue to accept the religion one grew up with because it has the ring of truth.
- One could reject the view one grew up with and become an adherent to a religion believed to be true.

- One could opt to embrace a less demanding, more convenient religious view.
- One could become a religious skeptic, concluding that, because the process of belief-formation is unreliable, *no* religion appears to really save.

Why should the view of pluralism be chosen instead of these other options?

An analogy from politics is helpful.[2] As with the multiple *religious* alternatives in the world, there are many *political* alternatives—monarchy, Fascism, Marxism, or democracy. What if we tell a Marxist or a conservative Republican that if he had been raised in Nazi Germany, he would have belonged to the Hitler Youth? He will probably agree but ask what your point is. What is the point of this analogy? Just because a diversity of political options has existed in the history of the world doesn't obstruct us from evaluating one political system as superior to its rivals. Just because there have been many political systems and we could have grown up in an alternate, inferior political system doesn't mean we are arrogant for believing one is simply better.[3]

Furthermore, when a pluralist asks the question about cultural or religious conditioning, the same line of reasoning *applies to the pluralist himself*. The pluralist has been just as conditioned as his religious exclusivist counterparts have. Alvin Plantinga comments:

> Pluralism isn't and hasn't been widely popular in the world at large; if the pluralist had been born in Madagascar, or medieval France, he probably wouldn't have been a pluralist. Does it follow that he shouldn't be a pluralist or that his pluralistic beliefs are produced in him by an unreliable belief-producing process? I doubt it.[4]

If all religions are culturally conditioned responses to the Real, can't we say that someone like Hick *himself* has been culturally conditioned to hold a pluralistic view rather than that of an exclusivist? If that is the case, why should Hick's view be any less arbitrary or accidental than another's? Why should his perspective be taken as having any more authority than the orthodox Christian's?

There is another problem: *The exclusivist likely believes he has better basis for holding to his views than in becoming a religious pluralist; therefore he is not being arbitrary.* John Hick holds that the religious exclusivist is arbitrary: "The arbitrariness of [the exclusivist position] is underlined by the consideration that in the vast majority of cases the religion to which a person adheres depends upon the accidents of birth."[5] But the exclusivist believes he is somehow justified in his position—perhaps the internal witness of the Holy Spirit or a conversion experience that has opened his eyes so that now he sees what his dissenters do not—even if he can't argue against the views of others. Even if the exclusivist is *mistaken*, he can't be accused of arbitrariness. Hick wouldn't think of his own view as arbitrary, and he should not level this charge against the exclusivist.

A third problem emerges: *How does the pluralist know that he is correct?* Hick says that the Real is impossible to describe with human words; It transcends all language. But *how does Hick know this?* And what if the Real chose to disclose Itself to human beings in a particular form (i.e., religion) and not another? Why should the claims of that religion not be taken seriously?[26] As Christians, who lay claim to the uniqueness of Christ, we are often challenged to justify this claim—and we rightly should. But the pluralist is *also* making an assertion that stands in *just as much* need of verification. He makes a claim about God, truth, the nature of reality. We ought to press the pluralist at this very point: "How do you *know* you are right? Furthermore, how do you know *anything* at all about the Ultimate Reality, since you think all human attempts to portray It are inadequate?"[7]

At this point we see cracks in Hick's edifice.[8] Although Hick claims to have drawn his conclusions about religion from the ground up, one wonders *how* he could arrive at an unknowable Ultimate Reality. In other words, if the Real is truly unknowable and if there is no common thread running through all the world religions so that we could formulate certain positive statements about It (like whether It is a personal being as opposed to an impersonal principle, monotheistic as opposed to polytheistic, or trinitary as opposed to unitary), then why bother positing Its existence at all? If all that the world religions know about God is what they *perceive*—not what they know of God as he really *is*, everything can be adequately explained through the human forms of religion. The Ultimate becomes utterly superfluous. And while It *could* exist, there is no good reason to think that It *does*. One could even ask Hick what prevents him from going one step further and saying that religion is *wholly* human.

Furthermore, when Hick begins at the level of human experience, this approach almost inevitably winds up treating all religions alike. The German theologian Wolfhart Pannenberg writes, "If everything comes down to human experiences, then the obvious conclusion is to treat them all on the same level."[9]

In contrast to Hick, the Christian affirms that *the knowledge of God depends on his gracious initiative to reveal himself*.[10] We read in Scripture that the natural order of creation (what we see) actually *reveals* the eternal power and nature of the unseen God. He has not left himself without a witness in the natural realm (Rom. 1:20; also Acts 14:15–18; 17:24–29; Ps. 19:1). God's existence and an array of his attributes can be known through his effects. His fingerprints are all over the universe. The medieval theologian-philosopher

Thomas Aquinas, for instance, argued in this way: "Hence the existence of God, insofar as it is not self-evident to us, can be demonstrated from those of His effects which are known to us."[11] What we know about God and an over-arching moral law in light of his creation, in fact, means we are without excuse (Rom. 2:14–15). (We'll say more about general revelation in Part IV.) So rather than *dismissing* the observable world as inadequate, why can't we say that what we see in the world serves as a *pointer toward God*?

Thus there is a role for Christian apologetics to play in defending the rationality and plausibility of the Christian revelation.[12] This role—especially in the face of conflicting worldviews—shouldn't be underestimated.[13] While Christians should be wary of furnishing arguments as "proofs," which tend to imply a mathematical certainty, a *modest* and plausible defense of Christianity—carried out in dependence on God's Spirit—often provides the mental evidence people need to pursue God with heart, soul, *and* mind.

Deflating "If You Grew Up in India, You'd Be a Hindu."

- The phenomenon of differing religious beliefs doesn't automatically entail religious pluralism. There are other options.
- Simply because there are many *political* alternatives in the world (monarchy, Fascism, communism, democracy, etc.) doesn't mean someone growing up in the midst of them is unable to see that some forms of government are better than others. That kind of evaluation isn't arrogant or presumptuous. The same is true of grappling with religion.
- The *same* line of reasoning applies to the pluralist himself. If the pluralist grew up in Madagascar or medieval France, he would not have been a pluralist!
- If we are culturally conditioned regarding our religious beliefs, then why should the religious pluralist think his view is *less* arbitrary or conditioned than the exclusivist's?
- If Christian faith is *true*, then the Christian would be in a *better* position than the pluralist to assess the status of other religions.
- How does the pluralist know *he* is correct? Even though he claims that *others* don't know Ultimate Reality as It really is, *he* implies that he does. (To say that the Ultimate Reality can't be known is to make at least *one* statement of knowledge.)
- If the Christian needs to justify Christianity's claims, the pluralist's views need just as much substantiation.
- If we can't know Reality as It really is, why think one exists at all? Why not simply try to explain religions as purely human or cultural manifestations without being anything more?

CHAPTER 14

"Mahatma Gandhi Was a Saint If Ever There Was One."

PLURALISTS USUALLY CLAIM THEY BUILD their pluralistic ideas from "ground level," from what they observe in the world's great religions.[1] And there's a key point a religious survey almost always settles for the pluralist: The saintliness of Christians is roughly on par with adherents to other religions. That raises some fair questions. If Billy Graham will be saved, why would God exclude people like Mahatma Gandhi? If other religions make people good, isn't it a form of religious snobbery to think God would only save people who adhere to the tenets of Christian revelation?

Viewing the capacity of religions to produce moral or saintly individuals indeed says something about those religions. But using those observations to judge all religions to be equally able to save can't be our prime factor in assessing religions. Let us respond to Hick's "saintliness criterion."

First, *Hick seems to be selective about what counts for starting at the ground level and what doesn't.* As we noted earlier, Hick attempts to explain away the deity of Christ, attributing this doctrine to a much later mythological development. He also denies the resurrection of Christ, passing it off as another mythological belief. Hick must reject these core tenets of Christianity—Jesus' deity and his resurrection—so that his project can succeed. But this contradicts the claim that Hick isn't making any prior assumptions about religions. An important part of starting from the ground up, it seems, is (1) to take a religion's claims at face value and (2) to take into account *the supporting evidence* for claims made by any religion.

Ironically, where Hick mythologizes Christianity, there are plausible and reasonable arguments that support the picture the Gospels paint of a divinely authoritative Jesus and of the bodily resurrection of Jesus[2] (the latter of which reinforces those claims). Why couldn't Hick plausibly draw conclusions based on such evidence, affirm the uniqueness of Christ, and from there work out the problems of Christian particularism—like the problem of hell or the fate of the unevangelized? Because Christians have reliable grounds for their beliefs, it's hardly implausible to ask pluralists to work out the implications of Christian particularism in the face of conflicting truth claims.

Second, *in the end, Hick's "ground-level" approach ends up being no less particularistic than the Christian exclusivist*: Hick considers certain Christian doctrines to be mythological or literally false, strictly speaking—such as Jesus' atoning sacrifice for sins, Jesus' deity and resurrection, or the Trinity. But, as we have seen, Hick believes *he* is correct and that the Christian or Muslim or Jew is in error by thinking he or she is truly worshiping the Ultimate Reality.

Third, *how does Hick* know *that genuine spiritual transformation is taking place?* Hick presumes that the world religions transform persons from self-centeredness to Reality-centeredness. Part of this process is making persons more moral than they would otherwise be. But given Hick's assumptions about religions—that religious belief is rooted in what we *perceive* about God and not in what God really *is*—all Hick can do is speak of how things *appear* to him. So while people may *look* more moral on the outside, Hick cannot, given his position, argue for *actual* spiritual transformation. Hick can only say, "Religions *appear* to spiritually transform their adherents, but I don't know if they *really* do." In other words, we can't judge a religion's effectiveness simply by *seeing* the actions of its adherents.[3]

Fourth, *religious pluralism may actually* diminish *moral transformation by judging the central tenets of religions to be false*. That makes the position of religious pluralism problematic from a *pragmatic* point of view. While a religious pluralist like Hick may be a moral person, moving from an exclusivistic religion to religious pluralism would have a detrimental effect on one's moral life—if not immediately, undoubtedly in successive generations. For all the pluralist knows, the Ultimate Reality, if personal, may be completely unconcerned about our moral transformation. (We could be hedonists for all It cares.) But for Christian exclusivists, say, to diminish the authority of Christ and the theological significance (and the corresponding moral ramifications) of his death and resurrection would in all likelihood proportionally affect their motivation to live morally.

Fifth, *why should a religion's capacity to save be judged* solely *by the moral fruits of its adherents?* Although this result isn't unimportant, it can't be taken as *the* distinguishing mark of a religion's legitimacy. In fact, there is nothing distinctively religious about moral fruits since *even atheists or agnostics* could display these moral virtues as well. Perhaps the pluralist could even accommodate atheism, since the atheist may be grasping at the Ultimate Reality in his own non-theistic way![4] Furthermore, there are other criteria that must also figure into the evaluation—the logical or internal consistency of a belief, its historical reliability, its philosophical defensibility, its experiential relevance (that it fits the facts of experience) and the like (which we will examine more closely in the last chapter of this book).

Take, for instance, the *historical reliability* of a religion's claims. I regularly attended a mosque for a couple of years while I was in college. At noon on every free Friday, I would listen to Omar, the *imam*, exposit the Qur'an, and then I would chat with my Muslim friends over lunch. A number of times the death of Jesus would emerge in these discussions. As a Christian, I maintained that Jesus died on the cross—a claim that enjoys strong historical support. But most Muslims deny such a claim, as is implied in the Qur'an in Sura 4:157. Both my Muslim friends and I couldn't be correct. If Jesus didn't die, then Christianity is finished. It won't do to simply moralize Christianity by reducing it to an ethical system. Jesus' message is so intimately tied to his person and mission that they can't be separated.

Or what of the *philosophical* aspects of a religious view? For instance, reincarnation is a commonly accepted view within many Eastern philosophies. The law of *karma*, the cosmic law of cause and effect, means that what we choose in one life—whether good or bad—is repaid in the next. This cycle of birth and rebirth continues until eventually reaching *nirvana* (when, the Buddhist believes, a faithful person achieves the eradication of desire), thus obtaining deliverance or liberation (*moksha*) from the imprisonment of birth. But there is a logical implausibility to this central tenet of many Eastern views: If one's life circumstances are the result of previous choices, how did this cycle begin in the first place? And if everyone eventually achieves release from the cycle of rebirths, *why*, given an infinite series of past opportunities, *hasn't this release already been achieved by all?*[5] An infinite past should offer ample opportunity for everyone to be freed from this cycle. The fact that we aren't already all freed from it is philosophically problematic for the reincarnationist.

A final example is the *experiential relevance* of a religion—that its claims fit the facts of experience. For instance, let's consider scientific experience. According to the best evidence, the universe began about 15 billion years ago—a beginning known as the Big Bang.[6] Previously there had been two other competing hypotheses, which have been dismissed by contemporary physics: (a) an eternal "steady-state" universe or (b) one which has undergone an infinite number of oscillations or expansions and contractions.[7]

Now, if the universe *began* to exist, it must have had a cause, since it simply couldn't have popped into being out of nothing. How then could it have come about? What triggered the physical beginning of the universe? Although I cannot elaborate on the matter here,[8] a personal agent—God—offers a sufficient explanation for the beginning of matter and space-time. This God brought about a state of change out of a changeless one. Many cosmologists are discovering that the Big Bang theory fits quite nicely with the Christian doctrine of Creation out of nothing. The beginning of the physical universe would thus be an argument for a *personal* God (as theism maintains) and against the typical Eastern religious viewpoint—that the Ultimate Reality (e.g., *Brahman*) is *impersonal*.[9]

Sixth, *since certain religions are intellectually preferable to others, all religions shouldn't be reduced to the same level of legitimacy*: Simply because there are similar moral fruits among religions, one can't thereby conclude that they are intellectually on par. What about pseudo-Christian cults like Mormonism or the Jehovah's Witnesses, which espouse similar moral virtues but are founded on dubious intellectual foundations and on charlatanry?[10] The examples of intellectually dubious religions and cults could be multiplied indefinitely. If these religions—whether the polytheism of ancient Rome or Jim Jones-like cults—were to somehow produce moral fruits in their adherents, would this legitimize what would otherwise be highly suspect?[11]

In light of the moral fruitfulness of world religions, we can affirm that Christians are called to help their disadvantaged brothers and sisters in Christ's name (Matt. 25:31–46) and that those who claim to know God must exhibit love (1 John 4:7–8). The Bible itself doesn't deny the possibility of virtue and moral goodness in pagans—what has been called "common grace"—but such relative goodness is insufficient to bring a person into right standing before a holy God. From the Christian perspective, what is foremost is *the need for reconciliation with God*—which Christianity proclaims takes place through Jesus, that "God was reconciling the world to himself in Christ" (2 Cor. 5:19).

We could add that Hick's assertion about the intrinsic and saving value of ethical goodness exhibited by, say, love or compassion actually runs *counter* to his own presuppositions. That is, Hick has no foundation for such a position. So we could ask, "Which religion's view of Ultimate Reality even affords Hick the basis for considering *love* or *compassion* to be the criterion for a religion's capacity to save or liberate?" Put another way, "Which religion or worldview best grounds the reality of love and compassion?" It is no secret that Hick himself rejects a *personal* "God" in favor of an *impersonal* Ultimate Reality.[12] Yet we have to wonder how a relational and personal quality such as love or compassion could be grounded in an impersonal Reality. Rather, doesn't theism or—even more so—a *Trinitarian* theism in which Father, Son, and Spirit enjoy a deep, loving communion ("perichoresis") from eternity provide such a basis? Ironically, the quality Hick utilizes to validate religious pluralism is actually found within the theistic tradition—especially that of Christian theism.

Hick's use of saintliness—or, in the case of Knitter, the capacity of religions to promote socio-economic, cultural, or spiritual freedom—to determine the equality or parity of the world's religions is hardly the only available criterion to judge a religion as able to save or liberate. Besides that, the virtue of love or compassion is simply *incompatible* with Hick's starting assumptions. And he himself seems quite aware that if Jesus believed himself to stand in the place of God, and if he rose bodily from the dead, this would be problematic for his thesis.

Deflating "Mahatma Gandhi Was a Saint If Ever There Was One."

- If the pluralist starts at "ground level" in assessing religions, why think that *moral fruitfulness* or *saintliness* is the ultimate criterion? On what basis should we accept this?
- Again, the pluralist view is no less exclusivistic than the Christian. The pluralist ends up downplaying or distorting certain Christian tenets in order to defend his pluralistic views.
- How does the pluralist *know* that genuine moral transformation is taking place? Perhaps it only *appears* to be so. Yet the pluralist gives the impression that he sees what the exclusivist hasn't seen.
- Pragmatically speaking, pluralism may *diminish* moral transformation within established religions by judging central religious tenets to be false. The beliefs that the faithful considered true and motivating toward ethical living are now considered "metaphorical" and literally false.
- Why should we judge a religion's capacity to save based solely on moral fruitfulness? Even atheists or agnostics could display these fruits.
  (1) What of the *historical reliability* of a religion's claims?
  (2) What of the *philosophical defensibility* of a religion's views?
  (3) What of the *experiential relevance* of a religion (for example, the scientific support for belief in Creation)?
  (4) What if a religion is built on *shaky or dubious foundations?*
- If love or compassion are the fruit of religion, it is *Trinitarian theism* that provides a foundation for such ethical values—not belief in an impersonal Reality.

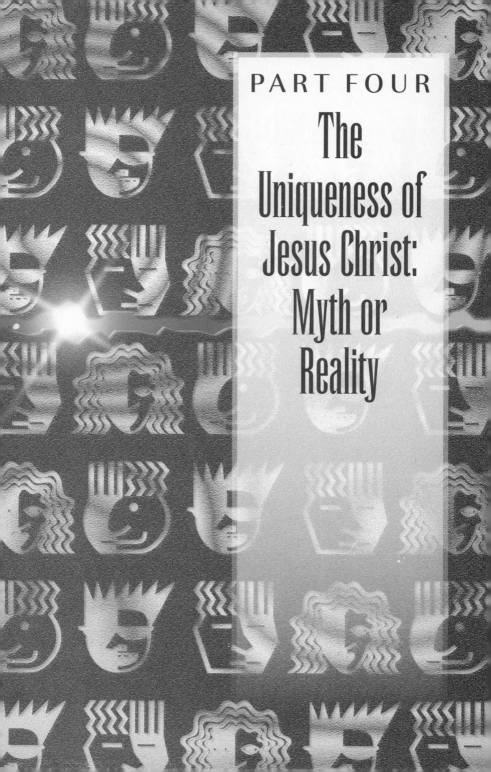

PART FOUR

The Uniqueness of Jesus Christ: Myth or Reality

I F JESUS IS TRULY GOD incarnate and his death alone is the sole basis of salvation, John Hick admits, "then the only doorway to eternal life is the Christian faith."[1] As he knows, the substitutionary Atonement and the uniqueness of Christianity presuppose Jesus' deity.[2] I'm not trying to single out Hick, but if pluralism is wrong and orthodox Christianity correct, then Hick is in a heap of trouble!

Like other non-Christians who knowingly reject the claims of Christianity, Hick denies certain basic assumptions that Christians take for granted. Hick asserts that New Testament scholarship has shown that "fragmentary and ambiguous are the data available to us" about Jesus. Moreover, the imaginations of individuals and communities have "projected" their own ideal of Jesus into the New Testament.[3] While Hick admits that Jesus was a real man who lived in first-century Palestine, he eventually became divinized or "apotheosized" by his followers, just like the historical person Gautama came to be revered as Buddha.[4]

Although Jesus' rising from the dead—and however this is to be understood is an ambiguous question, to Hick's mind—sets him apart from Gautama, there is no connection between his resurrection and his divinity any more than Lazarus or Jairus' daughter.[5]

Jesus was someone who was "intensely and overwhelmingly conscious of the reality of God," Hick claims. He was "powerfully God-conscious." So to be in the presence of the Nazarene was not to be literally in God's presence; rather, "We could catch something of that consciousness by spiritual contagion."[6] Throughout the ages, however, Jesus' devotees have believed a metaphorical idea. They have believed a story—a "myth"—that is not literally true, but rather "invites a particular attitude in its hearers."[7] Jesus himself, however, did not claim to be God; instead, his deity was a "creation" by the church.[8]

Hick's position illustrates to us that besides the alternative of Jesus' being "Lord," "liar," or "lunatic"[9]—the well-known trilemma most memorably expressed by C. S. Lewis—there is yet *another* alternative that many seriously entertain. The fourth alternative is that Jesus Christ as he is known by the

Christian community is not the Jesus of history but a "myth" or "legend." So we need to add to "Lord," "liar," and "lunatic" another L-word—"legend."[10]

As it turns out, the critic of Christianity who hides behind "Jesus as legend" takes refuge in a perspective that has not fared well recently. Virtually no reference is made to myth in the recent historical-Jesus literature[11]—although the Jesus Seminar has recently revived the notion of myth in the Gospels.[12]

On the contrary, New Testament scholarship has increasingly recognized that the Gospels offer reliable depictions of first-century Judaism as well as an accurate portrait of Jesus and his ministry. The philosophically driven view that the Gospels are myth is riddled with problems.

So who *was* Jesus? Was he a wandering *hasid*, or holy man, as Geza Vermes and A. N. Wilson propose? Was he a "peasant Jewish Cynic," as John Dominic Crossan alleges? Was he a magician who sought to lead Israel astray, as the Talmud holds? Was he a self-proclaimed prophet who died in disillusionment, as Albert Schweitzer maintained? Was he some first-century personage whose purported miracles and divinity were mere myths or fabrications by the early church—as David F. Strauss, Rudolf Bultmann, and John Hick suggest? Or was he, as the Gospels assert, "the Christ, the Son of the living God"?

Much can be said in defense of Jesus' uniqueness, and there is a vast amount of literature available about the historical Jesus;[13] we will merely be able to offer general remarks and some helpful pointers. In doing so, we will assume two things. First, we will take for granted that the study of history is not a relativistic undertaking; its "truth" isn't simply a cultural or psychological concoction of historians that will be remixed and reheated in the next generation. As Alexander Pope humorously captures it in his *Essay on Criticism*:

> We think our fathers fools,
> So wise we grow;
> Our wiser sons, no doubt,
> Will think us so.[14]

Admittedly, the recounting of historical events is to some degree *interpretative* and not merely rehearsing brute facts. So we deal with facts along with interpretation. It simply doesn't follow, though, that all attempts at history are doomed to relativistic or subjectivistic speculation. After all, we can often give plausible evidence that someone is doing *bad* history—such as the Holocaust deniers. Or during the Renaissance, Lorenzo Valla's historical research demonstrated the "Donation of Constantine" was a forgery because of certain anachronisms he saw in this document. Another example is that of the pro-Stalinist Claud Cockburn, former journalist of the *London Times* and editor of *The Week*, who had fabricated entirely imaginary news stories to promote communism. He believed that the cause for which a man "is fighting is worth lying for."[15] It's obvious that there is a significant contrast between a deceptive fabricator and a finite historian trying to make sense of the available data. As I will express later, there is a difference between *history* and *propaganda*.

Moreover, even if historical accounts are *incomplete*, that doesn't logically mean they are false or totally lacking in objectivity. It's the burden of the historical relativist to show *how* this necessarily follows. Furthermore, although the historical relativist maintains that no historian can shake free of his own subjective and cultural constraints to draw objectively true conclusions, he still always takes *his own* views more seriously than he does those of his counterparts![16] The historical relativist appears to speak absolutely and as an *objective* observer about the truth of historical relativism!

Second, we assume that *Jesus did exist*, that he lived in first-century Palestine, gathered a group of followers, was crucified under Pontius Pilate through the instigation of certain religious leaders, and that a significant religious movement began shortly after his death. These are facts that almost no serious historian would contest.[17] (One historian who denies Jesus ever existed is G. A. Wells. The arguments in his book *Did Jesus Exist?*,[18] however, are based on antiquated and/or unsubstantiated claims.[19])

But where does the Christian begin defending the uniqueness of Jesus in a post-Christian age? When we hear unorthodox and often unsubstantiated assessments about Jesus by Hick or the liberal Jesus Seminar, we can raise serious questions about their flawed historical methodology.[20] The Christian need not fear the results of historical research about Jesus, although he *should* be aware of the presuppositions that may be influencing it. As historian Paul Johnson has put it:

> A Christian with faith has nothing to fear from the facts. . . . The Christian . . . should not feel himself inhibited in the smallest degree from following the line of his inquiries—the line of truth—whithersoever it may lead. Indeed, I would say he is positively bound to follow it. He should, in fact, be freer than the non-Christian, who tends to be precommitted by his own rejection of Christian truth.[21]

CHAPTER 15

"You Can't Trust the Gospels. They're Unreliable."

THE CHRISTIAN HAS NO WAY TO REFUTE SKEPTICISM about the unique claims and deeds of the historical Jesus without first establishing that the *texts* that record his claims are generally reliable. If the Gospels are fictitious, then a defense of Jesus' self-understanding and unique role in salvation will also come under fire. So what follows are a few points to keep in mind when discussing the Bible's historical reliability.[1]

First, *the Christian doesn't need to start a discussion with a skeptic assuming that the Gospels are "sacred writings" or "inerrant."* He only needs to argue that they purport to be historical and that they can be shown to be reliable for historical purposes. The Christian can challenge the skeptical inquirer: "Treat the Gospels just like you would any other historical document. Subject it to the same criteria. Treat it just like Caesar's *Gallic Wars*, Josephus' *Jewish Wars*, or Tacitus' *Annals of Imperial Rome*. If you accept *them* as generally accurate, on what basis would you discount the reliability of the Gospels?" My experience has shown that few skeptics have assessed the Gospel accounts in this light. When I have talked about the testimony of Jesus in the Gospels, I have been told that certain esoteric or "secret Gospels" should be preferred over the canonical ones. Some of my Muslim friends have recommended the *Gospel of Barnabas* as the "real"—read, "Muslim"—Jesus. Others have placed more confidence in the Gnostic *Gospel of Thomas* or the New-Age Akashic records. When I have asked *why* they prefer these documents to the Gospels, they never furnish me with any good reasons to reject the Gospels' reliability. (This isn't to say that some critics won't attempt reasons for accepting such books, but it is a common tendency not to.) Rather than asking which historical hypothesis has the best explanatory power or is most plausible or how it fares in comparison to its rivals,[2] most skeptics, if they don't reject all such documents, place far greater confidence in spurious or dubious sources than they do in the Gospels.

Let's examine just one of these alleged sources for the life of Jesus in detail—the *Gospel of Thomas*. The media-alluring Jesus Seminar has wrongly presumed the *Gospel of Thomas* as a legitimate source of information about Jesus, being dated, we are told, at A.D. 50. This early date, however, is wholly unwarranted. *No* evidence supports a date earlier than A.D. 150.[3] Also, while one-third to one-half of the sayings in *Thomas* do have parallels in the Gospels, many of them are unorthodox sayings that reflect the "Gnostic" heresy. (Full-blown Gnosticism was a *second*-century phenomenon that had to do with salvation through enlightenment for an elite few. It emphasized the goodness of the spirit and the badness of the material or physical.) Now if *Thomas* were really written as early as A.D. 50 and authentic, at least some of these Gnostic sayings would have been found within the four Gospels. But what is apparent is that the Gospel writers are cited by *Thomas*, not vice versa. Moreover, *Thomas* lacks any historical narrative—a typical omission of second-century Gnostic texts, which weren't concerned with God's acting in history.[4]

Another claim that brings the Gospels under fire is the alleged anti-Semitism some Jewish scholars claim to find in the Gospels, especially the Gospel of John's references to "the Jews."[5] They take negative references at face value but at the same time overlook passages that speak *positively* of the Jews (for example, Jesus is "a Jew" [John 4:9] and salvation is "of the Jews" [John 4:22]), or they minimize or explain away passages that reveal Jesus' remarkable identity claims,[6] asserting that such passages are being put on Jesus' lips by the early Christian community.[7] As we look at the New Testament, however, we simply see no racial hatred. Jesus himself was *Jewish*, and he gathered a group of *Jewish* followers who would found the church in *Jerusalem* and contribute to the New Testament. The point of tension is not *race* but *theology*, and it arose *between* Jews, not between Gentile Christians and first-century Judaism.[8]

Another consideration is that the skeptic, in all likelihood, may be convinced that the Gospels offer us accurate historical information in some areas—such as archaeologically confirmed buildings or towns, but he may out-of-hand reject the idea that miracles—such as the Resurrection—can potentially explain other historical data. But this issue goes beyond the matter of historical evidence and shifts to the worldview one will allow. If a person rejects belief in God and the possibility of miracles outright, then no amount of evidence will persuade him to believe otherwise. "A dead man just *doesn't* come back to life," the skeptic assumes. So God's existence and, consequently, the possibility of God's interruption of the natural order, must be answered before that skeptic will entertain miraculous explanations.[9]

Second, *if the New Testament is textually flawed and unreliable, then it can be argued that every other book in antiquity is also unreliable.* In numerous discussions with Muslims, I have been told that we can't trust the Gospel accounts of Jesus. The original Gospel text had become so corrupted over the centuries that the true message of Jesus was distorted.

The only problem with this allegation is that it is wholly unjustified. In the first place, only 1 to 3 percent of the Gospel text is open to any charge of distortion at the hands of copyists. Only in a minute portion of Scripture are we uncertain as to what the original said. In other words, virtually *all* of the original text of the Gospels is recoverable.[10]

In the third place, *the New Testament boasts manuscript support vastly larger than any work of antiquity—close to 5,000 manuscripts and manuscript fragments.*[11] For instance, we accept the authenticity of Thucydides' historical work (460–400 B.C.) even though we have only *eight* manuscripts and a few papyrus scraps.[12] Typically, with many of the works of antiquity—Thucydides, Caesar, Tacitus, Sophocles, or Euripides—we have gaps of hundreds or even over a thousand years from the time of writing to the earliest extant manuscripts,[13] yet these texts are generally presumed authentic. By comparison, the gap between the writing of the New Testament books and the earliest manuscripts of the New Testament we possess is far narrower. Take, for instance, the famous John Rylands papyrus fragment of John 18:31–33; 37–38, which dates to around A.D. 140; the manuscript was written only *fifty* years after John wrote his Gospel. This is just one of many such examples. So from a textual point of view, the Gospels are excellent, reliable ancient documents.

Fourth, *as we do with other historical documents, we should assume the Gospels are reliable unless there are reasons to believe the contrary.*[14] Some scholars make a curious assumption about New Testament documents—namely, that they are unreliable unless this can be shown otherwise through independent corroboration. They assume distortion and error unless shown the contrary. But this approach leads to historical skepticism. Other works of antiquity, we noted, aren't handled in this way.[15] The proper approach to studying ancient documents for the purposes of writing history is to assume accuracy and truth-telling unless we are led to believe otherwise. That is, we should accept them at face value unless those sources or individual writers have something about them that makes them inherently suspicious.

The appropriateness of this approach seems obvious. In our everyday conversations, for example, we assume people are telling us the truth. If someone introduces himself to me as "Jeff," I don't ask to check his birth certificate or driver's license. I take for granted he is telling me the truth. We seldom presuppose a skeptical approach. If we assumed that everyone were lying until it could be proven otherwise, then there would be no point in lying! In a court of law, we presume innocence until guilt is proven, laying the burden of proof on the skeptic. The bare fact that a purportedly historical document can't be verified by another text shouldn't disqualify that document.

Deflating "You Can't Trust the Gospels. They're Unreliable."

- Without assuming that the Gospels are "holy books" or "inerrant," they can be shown to be reliable for historical purposes.
- Ask the person who rejects the Gospels' historical reliability, "On what basis do you reject their general accuracy?" If someone favors an unorthodox "Gospel" of Jesus (such as *Thomas*) over the canonical Gospels, ask why.
- If the New Testament is textually flawed, then so is every other work of antiquity. To the contrary, these manuscripts are quite reliable.
- Typically, we assume historical documents are reliable unless we have good reason to doubt them. Why should this procedure be reversed—making biblical texts false until proven true?

CHAPTER 16

"Jesus' Followers *Fabricated* the Stories and Sayings of Jesus."

WHEN MY WIFE AND I VISITED KIEV shortly after the breakup of the Soviet Union, we heard a standing joke bandied about concerning two of Russia's most prominent newspapers, *Pravda* and *Izvestia*. *Pravda* means "truth" and *Izvestia* means "news." Because of the well-known Communist propagandizing and serious distortion in reporting, we were told that there was no *pravda* in *Izvestia* and no *izvestia* in *Pravda*!

Some critics allege the same can be said about accurately recounting history: If an author has certain convictions or presuppositions, he can't accurately recount history. He is merely spewing propaganda. For instance, Thomas Sheehan, Loyola philosophy professor and author of *The First Coming: How the Kingdom of God Became Christianity*, maintains that "Jesus did not think he was divine," nor did he "assert any of the messianic claims that the New Testament attributes to him."[1] Although Jesus believed himself to be an eschatological prophet, within a half-century the church came to believe he was the divine Son of God. Sheehan argues for these claims in part by saying that because the Gospels are "religious testimonies," they cannot be trusted.[2] In the same vein, Hick maintains that "the documents [the Gospels] are all documents of faith."[3] The assumption is clear—a faith-perspective distorts history.

On the contrary, holding this view ultimately leads to historical skepticism—because *all* historians write with a purpose, and Sheehan, though not a historian, is no exception. Purposes extend even to the point of including certain materials and omitting others. If writing with a goal—whether it be evan-

100 • "TRUE FOR YOU, BUT NOT FOR ME."

gelistic, apologetic, or didactic—implies propaganda, then *all* recorded history is propaganda. But most of us recognize that *belief* shouldn't be confused with *reason for belief*. In other words, to hold a belief strongly doesn't necessarily imply that the belief is wrong. Instead, the *basis* for that belief should first be explored; a work shouldn't be dismissed simply because of the strong convictions of the writer.[4] Should we discount the factuality or reliability of the accounts of Nazi concentration camp survivors simply because they passionately recount their story? Aren't the Holocaust deniers and revisionists, who can hardly be called dispassionate, the ones who falsify history?[5]

Furthermore, this error of Sheehan, Hick, and others fails to distinguish between *innocuous* presuppositions and *vicious* ones. Innocuous presuppositions don't end up distorting historical evidence. They don't become the *basis* of accepting a historical hypothesis. Vicious ones, on the other hand, twist and warp the evidence in a propaganda-like manner. They override the evidence in order to inevitably conclude what was presupposed from the start. This ends up being a vicious circle.[6]

And when it comes to the Gospels, the question must be raised: What actually motivated the evangelists to write what and as they did? A good case can be made that it was their own experience with Jesus.

Now when it comes to actually examining the historicity of the Gospels, we see remarkable indications of accuracy. Take John's Gospel, which often isn't accepted as reliable history because it contains more developed theological reflection than Matthew, Mark, and Luke. Yet this Gospel reveals a first-century Palestinian background rooted in the Old Testament—as the discovery of the Dead Sea Scrolls confirmed this through, for instance, their reference to "sons of light" and "sons of darkness." It also offers exceptional topographical information that has been repeatedly confirmed archaeologically. John's mention of Jacob's well at Sychar (4:5), the pool of Bethesda (with five porticoes) by the Sheep Gate (5:2), the pool of Siloam (9:7), and Solomon's Colonnade (10:23) have had the strong support of archaeology. In light of the extensive usage of the "witness" theme in this Gospel, the author's emphasis is clear that the incidents included can be relied upon (see 21:24). John is even interested in chronology and specific times (1:29, 35, 43: "the next day"; 4:43: "after the two days"). John is also familiar with particular cultural understandings such as the relationship between Jews and Samaritans (4:27), the general view of women in society (4:27), or the nature of Sabbath regulations (5:10).[7]

So if the reliability of the Gospels can be shown historically and archaeologically, this can, in part, help defuse skepticism and inspire greater confidence regarding, say, the claims or resurrection of Jesus.[8] Our first point is this: *When engaging the skeptic, the Christian can offer good reasons for taking the Gospels to be historically reliable. This, then, may provide a platform for speaking about the claims and deeds of Christ.* As Craig Blomberg asserts, "Once a historian has proved reliable where verifiable, once apparent errors or contradictions receive plausible solutions, the appropriate approach is to give that writer the benefit of the doubt in areas where verification is not possible."[9]

Second, *the claim that the early Christian communities read back into Jesus' teachings their own concerns and controversies won't withstand scrutiny.* If such matters were invented and projected backward to Jesus to substantiate them, then why are issues such as spiritual gifts (e.g., speaking in tongues [1 Cor. 12, 14]); divorcing when deserted by an unbelieving spouse (1 Cor. 7:15); eating meat offered to idols (1 Cor. 8); or circumcision (Acts 15)—issues that received significant attention in early Christian communities—glaringly absent in Jesus' teaching? These disputes often divided many of the early Christian communities, but we don't find Jesus addressing them. Rather, the epistles and to some extent the book of Acts—*not* the teachings of Jesus—inform us of these controversies. So to allege that, in the midst of their disputes and concerns, early Christians fabricated sayings and attributed them to Jesus doesn't square with the New Testament evidence.

Third, *the Gospels—primarily Mark, Matthew, and Luke—offer a portrait of Jesus within one generation of his death, which tends to ensure the accurate transmission of the Jesus-tradition.* It's taken for granted in New Testament scholarship that Mark's gospel was written first and that Matthew and Luke independently follow Mark as their primary source.[10] Luke's gospel, then, was obviously written before its companion volume (Acts) was.

Now, a very good case can be made for the completing of Acts before A.D. 62–64,[11] when Paul was executed under Nero's order. At the end of Acts, Paul is still under house arrest in Rome. Luke, who was interested in significant events in early Christianity, such as the martyrdom of prominent Christians (e.g., Stephen and James), surely would have included Paul's death had he known about it. The best explanation for Luke's not having mentioned Paul's execution—or, for that matter, the siege and destruction of Jerusalem in A.D. 70 or the Neronian persecution—is that this event hadn't yet taken place. So Acts was in all likelihood written before A.D. 62.[12] So we can assert on good grounds that the Synoptic Gospels (Matthew, Mark, and Luke) may well have been written within thirty years of Jesus' death—a period in which the accuracy of these Gospels could be easily checked or challenged by eyewitnesses or inquirers.[13]

The early date of these Gospels, besides other factors, gives many conservative scholars confidence that what they recorded is trustworthy. Not only were the Gospel writers interested in recording accurate history (see Luke 1:1–4), first-century Palestinian Jews at the various levels of society were able to memorize large portions of Scripture. Given (1) the importance of memorization and oral tradition in first-century Palestine, (2) the practice of (occasionally) writing down and preserving the teachings of rabbis by their disciples, (3) the fact that the vast majority of Jesus' teaching was in poetic (and easily memorizable) form, (4) the importance and revered status of religious traditions in Palestine, and (5) the presence of apostolic authority in Jerusalem to ensure the accurate transmission of tradition (and to check potential heresy), we have good reason to believe that the material in the Gospels was carefully and correctly set down.[14]

Another factor that contributes to the conviction that the Gospels are reliable is the data of some of Paul's writings (Romans, 1 Corinthians, 1 Thessalonians) and James' epistle, all of which *pre-date* the writing of the Gospels (from the late A.D. 40s through about 57).[15] James' using much material from the Sermon on the Mount (Matt. 5–7) reminds us that Jesus' teachings were being accurately preserved. Besides his familiarity with Jesus' teaching from the Sermon on the Mount (for example, in Romans 12:17–21), Paul is familiar with Jesus' words on divorce and remarriage (1 Cor. 7:10; compare Mark 10:10–12) and with the tradition of the last supper (1 Cor. 11:23–25; compare Luke 22:19–20). Paul is also familiar with the historical Jesus: the virgin birth (Gal. 4:4), his Davidic descent (Rom. 1:3), and being born under the law (Gal. 4:4, which appears to highlight Jesus' circumcision and presentation in the temple [Luke 2:22–24]), the last supper/passion (1 Cor. 11:23ff.), and the plot to kill Jesus (1 Thess. 2:14–15)—not to mention the historicity of his resurrection in 1 Corinthians 15.[16]

What cannot be doubted is that many New Testament critics have approached the Gospels with an utterly unjustified skepticism—a skepticism that wouldn't be considered justified in any other branch of ancient history. New Testament scholar R. T. France declares that "at the level of their literary and historical character we have good reason to treat the Gospels as a source of information on the life and teachings of Jesus, and thus on the historical origins of Christianity."[17] The Greco-Roman historian A. N. Sherwin-White—evidently *not* a Christian—claimed: "It is astonishing that while Greco-Roman historians have been growing in confidence, the twentieth-century study of Gospel narratives, *starting from no less promising material*, has taken so gloomy a turn."[18]

Fourth, *the simple, unsophisticated nature of the Gospels attests to their reliability rather than to their being fabrications.* It isn't unusual to read skeptics who point out alleged contradictions or lack of harmonization in, say, the Gospel accounts of the Resurrection narratives.[19] But although the numbers of women, for example, differ from Gospel to Gospel, no evangelist asserts that *only so many* women went to the tomb. And even when it *appears* in

John's Gospel that only Mary Magdalene was at the tomb, she implies that she wasn't alone: "*We* don't know where they have put him" (John 20:2).

Now, even if actual discrepancies existed in the Gospels, no good historian rejects a document because of conflicts in secondary matters. What is beyond doubt is that there is a general core of agreement among the Gospels. In any event, it's clear that the Gospel writers were *not* plotting or fabricating these stories. Otherwise, they would have attempted to be more uniform in their accounting. For example, a fabricated account most likely would *not* have relied on women as the first witnesses of the Resurrection because of their typically lower status in Jewish society.

Critics may point to the sudden "shorter" ending of Mark's gospel—at 16:8, where the women leave the angel at the tomb trembling, bewildered, and not speaking to anyone (though various versions continue with verses 9–20, which were added later). Skeptic Randel Helms calls this "one of the strangest and most unsatisfying moments in all the Bible."[20] As we will see again later on, however, this ending meshes quite well with Mark's emphasis on the fact that the nature of Jesus' messiahship couldn't be understood apart from his death. While Jesus would warn people, "See that you say nothing to anyone," in order to not perpetuate misunderstanding, the women ironically "said nothing to anyone" (16:8), even though Jesus had fulfilled his mission on the cross and, according to the angel, had been raised from the dead. They kept silent when they no longer needed to! What Mark attempts to do in his gospel is call his audience, by way of pastoral encouragement, to persevere despite past failure and disobedience. So in spite of the failure and fear of the disciples throughout the book—which Mark highlights more than the other Gospel writers—they can derive courage and hope from the promise that Jesus is risen and will meet them in Galilee (16:6–7).[21]

An important criterion that helps us discern the authenticity of Jesus' sayings and deeds and thus the reliability of the Gospels is the "criterion of embarrassment"—actions or sayings of Jesus that would have embarrassed or caused difficulty for the early church. In other words, *why* would the early church fabricate what it knew to be potentially embarrassing incidents?[22] For example, Jesus submits to baptism by the "unworthy" John the Baptist (Mark 1:4–11).[23] Another example is that Jesus didn't know the time of his return (Mark 13:32). According to Christian orthodoxy, Jesus, being divine, *could* have known the date of his return before his death and resurrection, but he voluntarily relinquished this information as part of his earthly mission. So why would the early church take pains to *invent* a saying of Jesus that would bring possible embarrassment? We could also add incidents such as Jesus' cursing a fig tree (Mark 11:12–14), allowing unclean spirits to enter swine and immediately destroy them (Luke 8:32–33), his family's believing he was out of his mind (Mark 3:21), the sometimes unimpressive results of his ministry (Mark 6:5–6; John 6:66), and his refusal to do miracles (Matt. 13:58).

Furthermore, early Jewish Christians wouldn't likely have concocted stories of miracles to defend Jesus' messiahship; it simply wouldn't have helped their case. Most Jews expected the Messiah to be a king, a political deliverer, a shepherd over Israel—not a miracle-worker: "Messianic beliefs simply did not require a prospective Messiah to heal and exorcise demons. Therefore, one should hardly expect early Christians to find it necessary to create such a large number of miracle stories."[24] Not only this, but such a good crop of miracle stories probably didn't originate in the early church because Jesus periodically refused to perform miracles to simply astonish his audience (Mark 6:1–6; Matt. 13:58). This fact—an element of the criterion of embarrassment—could have been viewed, then, as his *inability* to perform them.[25] It is unlikely that the authors would have risked the "embarrassment" of recording such things if they weren't factually accurate.

At the beginning of this section, we argued that the Christian cannot simply say to the skeptic, "But the Gospels *say* Jesus made unique claims about himself" because the skeptic will no doubt raise questions about the very reliability of the Gospels. We have laid out some of the reasons for taking the Gospels to be generally reliable. Although much more could be said, the Gospels'—and New Testament's—massive manuscript evidence, their historical reliability, the straightforward and simple nature of the Gospel narratives, and other factors allow us to move forward to the claims of Jesus of Nazareth. Having noted the reasonable evidence to accept the Gospel tradition, we can move to issues surrounding Jesus' uniqueness.

Deflating "Jesus' Followers *Fabricated* the Stories and Sayings of Jesus."

- To say that one writes with an evangelistic or apologetical purpose doesn't mean what is written is unreliable. Passion or zeal—as with the Holocaust survivors—need not entail distortion of data.
- Point out places where the Gospels show themselves to be reliable historically and archaeologically. This lends credibility to what cannot be directly verified—Jesus' claims and deeds.
- Early Christians didn't read back into Jesus' teachings their own concerns and issues:
  (1) Many of the controversial issues in the epistles aren't even mentioned in the Gospels (circumcision, speaking in tongues, eating meat offered to idols, etc.).
  (2) Matthew, Mark, and Luke offer a portrait of Jesus within one generation of his death. Note the case of Acts, which was likely written

before Paul's death (*ca.* A.D. 64), which means that Luke's gospel was written earlier than this and that Mark, which Luke follows, was written even earlier.

(3) First-century Palestinian Jews were concerned about accurately preserving tradition, and this concern is reflected in the epistles—for example, themes from the Sermon on the Mount are reflected in James and the tradition of the Last Supper is mentioned in 1 Corinthians 11.

(4) The Gospels do not reflect a fabrication. There is a simplicity to them, making fabrications unlikely. (Note the women as witnesses of Jesus' resurrection despite their lower societal status, or the "embarrassing" points that would probably be deleted if the Gospel stories or sayings were fabricated—Jesus' baptism by John, his ignorance of the time of his own return, his not doing miracles in some places).

(5) Why invent so many miracle stories, when most Jews expected a political deliverer as Messiah, not a wonder-worker?

CHAPTER 17

"Jesus Is Just Like Any Other Great Religious Leader."

J ESUS WAS A WISE TEACHER, many pluralists will admit. Others prefer to call him a charismatic leader or a social reformer. But the farthest any pluralist wants to go in applauding Jesus is to say that he was "God-conscious." In other words, to the skeptic, Jesus was strictly human, not the God-man of orthodox Christianity. And most definitely of all, they say, Jesus didn't teach that he was divine. That notion "is a creation of the church, one that Jesus himself would probably have regarded as blasphemous."[1]

These are common assertions heard from scholars, co-workers, and classmates. They deserve some investigation.

First, *Jesus not only made claims that no other religious founder did, but the Gospels' portrait of him doesn't easily coincide with alleged parallels*: To hear people lump Jesus in the same category as the founders of other world religions is entirely common. Mahatma Gandhi said Jesus was "a great world teacher among others."[2] Because Jesus preached a religion of universal love, Gandhi could have Jesus in his heart just as he could Krishna or Rama.[3] His version of Hinduism had room for Jesus just as it did for Muhammad, Zoroaster (the founder of Zoroastrianism), and Moses.[4] For Ghandi, Buddha and Jesus were exemplary in their active spirituality and their avoidance of "idle meditation."[5] Yet Gandhi didn't see Jesus as any more or less worthy of praise than the founders of other religions.

However, when we analyze the personal *claims* that these founders made, we see a marked distinction between Jesus and the rest[6] (not to mention the evidence corroborating their respective claims). Whether in the Orient or the

Occident, the founders of the world's great religions made no claims as extravagant as Jesus of Nazareth did: to forgive sins, to be the judge of all, to always be present with his followers throughout the ages, to hear their prayers. For instance, according to Stuart Hackett, a philosopher well-versed in Eastern thought,[7]

> Oriental scholars generally admit that none of their seminal thinkers like Buddha, Confucius, or Lao-Tzu (Taoism's alleged founder) made any claims that parallel the astonishing claims to divine authority that Jesus did. Furthermore, Hindu claims of "avatars," or incarnate gods like Krishna, actually prove nothing since Hinduism, in its more reflective forms, is pantheistic (i.e., everything is God or Ultimate Reality). In a sense, then, *everything* is an incarnation of the Ultimate Reality, Brahma, although any particular distinctions between persons or things as well as the existence of the external physical world are typically considered to be illusory (*maya*).[8]

So, in Hinduism, we have no real revelation of the Ultimate Reality, as we do in Christianity. Although somewhat overstated, C. S. Lewis aptly illustrates our point:

> If you had gone to Buddha and asked him, "Are you the son of Bramah?" he would have said, "My son, you are still in the vale of illusion." If you had gone to Socrates and asked, "Are you Zeus?" he would have laughed at you. If you had gone to Mohammed and asked, "Are you Allah?" he would first have rent his clothes and then cut your head off. If you had asked Confucius, "Are you Heaven?", I think he would have probably replied, "Remarks which are not in accordance with nature are in bad taste." The idea of a great moral teacher saying what Christ said is out of the question.[9]

A further point needs to be made. It isn't unusual for some to claim that Jesus' birth, deification, or resurrection are beliefs paralleled in the pagan religions and cultures surrounding Palestine. Behind this claim is the assumption that Christianity must have been *influenced* by these beliefs, or at least that Christian beliefs are "just like" these other religious ones—a human concoction.[10] For example, John Dominic Crossan, co-founder of the Jesus Seminar, compares the birth and deification of Jesus to that of Gaius Octavius (b. 23 Sept. 63 B.C.), Julius Caesar's son. (Crossan calls this "a tale of two gods.")[11]

However, simply to lump together one similar-sounding belief with another rather than taking each claim on a *case-by-case* basis will not do. This phenomenon has rightly been called "parallelomania."[12] In fact, the once-influential "history of religions" school, which engaged in parallelomania by tying Christianity to paganism, was unable to muster much force precisely because its parallels were simply *too vague*.[13]

Deflating "Jesus Is Just Like Any Other Great Religious Leader."

- Jesus made *claims for himself* that no other religious founder did: to forgive sins, to be the judge of all people, to always be present with his followers, to hear their prayers, etc.
- The alleged "parallels" between Jesus and pagan deities that die and rise again are simply too vague to account for what we see in the Gospels—and it is a Jewish background that provides the necessary worldview to place Jesus in a proper context.

CHAPTER 18

"People Claim JFK and Elvis Are Alive, Too!"

ANYONE WHO HAS EVER STOOD in the check-out line at a grocery store has seen tabloids headlining rumors of John F. Kennedy or Elvis Presley reappearing after their deaths. While such rumors make for sensational stories, they become a pesky annoyance to Christians when skeptics toss out statements like "See, it's just like the resurrection of Jesus—a big hoax." More menacingly, critical scholars appeal to alleged parallels of "resurrections" in the ancient world to nullify the claim that Jesus rose from the dead.

How should we respond to these notions? We must call for *substantiation*. Anyone can *make* a claim, but to *justify* it is not so simple. When Christians make a claim that Jesus rose from the dead, they have a wealth of historical evidence on their side—quite unlike the rumors about the relatively recent deaths of JFK or Elvis. It is unfair to the historical evidence to throw the resurrection of Jesus in with crackpot claims. The person who equates Jesus with JFK or Elvis should be asked what *substantiation* there is for the allegation. Apologist Gary Habermas has investigated purported claims in the *ancient* world of a personage's resurrection or translation into heaven. He argues that such sources are generally late in their "recounting," put forth questionable or contradictory accounts, and aren't open to any sort of verification.[1]

The Christian can't allow the reality of Christ's resurrection to be side-tracked by these charges, either silly or serious.

Ironically, most skeptics of the Resurrection are far more critical of the Gospel accounts than they are of the claims of resurrection in other religions! But this is unfair and arbitrary, and we can take pains to point that out. Resurrection accounts of other religions are far different from the New Testament's common-sense defense of Christ's resurrection, which goes to great lengths to defend the historicity of this event, such as in 1 Corinthians 15.

As we have seen, those who lump Jesus together with all of the world religions' founders typically neglect to take into account the significance of Jesus' *claims* or his *self-understanding*. But, remarkably, they also fail to see the implications of Jesus' uniqueness in his bodily resurrection. This is a highly significant oversight: If Jesus rose from the dead as a vindication of his unique claims, *this provides evidence for Christianity's uniqueness among the world's religions.*

The skeptic might ask, "But isn't the Resurrection an extraordinary event that demands extraordinary substantiation?" Of course! But weighty evidence for this event *is* available. However, an important point needs to be understood: One's outlook or worldview may not allow for God's existence and/or the possibility of miracles. In this case, no matter how remarkable the evidence, it will no doubt be insufficient to overturn an anti-supernaturalistic worldview. But *if* there is no good reason to disallow it, then a supernaturalistic event like the Resurrection has much explanatory power. The Resurrection substantiates the facts surrounding the empty tomb, the boldness of the disciples, and the emergence of the early church. For instance, both Jesus' friends and enemies alike believed that the tomb was empty (Matt. 28:11–15). This implies that *something* happened to the body. The question remains, "Which explanation best accounts for the body's disappearance?"

The occurrence of Jesus' bodily resurrection from the dead is further reinforced by the fact that the first ones to witness the empty tomb were *women*, whose testimony would not be as readily accepted as that of men in first-century Palestine. Now, if the Resurrection appearances to women are a mere legendary addition, wouldn't this be expunged from the narratives—not to mention any reference to skepticism or doubt that the disciples might initially have had?

Furthermore, Jesus appeared not only to fully convinced believers—more than five hundred at one time, 1 Corinthians 15 affirms. His bodily resurrection convinced the *skeptic* Thomas, who cried out in response, "My Lord and my God!" (John 20:28); the *unbeliever* James, Jesus' half-brother, as well as the *enemy* and persecutor of Christians, Paul (1 Cor. 15:7–9). Furthermore, Jesus' followers didn't see a mere apparition. They observed Jesus eating fish and breaking bread. They touched him and grasped him.

Moreover, how could the early church get started so quickly without Jesus' resurrection? The disciples were a frightened, disillusioned lot. What transformed them into bold witnesses who were willing to die—and actually *did* die—for their belief in the resurrected Jesus? Why did they courageously defy Jewish authorities and face imprisonment for what could easily have been refuted if the disciples were up to some "Passover plot"? How could the early church begin in *Jerusalem itself*—not Rome—without Jesus' bodily resurrection to propel it into existence?

What we have here are three strands that reinforce the historicity of the bodily resurrection of Jesus: (1) the *empty tomb*, (2) *Jesus' post-resurrection appearances*, and (3) the *origin of the Christian church*. If the existence of God and the possibility of miracles aren't arbitrarily ruled out of bounds at the outset, and if God had a motive for more fully revealing himself (and there is a plausible expectation of his doing so),[2] these three factors furnish weighty evidence to affirm that God raised Jesus' body from the tomb.[3]

Below are some of the naturalistic—and woefully inadequate—explanations typically offered to explain away the bodily resurrection of Jesus. (I have already attempted to deal with the "late legend" view earlier in this section—though in another setting.) As much has been written in defense of Jesus' bodily resurrection,[4] I will offer only the briefest of responses:

- *"The disciples stole the body"*: As it happens, they were too confused, frightened, and dismayed for such a plan. In addition, the Gospel accounts, Acts, and the New Testament epistles bespeak a sincerity and integrity on the part of the disciples that rules out their being impostors. Furthermore, the disciples initially did *not* believe the women who reported that the tomb was empty (Luke 24:9–11). Moreover, if the disciples stole the body, why would almost all of them die martyrs' deaths for what they *knew* was a lie? And why start preaching in Jerusalem, where such a lie could most easily be exposed?

- *"Jesus' enemies stole the body"*: The problem here is that these enemies could easily have produced the body of Jesus to silence the bold preaching of the apostles. Also, the Jewish leadership began circulating the story that the *disciples* had stolen the body (Matt. 28:12–15), which meant that the Jewish leaders didn't have it.

- *"The women went to the wrong tomb"*: No, the women *knew* where the body had been placed (Luke 23:55), and the angel told them that Jesus was not in the tomb because he had risen. Peter and John went to the tomb and checked it out themselves because they didn't believe the women (Luke 24:11; John 20:3–8). And if the disciples had gone to the wrong tomb, Jesus' enemies would conveniently have pointed out the right one!

- *"Jesus didn't really die. He swooned, and the coolness of the tomb revived him"*: Roman soldiers knew when their victims were dead, and crucifixion meant a virtually certain death.[5] The water that flowed from Jesus' pierced side was probably the pericardial sac surrounding the heart, which fills up only when a person has died. To top this off, Jesus' tomb was sealed, covered with a large stone, and guarded by Roman soldiers. It's beyond farfetched to think that Jesus—who had been severely beaten and then crucified—could wrangle free of his linen wrappings, move the stone, slip past the guards, and then appear to the disciples looking as good as new.

- *"The disciples were hallucinating":*[6] The problem with this view is that hallucinations are only the result of what is already in the mind. And according to first-century Jewish thought, "resurrection" implied a *corporate* rising *at the end of human history*—not an individual resurrection within history. Nor were the disciples expecting a dying and rising Messiah.[7] No, the disciples had no category for a resurrection like Jesus'. Also, his resurrection was no wish fulfillment; the disciples simply were *not* expecting it and on at least three occasions didn't recognize Jesus. This would have been a strange sort of hallucination! Hallucination, besides being unlikely to be experienced by two or more people at the same time, *still* could not account for the empty tomb. Both friend and foe admitted Jesus' tomb was empty.

- *"Jesus rose from the dead even though his body remained in the tomb":* To the Jewish mind, an "empty grave" that contained a body would be a contradiction. Moreover, the disciples and hostile Jewish leaders acknowledged that the tomb was empty. Also, scholars who argue that the disciples saw *non-bodily visions* of Jesus (e.g., the Jesus Seminar) must *still* account for an empty tomb.

- *"Jesus' death and resurrection are just like the other ancient dying-and-rising gods":* Unlike mythical gods that died before winter and rose again in the spring, Jesus' death and resurrection were historical events that took place in early April of, probably, A.D. 30. Hebrews 7:27 reminds us that Jesus' death and resurrection took place once and for all. Furthermore, none of these pagan "savior" gods are purported to have died (1) *voluntarily*, (2) *as punishment for sin*, or (3) *for someone else*. And the Old Testament background to the Gospels provides the sufficient background to account for the theological significance of Jesus' death and resurrection.

Although we could give fuller responses to these naturalistic attempts to explain away Jesus' bodily resurrection, we can affirm that they typically fail to account for, say, the radical transformation of the disciples, the conversion of Jesus' half-brother James, the martyrdom of the disciples, or the virtually immediate emergence of the early church. What best explains these data? A supernatural explanation like the Resurrection fares better than a naturalistic one, offering a much more fruitful accounting of the evidence within the religious context of first-century Palestine.[8]

Deflating "People Claim JFK and Elvis Are Alive, Too!"

- The bodily resurrection of Jesus is *evidence* for the uniqueness of the Christian faith in the face of other world religions.
- Anyone can *claim* to make such parallels, but what is needed is *substantiation*.
- What evidence *best* accounts for (1) the empty tomb, (2) Jesus' postresurrection appearances, and (3) the origin of the Christian church?

CHAPTER 19

"But Jesus Never Said, 'I Am God.'"

I F CHRIST WAS MORE THAN HUMAN, why didn't he say it more plainly? If the belief that in Christ God became man and dwelt among us is such a crucial doctrine for his followers, why didn't Jesus spell that out more bluntly? These are questions that cut to the core of our beliefs as Christians. John Hick, for one, says that Jesus was simply a man very aware of God—a "God-conscious" man. It was Jesus' followers who later exalted Jesus to a status he himself would have thought blasphemous. As for Jesus, he was only a human—like the rest of us.

When Hick maintains that "Jesus did not claim to be God incarnate,"[1] he assumes that because Jesus didn't explicitly say, "I am God," this on the face of it dispenses with belief in Jesus' divinity. In the remainder of this section we will see that both in Jesus' self-understanding and in his followers' veneration of him we have good reason to affirm Jesus' deity.

First, *Jesus' own self-understanding was that he was indeed divine—not merely "God-conscious." He spoke and acted in the place of God:* Given the strong monotheistic belief of first-century Palestine, it is surprising that *Jews* first came to believe Jesus to be divine. As R. T. France indicates, such a belief couldn't easily be explained by wish fulfillment but "must have been caused by an overwhelming weight of facts and experience."[2]

It wasn't that Jesus went about the Galilean hills announcing, "I am God." (Thus we should maintain an "*implicit* Christology" rather than an *explicit* one.) As a matter of fact, given the political overtones of this loaded term in first-century Palestine, Jesus had to show remarkable reserve even about identifying himself as "Messiah." When he was identified by others as the Messiah or "the Son of God," Jesus almost always silenced those who rightly identified him—particularly in Mark—in order to not create an incorrect impression about his mission (Mark 1:24–25, 34, 43–44; 3:11–12; 5:43; 7:36).[3] Once Jesus' messianic mission on the cross was accomplished (Mark 9:9), only then could the Roman centurion announce that Jesus was "the Son of God" (15:39) without being silenced!

Now, in the New Testament the title "God" was generally reserved for the Father; although Jesus is called "God" (John 1:1, 18; 20:28; Rom. 9:5; Titus 2:13; 2 Pet. 1:1; Heb. 1:8), he is more often termed "Lord." This was to prevent confusion on certain fronts. First, even though the Father and Son are equal in nature—both have the same essence—the Father is greater in rank than the incarnate Son, who obeys his Father. By generally speaking of the Father as "God," the New Testament highlights the Son's subordination to the Father—as well as their distinction as persons. Second, if Jesus had regularly been called "God" by early Christians, this would have sounded to Jews as though Christians believe in two "Gods"—Yahweh and Jesus. To Gentiles, this would have sounded as if Jesus could easily be placed into their pantheon of gods. Finally, Jesus wasn't usually called "God" because it could easily compromise or eclipse his genuine humanity.[4] So to have asked Jesus during his ministry, "Are you God?" would have meant, "Are you the heavenly Father?"[5]

Although Jesus understandably didn't say, "I am God," he *said* and *did* a number of things that indicated not merely a God-consciousness or a more intimate relationship to his Father, but that he was much more than human (see, for example, Matthew 11:25–27). Interestingly, Jesus didn't so much *assert* his special status as *assume* it without needing to defend it.[6] For instance, he distinguished his own relationship with his Father from that of others ("My Father" *versus* "your Father" [John 20:17]). Just because Jesus didn't clearly assert, "I am God," hardly implies that Jesus didn't consider himself divine. One clear instance of this is when, under oath, he asserted that he was "the Christ, the Son of the Blessed One" (Mark 14:61–62), implying his vice-regency with God.[7] Jesus was clearly setting himself apart as one who stood in God's place. This didn't go unnoticed by those trying Jesus!

Immediately following this admission, he also referred to himself as "*the* Son of Man"—a title which probably reflects the lofty figure of Daniel 7:13–14. Now, there appears to be an intentional ambiguity associated with the term "Son of Man." As with Jesus' parables, this title both revealed and concealed. There was a sense of *authority* to the title, reflecting the majestic Son of Man in Daniel 7 who *reigned with God*—a messianic title that provoked the indignation of his opponents (Matt. 26:63–64). (Interestingly, the only place in the Old Testament that the two theologically loaded phrases "Son of Man" and "kingdom of God" appear together is in Daniel 7.)[8] Jesus implied this authority when he spoke of giving his disciples authority to eat at "*my* table in *my* kingdom" (Luke 22:29–30). His disciples picked this up as well when some of them wanted to sit with him in his "glory" (Mark 10:37). However, the title "son of man" also has the connotation of *frailty*—as with the prophet Ezekiel, who was called this. Jesus' own earthly mission combined both of these elements.[9] But what seems quite clear from the portrait of Jesus in Mark, Matthew, and Luke is his own belief that he was *the* Son of Man of Daniel 7, who would bring God's kingdom to Israel.[10]

Ben Witherington III has made an impressive case for the proposal that Jesus viewed himself as the embodiment of the Wisdom of God—a proposal that fares better than those that say Jesus was a social revolutionary, a wandering holy man, or the like.[11] Jesus wasn't merely a prophet, since this "leaves too much unexplained": he doesn't say "thus says the Lord" or other prophetic formulas, but rather "I say to you." He spoke, in other words, on his own authority (Mark 1:27). Unlike the prophets, Jesus often used parables, aphorisms, and beatitudes typical of the Wisdom literature of Judaism. Moreover, Jesus applies the language of Jewish Wisdom literature to *himself* (Matt. 11:16–19). Jesus claimed the privilege of revealing the mind of God to people: "No one knows the Son except the Father, and no one knows the Father except the Son *and those to whom the Son chooses to reveal him*" (Matt. 11:27). Jesus proclaimed himself to be greater than the wisest man who ever lived, Solomon (Matt. 12:42).

In addition to this self-understanding, *Jesus claimed certain functions and abilities that were reserved for God alone*. He said that he had authority to *forgive sins*—a claim understood to be a usurpation of divine prerogatives (Mark 2:1–12). He claimed that he was the *ultimate judge* of all, the one to determine every human's destiny (Matt. 7:21–23; 25:31ff.). He identified himself as *David's "Lord"* (Matt. 22:41–46). He used the language of *kingship* and expressed his intent to set up a new rule that included his disciples' ruling with him (Matt. 19:28). He *challenged others to follow him and required that their devotion to him surpass even familial commitments* (Matt. 10:34–39). Jesus draws a line of demarcation for all his hearers: the failure to hear, confess, and follow after Jesus jeopardizes our status before God (Matt. 10:32–33). We could even be persecuted for *Jesus'* sake—not merely the cause of righteousness (Matt. 5:11–12). He maintains that his words will never pass away (Mark 13:31)—a claim made about God's words in Isaiah 40:8.[12]

Related to the identity of Jesus is the important question "Why did Jesus die?" It is very difficult to believe that he died because he was a "superb moral teacher," or because he had legal squabbles with the Pharisees over the finer points of interpreting the Law. He died because he was a threat to the religious

(Jewish) and political (Roman) establishment.[13] This is why he was crucified as "King of the Jews." A person who spins out insightful parables or wise sayings and who calls people to live morally and to observe the lilies of the field would, as John Meier correctly argues, threaten no one. Most attempts to portray Jesus as a wise teacher don't do justice to the fact of his execution. Jesus' words and actions had the effect of dividing (Matt. 10:34–37): "A Jesus whose words and deeds would not alienate people, especially powerful people, is not the historical Jesus."[14] *Why crucify Jesus?* His being a social revolutionary could possibly provoke this, but it seems highly dubious that the church would have started on this basis, because the following Jesus had gathered was hardly a bunch of social revolutionaries.[15] Jesus' divine self-understanding— his belief that he was acting in God's stead—would better explain his crucifixion.

Quite a number of features of Jesus' self-understanding and mission reveal something far greater than a mere man. Whatever theory we espouse of Jesus, it must take into account certain important factors:[16]

- Jesus' independent approach to the law of Moses;
- his feeding the 5,000, which led to an attempt to make him king;
- his interpretation of his own miracles;
- his announcing the reign/kingdom of God as present and evidenced in his ministry;
- his choosing twelve disciples (rather than being sought out by them);
- his use of the title "Son of Man";
- his use of the term *amen* ("*Truly*, I say to you"), which denotes authority;
- his use of the term *abba* ("Father")—for Judaism, an unheard-of manner of addressing God;
- his distinguishing himself from his contemporaries (John the Baptist, the Pharisees, revolutionaries, and even the disciples);
- his belief that our future standing before God hinges on how we react to his ministry;
- his understanding that it was necessary to die, to undergo a "baptism" to rectify matters between God and God's people;
- his sense of mission to the whole of Israel, but especially the undesirables and outcasts;
- his raising messianic expectations through controversy.

Ben Witherington writes, "[Jesus'] action in the temple, the trial of Jesus, and his crucifixion as king of the Jews, all are more adequately interpreted as evidence that Jesus did not simply see himself as yet another prophet or teacher."[17]

Another important point in support of Jesus' deity is *the worship of the earliest churches, which reveals a remarkably exalted view of him.* We have seen that Jesus didn't go about Palestine saying, "I am God." There was a guardedness about making such assertions. However, we have also noted Jesus' *assumption* of divine standing, of being God's co-regent. As we read the Gospels, it often appears as though Jesus didn't need to explicitly assert his divinity because his words and deeds and self-understanding assumed his divine status.

However, we can look beyond Jesus' self-understanding to the worship of the early Christian communities to gain a greater awareness of Jesus' uniqueness. The German New Testament scholar Martin Hengel writes, "The discrepancy between the shameful death of a Jewish state criminal and the confession that depicts this executed man as the preexistent divine figure who becomes man and humbles himself to a slave's death is, as far as I can see, without analogy in the ancient world."[18] The early Christians assumed what the Gospels depict about Jesus' exalted status, and this similarity should not go unnoticed. We see this quite evidently in 1 Corinthians, which Paul wrote in the early A.D. 50s.[19] Just twenty years after Jesus' death, we read a firmly monotheistic Jew including devotion to Jesus alongside God the Father. In the context of idol worship, Paul writes in 1 Corinthians 8:5–6:

> For even if there are so-called gods, whether in heaven or on earth (as indeed there are many "gods" and many "lords"), yet for us there is but one God, the Father, from whom all things came and for whom we live; and there is but one Lord, Jesus Christ, through whom all things came and through whom we live.

Paul has adapted the Jewish monotheistic creed, the *Shema* of Deuteronomy 6:4–9, to include Jesus as the one "Lord" ("one Lord, Jesus Christ") while *excluding any pagan deities* as objects of worship. Larry Hurtado points out that there is "no hint of controversy [in the New Testament] over this matter" of including Christ in worship.[20] Yet this is clearly an early Christian tradition. The exalted status and titles ascribed to Jesus by the early Christians came about *through the worship or veneration of Jesus, not vice versa.* In fact, Paul's own persecution of Christians was prompted by the reverence Christians gave to Jesus.[21]

A further reinforcement of the primitive tradition of offering worship to Jesus is found in the Aramaic phrase *Marana tha*—"Come, O Lord!"—in 1 Corinthians 16:22.[22] Here we have a Greek-speaking gathering using an Aramaic utterance as a prayer to the risen Christ. The reason we witness this liturgical formula in Greek-speaking churches is that it originated from the earliest Jewish Christians and was passed on to Gentile Christians.[23] Hurtado lists other indicators of an early Christian worship that incorporated devotion to Christ: Christian hymns about Christ, prayer to Christ, using the name of Christ ("Jesus is Lord") as a confessional and/or baptismal formula, prophecy that is in the name of Jesus and inspired by the "Spirit of Christ." Given Judaism's concern with blasphemy and what counts for proper worship,[24] the "acceptance of Christ with God as worthy of cultic veneration within the early years of Christianity and among Jews sensitive to the scruples of their ancestral religion can only be regarded as a most striking phenomenon."[25]

Can a Jewish background by itself account for such veneration of Jesus? While Jews *did* recognize that God utilized certain "chief agents" such as Wisdom or Logos (personified divine attributes) or exalted patriarchs (like Moses and Enoch) or principal angels (like Michael), *none of these chief agents was worshiped*, nor was Jesus' burial place venerated as were those of holy men (Acts 2:29). So early Christianity—in its devotion or religious practice— moved significantly beyond Jewish tradition. And they did so suddenly.[26]

So when someone like John Hick asserts that Jesus eventually came to have an exalted status among his followers—implying that a long period of time elapsed so that a distorted tradition developed—he is far from accurately describing early Christianity. From the outset, we see signs within the primitive church indicating that Jesus was the object of its worship.

We are left to ask which picture of Jesus and the events surrounding the emergence of the early church *best* explains the available data. Which portrait of Jesus—wandering holy man, social revolutionary, Son of God—is the most plausible one? The Christian has good reason to believe that the traditional Christian understanding of Jesus makes the best sense of the available evidence—even if some of the evidence is *implicit* rather than *explicit*. Granted, the evidence presented shouldn't be taken as having some sort of mathematical certainty that will compel the belief of all reasonable people. Moral, cultural/ worldview, or philosophical considerations are part of the equation as well. However, what we have discussed can hopefully remove intellectual barriers to the Christian faith and can, as Paul Johnson puts it, "place [these] Christian notions in a plausible context."[27]

Deflating "But Jesus Never Said, 'I Am God.'"

- We argue for an *implicit* Christology. Although Jesus doesn't say, "I am God," he speaks and acts as one standing in God's place.
- For Jesus to call himself "God" would have caused confusion—that there were two "Gods," Yahweh and Jesus. Although Jesus is called "God" in the New Testament, the more frequently used title is "Lord."
- Jesus referred to himself as the "Son of Man," which seems to reflect Dan-

iel 7. His opponents recognized this title as highly significant (Matt. 26:63–64).

- Jesus presents himself as the embodiment of the *Wisdom* of God.
- Jesus claims certain functions and abilities that were typically reserved for God alone—for example, calling for allegiance to him that would surpass family commitments, people being persecuted for *his* sake.
- Why was Jesus executed? If Jesus were only a moralizer or storyteller, he would threaten no one. His belief that he was acting in God's stead would better explain his crucifixion.
- So many factors point to the fact that Jesus was more than a God-conscious man—announcing that the kingdom of God is present and evidenced in his ministry, calling himself "the Son of Man," and his awareness that he must die as part of his mission.
- The *worship* of Jesus in the early church—early A.D. 50s—reflects an exalted view of him (1 Cor. 8:5–6). He is prayed to and is part of the Christian confession. Though his first believers were Jews, there is no dispute about "blasphemy."

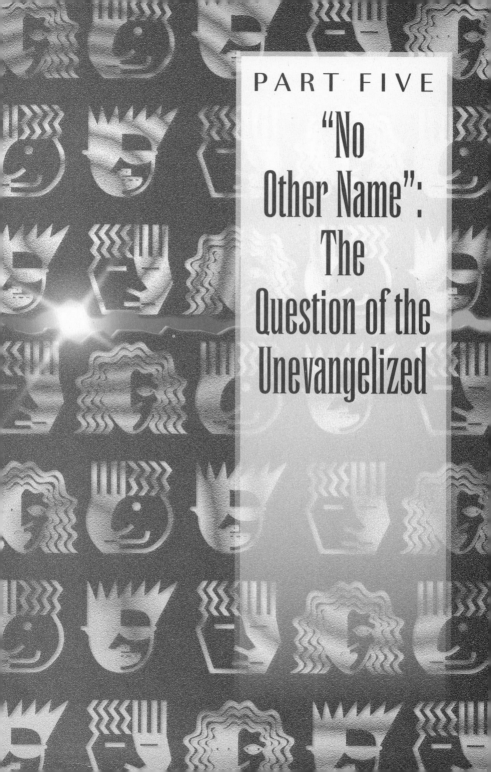

PART FIVE

"No Other Name": The Question of the Unevangelized

CHRISTIAN POET AND HYMN WRITER WILLIAM COWPER (1731–1800), contemplating the destiny of the unevangelized, considered their presumed condemnation grossly unjust. He held out the hope that some beyond the reaches of the gospel could be saved:

> Is virtue, then, unless of Christian growth,
> Mere fallacy, or foolishness, or both?
> Ten thousand sages lost in endless woe,
> For ignorance of what they could not know?
> That speech betrays the bigot's tongue,
> Charge not God with such outrageous wrong.
> Truly not I—the partial light men have,
> My creed persuades me, well employed, may save.[1]

Throughout the centuries, many Christians have maintained with the church father Cyprian that "outside the church there is no salvation [*extra ecclesia nulla salus*]." The view that salvation cannot be acquired through what we can see of God in the world—general revelation—is what has been called the *restrictivist* view.[2] But this position raises a host of questions that trouble both Christians and non-Christians: Are those who have never heard of Jesus Christ really *inevitably* lost? Are they *utterly* without hope? Is God's general revelation in nature and conscience of any saving use to the unevangelized?

We have briefly weighed religious pluralism on the scales and found it wanting. We have also examined the identity claims of Jesus of Nazareth, arguing that he alone is the unique revelation of God and mediator between God and humanity. Now we must squarely face the question that often emerges in discussions about the exclusive nature of Christianity: "If Jesus is the only way to salvation, what about those who have never heard of him? Are they eternally condemned to hell?" The implication of the inevitable lostness of hundreds of millions outside the reach of the gospel appears to strike at the very character of God. John Hick, for instance, finds the fate of non-Christians—according to the "old exclusivist view"—to be "unacceptable" since it is incompatible with the limitless love of God.[3]

Evangelical theologian Alister McGrath maintains that this issue is a matter of the fairness of God, but he remains agnostic about the issue.[4] Several prominent evangelical leaders see nothing rationally problematic with being agnostic about the problem of the unevangelized—with saying, "I don't know, but I trust a good and just God with their fate." However, I believe that we can move beyond the agnostic position and offer a plausible alternative to it. I will assume familiarity with the restrictivist position, which holds that salvation *cannot* be obtained through general revelation alone—that salvation comes through the hearing and believing the Gospel's claims. One must explicitly embrace Jesus to be saved.

I will present two models that attempt to deal with the matter of the unevangelized: (1) the *middle-knowledge* or *accessibilist* view and (2) the *wider-hope* or *inclusivist* view. Remember: both models attempt to offer *biblically compatible* hypotheses in an attempt to offer an *apologetic* or defense of Christian uniqueness in the face of charges of divine injustice. Both of these hypotheses attempt to show that Christian particularity or uniqueness doesn't entail God's injustice toward the unevangelized.[5] Both views fully recognize the fallenness of the whole human race and that only grace extended on God's part allows anyone to be saved. As challenging as these views may sound— particularly inclusivism—both root salvation in Christ's finished work on the cross. After examining both of these alternatives, I shall point out some shortcomings in the inclusivist model—despite a number of its merits.

Of all the difficult topics in this book, questions of the fate of the unevangelized are likely the point where evangelical Christian readers themselves most struggle. Christians need to feel at least minimally secure in their grasp of this difficult issue before they rush to offer an apologetic to non-Christian friends. When all the arguments have been heard, what we must cling to is the certainty of God's infinite justice, infinite love, and infinite wisdom.

CHAPTER 20

"If Jesus Is the Only Way to God, What About Those Who Have Never Heard of Him?"

R ESPONSE #1: THE ACCESSIBILIST OR MIDDLE-KNOWLEDGE PERSPECTIVE

Have you ever wondered, "What if I had grown up in another culture that had no Gospel witness? What if I were a Mongolian or a Sundanese Muslim in Java? Would I have been separated from God forever?" Some Christian thinkers won't consider such a hypothetical situation. You weren't born there, they say, and God doesn't work that way. He obviously intended you to be saved. But if we are willing to entertain such a contrary-to-fact scenario, the middle-knowledge view offers a plausible response to this question. It could be that those who would respond to the Gospel in any *possible* world are given the opportunity to do so in this *actual* world. God engineers the world in such a way that those who would freely receive Jesus Christ would be placed in the position of hearing about him.

This accessibilist or middle-knowledge view attempts to defend the goodness of God and the necessity of hearing the Gospel to be saved—in the face of vast unevangelized multitudes.[1] We use the term *accessibilism* because this view indicates that anyone *can* access salvation regardless of historical or geographical circumstances. (For our purposes, we are distinguishing this position from the traditional view of *restrictivism*, which as we noted maintains that salvation is available only through hearing the Gospel and responding in faith to Christ.)[2] Moreover, this alternative is concerned with "possible worlds"[3] and it is thus called, as we shall see below, the "middle-knowledge" view. As I mentioned earlier, this is a *rationally plausible* suggestion with significant explanatory power, defending God's character in the face of apparent injustice.

The view of middle knowledge[4] maintains that there are three aspects (or logical moments) of God's knowledge—*natural, middle,* and *free.* The distinctions are important:

1. *Natural knowledge:* God knows all *necessary truths* (such as laws of logic). God doesn't command or will them to be true. They simply *are* true by virtue of God's nature.
2. *Middle knowledge:* God knows what every possible free creature *would* freely do under any possible set of circumstances—and, hence, he knows what people would do in any of those possible worlds that God can make actual.
3. *Free knowledge:* This pertains to the knowledge God has of the *actual world* he makes.

The middle-knowledge perspective assumes that there are other worlds God *could* have made but did not. It also assumes God's full knowledge of what free creatures *could* and *would* freely choose if placed in a particular circumstance rather than another. In the actual world, no one is condemned because he or she was unable to hear the Gospel due to the accidents of birth or geography.

Here's why, according to the middle-knowledge perspective: God has arranged this world in such a way that those who never hear the Gospel would not have responded to it even if they had heard it. Those who are beyond the reaches of the Gospel in the actual world could be those who would never have responded to the Gospel in any possible world. So if I *could* have been born in an unevangelized region and *would* have responded to the Gospel had I heard it, then God ensures that I am born into a time and place in which the Gospel is proclaimed so I can respond to it.

Having outlined the basic approach of this possible-worlds perspective, we'll expand on it a bit in light of the problem of the unevangelized.

1. *God judges the unevangelized on the basis of their response to natural revelation:* The advocate of the middle-knowledge perspective freely admits that God's ("general") revelation in nature and conscience affords *a real opportunity* of salvation for the unevangelized. In contrast to the restrictivist, this view maintains that the revelation to the unevangelized doesn't damn them without furnishing genuine opportunities to be saved. Instead, God offers them grace to respond to this revelation. All they need to do is humble themselves before God and repent. God is not only *just* in his judgment of them but is also *gracious* in genuinely offering them salvation.

However, passages like Romans 1 appear to give little hope that many will be saved through God's general revelation. Perhaps a few among the unevangelized are responsive to this revelation, but the accessibilist believes that there is little room for optimism that vast numbers will be saved. It would be wonderful to find many a Socrates or an Aristotle in heaven, but Scripture doesn't furnish us with much encouragement that this will be so.

2. *God can't make persons freely choose to respond to the Gospel:* Over ten years ago, my sister Lil met an embittered atheist I'll call Elliot. Our family eventually befriended Elliot. We talked about the existence of God, ancient Near East history and archaeology, and the problem of evil—the most troublesome question for Elliot. At times he would get so red-faced with anger, that the rest of us held our peace until the storm subsided. Although he had some legitimate intellectual questions, it eventually became clear that no matter how good an answer he was given, he would never embrace God. His will was resolutely set against God, and he eventually cut off all contact with our family. C. S. Lewis captured this type of situation well when he wrote: "I believe that the damned are, in one sense, successful rebels to the end; that the doors of hell are locked on the *inside*."[5] If a million chances were likely to do any good, they would be given, he contended.[6]

No matter how many miracles or answers to prayer some may see, no matter how much prevenient grace is given by the Holy Spirit, some still refuse to submit to God. According to Lewis, there are only two kinds of people—those who say to God, "*Thy* will be done," and those to whom *God* says, "*Thy* will be done!" As in Stephen's day, some "are always resisting the Holy Spirit" (Acts 7:51). God can't force persons to freely receive the Gospel no matter how wonderful the news is. So one should not be surprised if vast numbers of persons persistently refuse to embrace Christ. Their lostness doesn't stem from any unfairness in God but from their own stubborn rejection of him.

3. *God knows all future possibilities and the free choices of human beings:* Because God is God, he knows all *possible* future events and human choices—not to mention what actually *will* take place in the future. So no wonder Jesus could tell Peter that he would deny him three times (Luke 22:34) or that Judas would betray him (Mark 14:17–21). No wonder Jesus could tell his disciples in great detail what they should do to prepare for the Passover (Luke 22:7–13) or to obtain a donkey for him so that he could ride it into Jerusalem (Mark 11:1–6). Thus God has knowledge of future free decisions and events.

Let's look at the example of Peter. God knew that he would freely choose to deny Christ under certain circumstances. But these circumstances weren't divine manipulation in which Peter would inevitably deny Christ. God's knowledge of what Peter or anyone else would do in certain circumstances isn't divine tampering. Not only are human beings free agents who could choose to act oppositely; God is also loving and gracious, desiring what is best for his creatures. Because God knows what free creatures would do in any circumstance, he creates situations in which these agents won't simply carry out God's designs—and God could even use the sinful acts of evil persons to serve his purposes—but they will do so freely.[7]

4. *It is possible that God could not create a world with only persons who would freely choose Christ*; so he chose a world containing an optimal balance of the fewest lost and the greatest number saved. Frequently Christians are asked, "Why didn't God create a world in which everyone chose to love him?" It seems that the simple response is that there is no such feasible world for God. While such a world is *possible*, it simply wouldn't be realizable for God to create it without violating creaturely freedom. If such a world were feasible, God would have brought it about:

> It's possible that in every world which God could create, someone would freely reject Christ. Again, God could force them [sic] to believe, but then that would be a sort of divine rape. Love for God that is not freely given is not truly love. Thus, so long as men are free, there can be no guarantee that they will all freely believe in Him.[8]

The triune God created human beings not because of any inadequacy or lack within the Godhead but so we could participate in the joys of union with him. Given God's desire that as many as possible repent and be saved rather than perish (2 Pet. 3:9), it seems reasonable to believe that God would want a maximal number of persons saved and a minimal number of persons condemned. He wants heaven to be as full as possible and hell to be as empty as possible. Therefore, God doesn't merely desire just a few persons to be saved and even fewer to be damned, lest heaven be significantly underpopulated.[9] He wants *as many as possible* to be saved and as few as possible to be damned. Why could it not be that this world is the one that achieves this optimal balance?

5. *In the middle-knowledge perspective, some persons possess "transworld depravity" or "transworld damnation" and would have been lost in any world in which they were placed.* Many such persons, according to God's providential arrangement, would be unevangelized anyway. The middle-knowledge or possible-worlds perspective stresses that no one is eternally lost because he was born in the wrong place at the wrong time. Everyone who would have responded to the Gospel of Jesus has the opportunity to hear it. On the other hand, those who suffer from transworld depravity and thus would refuse to receive the Gospel and submit to Christ in any world in which they could be placed may be providentially placed in a location where the Gospel would not come anyway. Those who are lost *in actuality* would be lost in any possible world. They would always refuse the Gospel if they heard it.

God, however, would in no way be unjust or arbitrary in condemning those who freely reject him—if he provides sufficient grace and opportunity for them to respond. In fact, those who reject the Gospel and are thus condemned may receive even *greater grace* than those who are saved. God is hardly less loving if he has extended a gracious offer to many who reject it rather than to merely a few who reject it. In the end, there simply *would be no person who, although rejecting the light he does have, would have believed if he had received more light.* William Craig writes:

> God in His providence has so arranged the world that those who would respond to the gospel if they heard it do hear it. Those who do not respond to God's revelation in nature and conscience and never heard the gospel would not respond to it if they did hear it. Hence, no one is lost because of a lack of information or due to historical or geographical accident. Anyone who wants—or would want—to be saved will be saved.[10]

Craig urges that the motivation for missions is in no way diminished since God has also providentially arranged that it is through human messengers that the Gospel will come to the people God knew would accept the Gospel if they heard it.[11] If *no one* were to go to, say, a particular tribal group in Papua New Guinea or in Gambia, West Africa, then God would place some of those afflicted with transworld damnation there. On the other hand, if God knew that a missionary would go to this tribe, then he would place people in the tribe who would have accepted the Gospel. Persons then can be *saved* through the labors of missionaries, but they are not *condemned* through the slackness of missionaries since, in the latter case, God would have placed *different* people—those suffering from transworld depravity—where there is no Gospel witness.[12] So, in the end, no one is condemned because of the accidents of geography and birth.[13]

Deflating "If Jesus Is the Only Way to God, What About Those Who Have Never Heard of Him?"

- Unlike restrictivism, this view allows for people to savingly respond to God's natural revelation—even if relatively few do so.
- No one is born at the "wrong place" and at the "wrong time." God knows which people *would* respond to the Gospel in any possible world and then places them where they will hear the Gospel.
- God can't *make* persons *freely* choose to respond to the Gospel. If there were a world in which all people would freely respond to him, he would have made it. But because there are many who will *resist* God's claim on their lives, God could not have made such a world.
- God, knowing all future possibilities and future free choices of human

beings, creates a maximal balance of the fewest lost and the most saved.

- Yet there are still people who possess the property of "transworld depravity." No matter how many opportunities or how much grace they receive, they steadfastly refuse the invitation of salvation. In his sovereignty, God could place these persons in places where they would not hear the Gospel and thus bring greater condemnation upon themselves.

CHAPTER 21

"If Jesus Is the Only Way..."

RESPONSE #2: THE INCLUSIVIST OR WIDER-HOPE VIEW
My great-uncle, Walter J. Schweitzer, was a missionary in Europe before and after World War II. Before the war, he regularly visited a sanatorium in his homeland of Lithuania to preach and sing hymns among his hearers. One Jewish patient, just before he died, told the others, "Friends, all that the man said and preached to us is true." Two men, Romanowski and Kozlow, took him seriously and expressed an interest in the message of Christ. They asked Walter to secure a Bible for them, and then they began to read it very attentively. One Sunday, my great-uncle strongly felt that he should visit these men, but he put it off. Then the following Tuesday, his wife, Raisa, passed by a Greek Orthodox service. The doors of the church building were open, and candles were burning inside. So she entered the sanctuary to see what was going on. Inside was a wake for a deceased person. Raisa looked in the coffin. In it was Kozlow's body! At the funeral the next day, Kozlow's brother told Walter, "My deceased brother waited all day Sunday for you to come; he continued to ask for you because he earnestly desired to speak with you before his death." This was an experience my great-uncle could never forget.[1]

Walter's experience prompts us to ask, "Assuming that Mr. Kozlow hadn't heard the Gospel clearly presented, did he need to hear the Gospel from my great-uncle—or whomever—before he died in order to be saved? On that Sunday, was his eternal destiny in the hands of a missionary who didn't respond to an inner prompting? Or would Kozlow's casting himself upon God's mercy suffice even if he lacked knowledge about Jesus' substitutionary death and failed to formally receive Jesus as his Lord and Savior? Could it be that God was more interested in the *direction* Kozlow was headed than his spiritual *"location"*—how far he had progressed on his spiritual pilgrimage?

The wider-hope or inclusivist[2] approach has people like Kozlow in mind. Perhaps they are *not* inevitably lost, the inclusivist submits. Some restrictivists or accessibilists may assert that we can't speak definitively about any individual's situation. For example, we can't know that Kozlow would eventually have responded to Christ had he not died unexpectedly. We also simply cannot prove or know exactly what was going on in Kozlow's heart before his death.

While this often may be true, it is not always so, the inclusivist asserts. The inclusivist is more willing to forthrightly say a particular individual will be saved. For example, former missionary and writer Don Richardson has often told the story of a modern-day Melchizedek.[3] When he was speaking to a church in San Jose, a young black Kenyan by the name of Joseph introduced himself. Joseph had gone to an evangelical seminary and worked with the mission Overseas Crusades. He told Don about his grandfather, Arap-Sumbei, who took him by the hand one day when he was seven years old to show him something from a hilltop. Arap-Sumbei told Joseph, "Look at everything you can see—the grasslands, the river, the lake, zebras, the sun, this hilltop, your body and mine. Who created all this? Who made all you see?"

Joseph replied that he didn't know.

His grandfather said, "*Chepta-lel* did" and went on to describe him as the spirit who created everything. "You can't see him who is everywhere. He sees you. He knows your thoughts before you think them. If you do what is good, he will be pleased with you. If you are evil, he will hold you accountable."

Joseph was impressed with his grandfather's reverence for and knowledge of God. Joseph would observe his grandfather's occasionally offering sacrifices to *Chepta-lel* on behalf of the village. He was a highly respected man in his community. However, his grandfather never had the privilege of hearing the Gospel and responding to it.

After telling Don about his grandfather, Joseph asked him if he thought he would see his grandfather in heaven. Don replied, "I see no difference between him and Job, who discussed general revelation with his friends. Had Arap-Sumbei heard the Gospel, he would have recognized that what he had done had been 'wrought in God' " (John 3:21).[4]

This story may or may not make a restrictivist nervous. But it would be a caricature of inclusivism to say it holds that every pagan burning animals to a deity will be saved. Rather, for the inclusivist, this example seems to illustrate what Romans 2:7 declares: "To those who by persistence in doing good seek glory, honor and immortality, [God renders to them] eternal life." *If* it is possible that God's Spirit works in the hearts of unevangelized persons to the extent that they abandon self-effort and throw themselves upon God's mercy—and the example of Arap-Sumbei seems to bear this out—*and* thus find salvation, then perhaps this inclusivist model could answer charges that God is unjust.

The inclusivist perspective maintains "two essential truths"—one inclusive and the other exclusive:[5] Salvation is *inclusive* in its *intended scope* in that God desires all to be saved rather than perish (1 Tim. 2:3–4; 2 Pet. 3:9; cf. also John 3:16–17),[6] and it is *exclusive* in its *source*—Christ alone (John 14:6; Acts 4:12), who is the full and final revelation of God (Heb. 1:3).

This wider-hope/inclusivist view holds that the opportunity for salvation is universal and that the unevangelized aren't inevitably condemned. God has a universal will to save. Although some do resist this desired will of God and his purposes for them (Matt. 23:37; Luke 7:30; Acts 7:51) and thus bring condemnation upon themselves, God has made salvation possible for all—even apart from the standard means of missionary preaching.

This contrasts with the restrictivist position, in which the unevangelized have no hope of salvation unless they hear and respond to the Gospel by faith. Taking the restrictivist position, Harold Lindsell puts it this way: "The knowledge that the man who has never heard of Christ is separated from God is a prime factor in stimulating conservative missionary zeal."[7] Those who maintain this view cite verses that tell us that all who call upon the name of the Lord will be saved (Rom. 10:13); that no one comes to the Father except through Jesus (John 14:6); that it is only the name of Jesus that saves (Acts 4:12); that the one who does not have the Son does not have life (1 John 5:11–12); that people cannot believe without a preacher (Rom. 10:14–15).[8]

Those from the restrictivist position maintain that even though most Gentiles know that a powerful, perfect God exists through nature (Rom. 1:20) and conscience (Rom. 2:15), they *invariably* reject this knowledge of God. R. C. Sproul states that a person who has never heard of Christ won't be punished for not having heard of him. But he'll certainly be punished for not having responded to what he already knew about God.[9]

The inclusivist raises questions against the traditional restrictivist view: "What about Old Testament saints who didn't know about the historical Jesus and his sacrificial death? And what about infants and the mentally deficient who are unable to grasp the message of the Gospel? Furthermore, if God desires the salvation of each person and Christ died for each one, will the salvation of some be *jeopardized* because missionaries haven't yet reached them?" The respected Christian statesman John Stott has written, "I have never been able to conjure up (as some great evangelical missionaries have) the appalling vision of millions who are not only perishing but will inevitably perish."[10] Although Stott says that we must remain agnostic about the destiny of the unevangelized but certain about the urgency and duty of evangelism, he remains hopeful that God will somehow redeem a large proportion of humanity.

How the "Untold Millions" May be Saved: The Inclusivist's View on Christ's "Name"

Below I will present the inclusivist case and then offer some cautions, citing shortcomings of this view. In presenting the inclusivist case, I will contrast it with *restrictivism*, since the middle-knowledge or accessibilist position answers a number of problems that the inclusivist raises against restrictivism. As inclusivism is sometimes unfairly portrayed, I will try to bring clarity to the discussion—even though I do not wholeheartedly endorse this position. Let us now explore some of the tenets of inclusivism.

Tenet #1: *Human beings are guilty and helpless before God, separated from him, and cannot be saved apart from Christ:* Restrictivists, accessibilists, and inclusivists all agree about Scripture's clarity (Romans 1–3, for example) concerning everyone's having sinned and therefore being justly condemned before God.[11] Everyone is held accountable before God so that "every mouth may be silenced." We have willfully failed to do what is right before God.

Moreover, we are helpless to save ourselves. No matter how sincere, devout, or morally upright a person is, he or she can't find favor before God because of these qualities. It is God's gracious gift of salvation that brings a person into right standing before God (Rom. 5:1–2; Eph. 2:8–9). If anyone is *ever* saved, it is by grace on the basis of the cross-work of Christ. Jesus is the means of human salvation and the *only* mediator between God and man (Matt. 11:27; John 14:6; Acts 4:12; 1 Tim. 2:5). And whether a person lived *before* or *after* the time of Christ, his reconciliation with God comes through Christ. So then, anyone who hears and understands the Gospel but nevertheless repudiates it cannot be saved (John 3:36; 1 Cor. 16:22). Those who willfully reject Christ's sacrifice are clearly condemned by Scripture.[12]

Tenet #2: *God desires for all to be saved, which seemingly implies that he makes salvation available to all:* Michael Green, commenting on 2 Peter 3:9 ("The Lord is . . . not wanting anyone to perish, but everyone to come to repentance"), asserts that the "plain meaning" of the text is that God wants all people to be saved.[13] The same thought is expressed in 1 Timothy 2:4: "[God] wants all men to be saved and to come to a knowledge of the truth." (Although some may argue that God desires the salvation of all *kinds* of people—all without distinction—race or class—the more natural sense seems to refer to all, without exception—that is, every individual.)[14] It is difficult to believe that God would *desire* the salvation of all without actually making salvation *available* to them.

God, of course, owes no one salvation (as we noted in Tenet #1). So the inclusivist's reference to God's fairness or justice shouldn't be understood in a *retributive* sense, which is where the substitutionary death of Christ as the punishment for sins enters in. But given the fact that God *does* love all individuals and wants all individuals to repent and find salvation, it would seem strange that those who might have responded to the Gospel would be deprived of salvation because no missionary ever came to them. In light of God's love for the world, his making salvation within the reach of all who would embrace it—even if some are without the Gospel message—is in keeping with his character. In light of this truth, the inclusivist appeals to God's *distributive* justice: Given his love for everyone, his salvific provision for everyone, and his desire for everyone to be saved, it would be in keeping with such a desire to make salvation universally obtainable. The inclusivist John Sanders states: "God's distributive justice seeks to distribute the good of Jesus' redemption to all of humanity, not just a few. Hence God makes the salvation of Jesus . . . accessible to every single individual who has ever lived."[15]

The inclusivist points to a book such as Jonah, in which God expresses his deep concern for the Ninevites. The Assyrian capital, Nineveh, was not only "great" (1:2) in terms of its large population (4:11) but because it was important to God. It had great value in God's eyes. Jonah knew that it was God's nature to show mercy and compassion and that he could extend it to the Ninevites.[16] The story of God's loving attitude serves as a reminder that despite human sin and misery, there is "a wideness in God's mercy"—a wideness that extends salvation to all even though many reject it and bring eternal wrath upon themselves.

Given the assumption of God's desire that all be saved, the inclusivist thinks it reasonable to discover ways in which God might fulfill this desire.[17] Stuart Hackett puts the connection this way:

> If every human being in all times and ages has been objectively provided for through the unique redemption in Jesus, and if this provision is in fact intended by God for every such human being, then it must be possible for every human individual to become personally eligible to receive that provision—regardless of his historical, cultural, or personal circumstances and situation.[18]

If Old Testament saints were saved only through Christ but without a knowledge of the historical facts about Jesus, why couldn't this be true for the unevangelized? The inclusivist maintains that while Jesus is *ontologically* necessary for salvation, he is not *epistemologically* necessary.[19] That is, just as Abraham and other Old Testament saints did not *know* about the atoning death of Jesus Christ ("epistemologically"), the *fact* of their salvation was accomplished through him ("ontologically").[20]

Tenet #3: *Inclusivism claims that salvation through the "name" of Jesus doesn't necessarily imply knowing the historical facts about Jesus' sacrificial death:* Drawing on family history once again, my father appears to fit the scenario advocated by inclusivists. Born in 1925, my father grew up in a small Ukrainian village in the Petrova region. When he was five, his father—a simple farmer—was forcibly taken by Soviet soldiers to work in one of Stalin's labor camps, where he would eventually die of starvation. Then during World War II, my father was forced to dig trenches, first for the Soviet Army and then for the Germans. Some of his co-workers, despairing of the seeming hopelessness that the war wrought, would drink their minds into oblivion. My father, however, turned his thoughts to a God he barely knew, asking for help in his distress. At once he was at peace, sensing that he had been divinely granted a new start and a bright hope in darkness.

It was only later, though, that a Bible came into his hands through the kindness of a German officer, by which my father came to understand what Jesus had done for him. He was then baptized in a partly frozen stream near the Ingul River in Hungary in November of 1944. Like the tax-gatherer in Christ's parable, he had cried out, "God, be merciful to me a sinner," and, looking back, he could see that it was the Spirit of Christ at work within him even though he had minimal doctrinal content to go on. But what if he had died before knowing about the Jesus who died for him? Some may contend that it is difficult, if not impossible, to argue from a contrary-to-fact situation. However, my father's example, the inclusivist suggests, seems to show that God was concerned more with the *direction* of his life than his being in the *position* of clearly grasping the Gospel.

As I have mentioned, the inclusivist view agrees that anyone who is saved is saved by Christ's "name" (Acts 4:12). But does everyone who receives salvation have to know that *Jesus of Nazareth* died in his place and rose again? Certainly Abraham received right standing before God by faith (Gen. 15:6) but *without* any knowledge of Christ. On what basis, then, did Abraham receive salvation? Ultimately, Christ's death alone brings forgiveness for the sins of all pre-Christian saints (Rom. 3:25). Even though they were saved by faith in *God* (see Hebrews 11) and not by faith in the historical Jesus—they weren't aware of him or of his future substitutionary sacrifice—the *basis* of their forgiveness was his atoning death.

But aren't we saved by the *name* of Jesus? Yes, the inclusivist agrees, but he argues that the word "name" in Scripture can be used more broadly than a person's literal name. It can represent the *character, reputation,* or *authority* of a person or political state—such as a law enforcement officer at the door of a crack house demanding, "Open up in the *name* of the law!" It is the same idea as when we as believers pray in Jesus' name—on the authority of Jesus' person and work. When God swears by his *name* (Jer. 44:26), his character and authority are behind his oath. When those who lived in ancient Babylon tried to make a "name" for themselves (Gen. 11:4), they weren't merely thinking of what they would be called but of the great reputation they sought to acquire. Similarly, the inclusivist argues that a person who receives salvation through Christ's *name* does so through the person and work of Christ even if he has not heard of him—just as with the Old Testament saints.

Tenet #4: *Natural revelation can have a positive role and may be used by God's Spirit to show the unevangelized their need for him:* As distinguished from God's special revelation through the prophets and apostles, the Scriptures, and Jesus Christ, God reveals himself generally to all through creation (Rom. 1:18ff.) and conscience (Rom. 2:14–15) so that all are without excuse before him. General or natural revelation (1) establishes God's existence, (2) unfolds God's character, and (3) reveals God's moral requirements. Thus people generally know *innately* or intuitively—through conscience—that a moral Lawgiver exists and that they are accountable to him, and they know *inferentially*—through rational reflection upon the created order—God's power and eternity.[21]

So the person who rejects the validity of basic moral intuitions and abandons the goads of his conscience is rightly called morally bankrupt. To reject the intuition that murder and rape are objectively wrong is to reject what is fundamental to humans. There is no point in talking about ethics with such a moral corkscrew.

Or take the world's natural beauty. Those who fail to appreciate the vast abundance of beauty in this universe are also somehow defective. The beauty of a starry night, the majestic Alps, or a fiery sunset over the ocean points beyond itself to something transcendent.[22] And God holds humans responsible for recognizing what is both *innate* and *inferred* from conscience and the created universe that we might seek him, submit to him, thank him, and depend upon him.

Scripture indicates that the following things can be known to varying degrees about God through general revelation: God exists (Ps. 19:1; Rom. 1:18–20); God is transcendent, uncreated, and universal Lord (Acts 17:24); God is immanent (Acts 17:26–27); God is wise (Ps. 104:24); God is Creator (Acts 14:15); God is eternal (Ps. 93:2); God is good (Acts 14:17); God is righteous (Rom. 1:32); God is self-sufficient (Acts 17:25); God has a sovereign will (Acts 17:26); God is the standard of goodness (Rom. 2:15); God should be worshiped (Acts 14:15; 17:23); God will judge evil (Rom. 2:15–16); humans should perform what is good (Rom. 2:15).[23] Such knowledge, however, can be greatly distorted through human sinfulness.

"Can the Spirit Work Where the Gospel Isn't Preached?"

The discussion of the fate of the unevangelized clearly isn't without certain prior theological commitments. Presuppositions inevitably color our answers to this question.[24] For example, what does God's *love* for all people mean—that he actually *offers* them grace to find salvation, as the inclusivist believes, or only that he *desires* everyone be saved, as many restrictivists hold? Another matter of presuppositions relates to beliefs about the clarity of Scripture: Must the inclusivist point of view be *explicitly endorsed* in Scripture to be acceptable? That is, if the New Testament doesn't *specifically* address the question of the unevangelized, are we warranted in appealing to general biblical principles that might help us deal with this question?[25]

Another important matter that often divides inclusivists and restrictivists is the potential role general revelation has for the unevangelized. Apart from its pre-evangelistic value—in defending the existence of God—is this revelation only *bad* news for those who have never heard of Jesus, as restrictivists tend to maintain? The inclusivist contends that it seems strange that God would give a person enough of a revelation of himself to condemn him but not enough to save him, to give him enough knowledge of God to leave him without excuse but not enough to help him. Are the unevangelized literally "damned if they do and damned if they don't"?[26]

Scripture's discussion of natural revelation says that all people aren't left without a witness to God's greatness and goodness—a witness that satisfies human hearts with food and gladness (Acts 14:17). Paul told the Athenians that God is "not far from each one of us" (Acts 17:27). John 3:21 refers to the one who "lives by the truth" and *then* "comes into the light," which seems to be the light of God's special revelation in Christ (John 1:9). Having done good works, apparently in response to general revelation, he responds to Christ and it becomes clear that his previous works have been "wrought in God." (I should point out here that the question still remains as to how many actually *do* respond to general revelation. Is it really "multitudes," or only a precious few like Arap-Sumbei?)

It cannot be denied that some inclusivists are less than careful in their use of Scripture to justify their claims.[27] For instance, the examples of responsive pagans chosen by inclusivists aren't always clear or obvious—such as Balaam or the Ninevites who repent through Jonah's preaching—and restrictivists rightly contend that "these figures are not among the untold, strictly speaking."[28] Nevertheless, inclusivists believe they are on firm ground when they refer to those in the New Testament who are "informationally B.C."[29] such as the Magi (Matt. 2:1–12) or Cornelius (Acts 10). And they also refer to model "pagans" who are responsive to the true God before the time of Christ—

Enoch (Gen. 5:22), Abimelech (Gen. 20), Job (Job 39–42), Melchizedek (Gen. 14:18–20), Jethro (Ex. 18:11), Naaman (2 Kings 5:15), or Nebuchadnezzar (Dan. 4:34–37).

Can it not be said that *Melchizedek* was someone who clearly had a saving relationship with the true God even though he was an outsider? And *Job* too was clearly in God's favor as an upright and blameless man (Job 2:3)—without, as far as we know, any special revelation. In addition, *Job's friends*, misguided though they were, also had a knowledge of the true God. Moreover, *Rahab*, having heard of what God had done for the Israelites, seemed to be a believer in the true God *before* she ever became a part of God's people (Josh. 2:9–14; Heb. 11:31). *Cornelius* himself (Acts 10:1–2, 4, 22, 34–35) seems to exhibit the working of God's Spirit and grace in his life. Insofar as he was able, he did all he could to honor God. He was considered "righteous," "devout," and "God-fearing." Even before he heard of Jesus, his prayers had been answered by God, and his almsgiving and prayers had "come up as a memorial offering before God"—the very language used of acceptable sacrifices under the Mosaic Law (e.g., Lev. 2:1–2, 9, 16, etc.).[30]

In these cases, to the inclusivist it seems apparent that God's Spirit was clearly at work apart from the proclamation of the Gospel. So what prevents such a scenario from being a possibility in our day for those who haven't heard of Jesus? Perhaps there are unevangelized persons who, prompted by the Spirit, respond as best they can—even though the Gospel may never reach them.

At this point, the restrictivist brings into the argument the fact that pre-Christ believers are those who generally enter into a covenant relationship with God—who has disclosed himself—and that the covenant community of Israel embodies institutions that point toward their fulfillment in Jesus Christ.[31]

So the inclusivist argument appears blunted. But apart from the fact that this isn't always the case (Job and Melchizedek, for example), the inclusivist would argue further that this objection *shifts* the issue from *specific knowledge* of Jesus to the broader category of *special revelation*. That is, the fundamental question is whether explicit belief in Jesus is necessary for salvation. And clearly Old Testament believers did *not* have any such belief—not even an implicit belief in some future substitutionary sacrifice for sins. There seems to be, according to the inclusivist, a continuity between such Old Testament saints and the unevangelized in *this* important sense: *neither group has the full revelation of God in Christ*.[32] Although, for instance, the priestly and sacrificial institutions of Israel point to Christ—as the author of Hebrews makes clear—even Jesus' own disciples couldn't fathom a dying Messiah as a sacrificial lamb

(Matt. 16:21–23). They had political aspirations for the Messiah and a distorted vision of what he should be.

Now, the inclusivist argues that it is faith in God (Heb. 11:6) that saves—not simply a required minimum amount of information about Jesus' life and death in addition to it.[33] The inclusivist tends to assert that *the direction of the heart toward God* is more important than what a person knows intellectually. On the other hand, the restrictivist might respond that in the New Testament faith has *content*, not only an *object*, and that the direction of the heart must be directed by some content.[34] After all, one can have a "zeal without knowledge" (Rom. 10:2).[35]

The inclusivist need not deny, however, that certain doctrinal beliefs may be required for salvation, even without special revelation. Hebrews 11:6 insists that at least belief that *God exists* is a requirement; if general revelation makes one thing plain, it is this fact (Ps. 19:1–2). Moreover, in light of the above list of what can be known about God through natural revelation, what may be available to a person apart from special revelation—in varying degrees—are facts of God's goodness, creatorship, moral purity, sovereignty, and the like. These afford some content about God. Through the working of God's Spirit, a person could infer that God is personal (as opposed to impersonal), just, worthy of worship, the One to whom he is morally accountable, and the One who holds his destiny and spiritual well-being in his hands.

Also, salvation by *faith* implies that one has come to trust in and to commit oneself to a personal being (see John 2:23–24). In other words, whether a person has special revelation or not, he must cast himself on the mercy of God rather than rely on his own efforts. In light of God's moral standards, he recognizes his own sinfulness and inability to save himself. He knows that if reconciliation with God could ever come about, it must be through God's kindness and *grace*. Such a person would, then, need to turn from sin in repentance and seek to live according to what he knows about God. So both *actually* and *potentially*, content has some bearing on the discussion of the fate of those who have not heard.

One evangelical theologian suggests the following point:

> If they [i.e., persons of Rom. 1:20, who have a knowledge of God through nature, even if rejecting it] are condemnable because they have not trusted God through what they have, *it must have been possible somehow to meet this requirement through this means*. If not, responsibility and condemnation are meaningless. . . . Perhaps there is room for acknowledging that God alone may know in every case exactly whose faith is sufficient for salvation.[36]

Although the human tendency to suppress the truth is great (Rom. 1:18), the inclusivist asserts that we ought not exclude the possibility that God's gracious light shines in the dark corners of the world's unevangelized areas.[37]

Tenet #5: *The wider-hope view offers a positive outlook about the number of the redeemed:* Restrictivists, taking their cue from Matthew 7:14 ("But small is the gate and narrow the road that leads to life, and only a few find it"), assume there will be few who are redeemed in proportion to the unsaved. This shouldn't surprise us, the restrictivist argues, because we often see few saved and many more judged in Scripture (as in the flood of Genesis 7, in which only Noah and his family were spared).[38] However, the inclusivist argues that the "few" of Matthew 7 may refer to the nation of Israel in light of Christ's ministry.[39]

After all, Jesus says that "many" would come from the four corners of the earth to join the Jewish patriarchs in God's kingdom (Luke 13:29). Moreover, when we read of God's promise to Abraham in Genesis 12:3 and 15:5 of countless multitudes and in Revelation 7:9 of the redeemed that no one can number, we can be confident that vast throngs will be saved. (However, we must understand that large numbers of people *versus* significantly fewer people saved is *not* the chief concern in our discussion. If the human will, despite the Spirit's gracious promptings, freely rejects God's universal offer of salvation, then the *number* of saved becomes a moot point.)

The inclusivist holds out the hope that the great salvation of God doesn't depend *solely* on the efforts of missionaries—as important as this is. An agnostic on the fate of the unevangelized, Alister McGrath says that "we must never think that it is by preaching the Gospel that we are somehow making salvation available or impossible."[40] As with Cornelius, the work of God's Spirit can extend *beyond* the work of human agents. Even though the Spirit will often work *through* missionaries, the inclusivist maintains that their failure or inadequacies shouldn't be thought to somehow inhibit the sovereignty of God and his saving purposes.

Deflating "If Jesus Is the Only Way, What About Those Who Have Never Heard?" from a Wider-Hope or Inclusivist View

- According to inclusivists, God is reaching out in saving ways even to the unevangelized—implying that he is in no way guilty of the skeptic's charges of injustice.
- The inclusivist argues that the salvation of the unevangelized isn't—the movement of God's Spirit aside—*solely* in the hands of missionaries.
- Given that God desires that everyone be saved and that salvation is only through Christ, any who by God's Spirit are receptive to God's general revelation among the unevangelized (like Arap-Sumbei's faith in *Cheptalel*, the Creator) could be compared to the Old Testament saints in this

way: Both groups have saving faith but have no knowledge of Jesus of Nazareth. Neither group has the full revelation of God in Christ. So the inclusivist says that the unevangelized are "informationally B.C."

- Human beings are guilty and helpless, separated from him, and cannot be saved apart from Christ. However, if God desires everyone to be saved, it seems to the inclusivist that God would make the opportunity for salvation available to all.

- According to inclusivists, Jesus of Nazareth is *ontologically* necessary for salvation (his death alone makes every person's salvation possible), but it is not *epistemologically* necessary (as with the Old Testament saints, who never heard of Jesus or even had any idea of a future sacrifice for sins).

- The inclusivist argues that the word "name" in Scripture is often broader than a title. It refers to one's character, reputation, or authority. Being saved through Christ's name implies a wider opportunity for salvation than has traditionally been taught.

- For inclusivists, natural revelation may have a positive role besides serving as an apologetic for theism. God's Spirit can use it to show people their need for him through creation and conscience. For the unevangelized, natural revelation need not be only *bad* news ("damned if they do and damned if they don't").

- People like Melchizedek, Job, Job's friends, Rahab, and Cornelius seem to offer the inclusivist hope that the unevangelized aren't inevitably lost. If they are saved, it is still by grace through faith on the basis of Christ's death.

CHAPTER 22

"It Doesn't Matter What You Believe— as Long as You're Sincere."

SURELY *HE* IS ACCEPTABLE TO GOD," it isn't uncommon to hear. "Why does it matter if he's a Buddhist? He's seeking God in his own way. He's absolutely sincere."

During his conversion *away* from evangelical Christianity, John Hick felt he could observe followers of a variety of faiths all doing the same thing— moving away from self-centeredness and responding to the same Ultimate Reality. Muslims and Hindus exhibited the same degree of fervor and determination as the best of Christians. How can Christians criticize such sincerity? Doesn't a committed heart count for a lot?

Two answers are vital. First, remember that sincerity is *necessary* but still not *sufficient* for salvation. To say that "it doesn't matter what you believe as long as you are sincere" is a horrible line of reasoning; if it were true, then the sincerity of any stalwart Nazi or Stalinist would be commendable. The idea that God applauds the sincerity of the Satanist doesn't fit anything we know to be good and right.[1] After all, Jesus was crucified by sincere religious leaders, and Paul had been quite sincere as a persecutor of the church prior to his conversion. So while sincerity may be an ingredient in saving faith, it isn't enough by itself.[2]

Second, relying on sincerity for acceptance before God robs us of God's great gift: salvation by *grace*. The skeptic assumes that sincerity *merits* salvation. But God doesn't save us because of our sincerity. If sincerity has any connection with a person's salvation, it is a result of divine grace, not the basis of salvation. The same reasoning would apply to the argument that "Gandhi was a good person." The goodness Gandhi possessed was only a relative human goodness, which is significantly distinct from God's absolute goodness. That is, even "really good" people fall short of God's perfection. Relying on any degree of *human* goodness to merit God's favor is the opposite of embracing *God's* free offer of favor. Any tolerance or acceptance God could offer us based on our sincerity is nothing compared to the undeserved kindness he offers us in Christ.

In light of this "sincerity factor," the restrictivist J. I. Packer offers three points about the salvation of any unevangelized person—*if* the wider-hope view is correct. First, if there is any "good pagan" who reaches the point of casting himself on God's mercy, it was God's grace that brought him there—not any human-generated sincerity. Second, God will certainly save anyone he's brought to that point. And, finally, anyone saved in this way will learn in the next world that his acceptance came through Christ.[3]

Deflating "It Doesn't Matter What You Believe—as Long as You're Sincere."

- Sincerity is *necessary* but not *sufficient* for salvation. Jesus was put to death by sincere religious people.
- If you *rely on* sincerity for acceptance before God, you set aside God's saving grace. Sincerity as the basis of acceptance before God is a form of works-salvation.
- If any sincere "good pagan" has hope, it's because God's Spirit has already been at work within him.

CHAPTER 23

"Who Needs Jesus? And How Are They Going to Find Out About Him?"

H AVING OUTLINED THE ACCESSIBILIST and inclusivist views and having offered some suggestions that may be helpful in explaining God's heart for those who have never heard, I think it will be helpful to look hard at issues *Christians* raise about the unevangelized and our efforts to reach them.

Opponents of the inclusivist view have argued that accepting such a view would radically diminish missionary urgency. For example, Lorraine Boettner asserted, "In fact, the belief that the heathen without the Gospel are lost has been one of the strongest arguments in favor of foreign missions. If we believe that their own religions contain enough light and truth to save them, the importance of preaching the Gospel to them is greatly lessened."[1]

While inclusivists agree that other religions don't "contain enough light and truth to save" their adherents, they contend that Boettner's approach is a *pragmatic* (and possibly a *political*) one.[2] But this, they say, is distinct from whether or not the view is true. Just because something *works* is not necessarily an argument for its *truth*.

Inclusivists also point to various prominent thinkers who have been either sympathetic with or have endorsed their views—Don Richardson, Sir Norman Anderson, John Sanders, John Stott, I. Howard Marshall,[3] or Stuart Hackett— thinkers who are hardly unsympathetic toward world missions. Furthermore, the inclusivist points to many missionaries today—who generally pay a high personal cost to be on the mission field—who maintain an inclusivist perspective. For instance, John Sanders, author of *No Other Name*, has been told by a good number of evangelical missionaries that they readily share his inclusivistic views on the unevangelized.[4]

Regarding the importance of missions, the inclusivist contends, first, that *Scripture commands us to proclaim the Gospel and make disciples of all nations* (Matt. 28:19–20). What greater motivation do we need than this? The believer's primary stimulus to proclaim the Good News isn't compassion but Christ's command.[5] If a believer is ever deterred from proclaiming the Gospel— whether by optimism about God's sovereignty (as would-be missionary William Carey was told, "God will [save the heathen] without your help or mine") or by his hopefulness about the state of the unevangelized—then such a person has *greatly erred* and *disobeyed* Christ's clear command. Inclusivists, moreover, point out that we face this question daily. People ask, "Why *do* we proclaim the Gospel to a next-door neighbor or a college roommate who may have been exposed to the Gospel numerous times? These people have enough 'information' about Jesus. So why should we try to witness to them, anyway?" Inclusivists—like restrictivists—can answer: Because Christ has commanded us to witness. Analogously, why should we be deeply concerned with world missions and the unevangelized? Because Christ has commanded us to be concerned and active.

The normative means of reaching people is, indeed, the proclamation of the Gospel.[6] No one can bypass the utter importance of evangelism and missions. In fact, some inclusivists hold that the proclamation of the Gospel *strengthens* the influence that general revelation can have on someone. Stuart Hackett points out: "[A] person who, for whatever reason, did not find motivation of the natural revelation decisive, might find the requisite additional motivation in the adequate presentation of the historical Gospel."[7]

Second, inclusivists maintain that *those who may find God's mercy apart from the proclamation of the Gospel still need teaching, heart assurance, and a message they can communicate to others and eventually transform their culture.*[8] The essential assumption behind the charge that the inclusivist view will diminish missionary urgency is that there is only one purpose for missions (apart from the glory of God): to bring people into a right relationship with God. But there are other important purposes for missions for the inclusivist:

1. *How can we deny others the present experience of peace, joy, and power that comes through an awareness of the Gospel?* The fact that some have cast themselves upon the true God in faith and repentance apart from the Gospel can also be a motivating factor in that they "are waiting eagerly to hear more about [Christ]."[9] Most likely, they still lack any understanding of the basis for forgiveness, are uncertain about their destiny, feel condemned and burdened because of sin, and so on.

2. *The responsive unevangelized need a message to tell others:* A person

like Arap-Sumbei may be a good moral example to others, but without the Gospel, he can't be a soul winner or church planter. He can only try to persuade with the general revelation available to him.

3. *The Gospel has the power to transform a culture.* Clearly, Christianity has exerted an influence on Western culture in fundamental ways—human rights, abolition of slavery, women's rights, religious and economic freedom, the beginnings of modern science. The power of the Gospel to "uplift" a society is another important reason for missions.

Inclusivists add another point: *Christians can be as sacrificially minded for the sake of known fellow believers as they can be for the unevangelized who have responded to God as best they know how.* In recent years, many Christians in the West have at great personal cost dedicated their lives to getting Bibles or hymnals or translated Bible study tools into the hands of believers in Communist China or the former Soviet-bloc countries. They gladly and sacrificially—and with a sense of urgency—dedicate themselves to the spiritual well-being of fellow Christians. Such a mindset reflects what John himself said—that he had "no greater joy than to hear that my children are walking in the truth" (3 John 4; cp. Gal. 6:10). If such high personal price is paid for those who have already embraced the Gospel, says the inclusivist, how much more should it be for the unevangelized who have responded to God as best they are able, but are in far more desperate straits.

A third reason the inclusivist gives for missionary urgency and involvement is that *ignorance and risk can be as compelling a reason for action as knowledge and certainty:* Simply because one *thinks* that the wider-hope view is correct doesn't one feels the gravity of these problems any less than those who hold a restrictivist view. Ignorance or tentativity hardly negates this urgency. As Kreeft and Tacelli put it, "If you think your child *may* be dying, you will rush to the doctor at the same speed as if you *know* your child is dying."[10]

So inclusivist theologians believe they can without inconsistency admit the urgency and necessity of missions and be committed to fulfilling Jesus' mandate to reach the world with the Gospel. Inclusivists, however, ought to humbly acknowledge that their views on the unevangelized are a *possible* hypothesis that appears to be harmonious with Scripture. Their views, which attempt to avoid the problems of the restrictivist's views, could be wrong and thus need revision.

Some restrictivists, though, contend that holding this view with *tentativity* is an irresponsible dodge. But inclusivists respond that the position—even if not conclusively demonstrated—seems in keeping with various scriptural themes and texts and also seems more likely true than the traditional restrictivist position. Furthermore, this model has helped resolve questions for many

Christians and has furnished them with a view that has significant value in defending the character of God from charges of injustice raised by non-Christians.

John Stott himself sees this view as, first, preserving the necessary biblical safeguards (all humans are perishing apart from God's mercy; they cannot save themselves; and Jesus is the only Savior). Second, this position claims biblical warrant (such as Old Testament believers being saved with little or no knowledge of what the Messiah would do). For this reason, Stott is "attracted" by this concept although he believes that "the most Christian stance is to remain agnostic on the question."[11]

In his book, *The Contemporary Christian*, Stott summarizes the inclusivist view for us:

> What we do not know, however, is exactly how much knowledge and understanding of the Gospel people need before they can cry to God for mercy and be saved. In the Old Testament, people were certainly "justified by grace through faith," even though they had little knowledge or no expectation of Christ. Perhaps there are others today in a somewhat similar position. They know they are sinful and guilty before God, and that they cannot do anything to win his favor, so in self-despair they call upon the God they dimly perceive to save them. If God does save such, as many evangelical Christians tentatively believe, their salvation is still only by grace, only through Christ, only by faith.[12]

Drawing Conclusions About Inclusivism

At the least, these suggestions may enable the Christian to fend off skeptics' criticisms that the God of Christianity is ill-willed toward the human race. All of us must agree—and explain—that God is not unfair: "The Lord is gracious and compassionate, slow to anger and rich in love. The Lord is good to all; he has compassion on all he has made" (Ps. 145:8–9).

Having presented the inclusivist case in some detail, however, there remain some lingering concerns. While the inclusivist view attempts to resolve questions restrictivism raises, it isn't wholly satisfying.

First, *Romans 1 seems to argue against the inclusivist position*. Romans 1 appears to speak about sweeping condemnation of humanity despite the witness to God in creation and conscience. Moreover, the fact that even in places where the Gospel has permeated society, usually only a minority are saved. If inclusivism is true, then this would imply that only a *small* number would have responded to general revelation—not the vast numbers of unevangelized that inclusivists seem to imply.

Second, *there are people who don't respond to general revelation, yet respond to the preaching of the Gospel*. It probably needs no argument that great numbers who have been unconcerned with and unmoved by general revelation *do* in fact respond to proclamation. Inclusivists must be able to explain this phenomenon: Why do many *reject* general revelation and then *respond affirmatively* to the Gospel when they hear it? The accessibilist would argue that special revelation has an efficacy far greater than general revelation, which gives only a vague knowledge of the God of nature. Special revelation also addresses the spiritual needs of humanity and tells of God's loving condescension to us.[13]

Third, *the inclusivist argument in support of missionary activity, even if true, still* may *deter missions, and this can't be taken lightly.* While increasing or decreasing missionary motivation can't be taken as a complete measure of truth, ideas have consequences. If we embrace inclusivism, are we more, equally, or less motivated toward missions? It is highly doubtful that for most people inclusivism *increases* evangelistic fervor. Thus the inclusivist should present his views with utmost tentativity and care so that it in no way quashes missionary endeavor.

Fourth, *inclusivism can come close to endorsing non-Christian religions:* The official Roman Catholic position has taken inclusivism too far, as one can see in *The Documents of the Vatican II*.[14] Note the following statements:

- "Those who have not yet received the Gospel are related in various ways to the People of God. In the first place, there is the people to whom the covenants and the promises were given and from whom Christ was born according to the flesh. . . . This people remains most dear to God."
- "The plan of salvation also includes those who acknowledge the Creator"—for example, Muslims who "along with us adore the one and merciful God."
- "Nor is God himself far distant from those who *in shadows and images* seek the unknown God."

Unfortunately, an inclusivism-gone-too-far hasn't left evangelicals unaffected. For instance, evangelical theologian Clark Pinnock said back in 1992, "I am appealing to evangelicals to make the shift to a more inclusive outlook, much the way the Catholics did at Vatican II." Pinnock optimistically asserts that "God will find faith in people without the persons even realizing [they] had it."[15] But this is precarious and can significantly undercut the basis for Christian missions.[16]

We can't view other religions as though they differ only in *degree* from the Christian faith. In light of the unique claims of Jesus, they differ in *kind*. So while we can appreciate many positive qualities in the various religions, we must guard against the tendency to baptize these religions as—in whatever sense—vehicles of salvation, thus cracking the foundation of Christian missions.

It seems that inclusivism goes quite a way, but it does not go far enough. While it is motivated by the concern of God's fairness toward those who through no fault of their own never hear the Gospel of salvation, the claim that people can be saved, without hearing the Gospel, through general revelation *still doesn't deal with the millions who do not respond to general revelation but yet would respond to the Gospel if they were to hear it.* Contrary to the inclusivist's assertion, there could be a legitimate claim to divine *in*justice on this point. Many could complain that they were "born in the wrong place at the wrong time," having only the dim light of natural revelation, while others who are no more worthy were fortunate enough to be born in a time and place where they were able to hear the Gospel and be saved. And *this* is the problem that inclusivism was trying to solve in the first place.

The middle-knowledge view, we see, does not directly address the question about the status of Old Testament saints, who were saved on the basis of what Jesus Christ would do without having any knowledge about his sacrificial death. Still, this view grants that a person *may* be saved through general revelation—and how much more so through God's special revelation to Israel!—though those who are saved through general revelation would be few in number. Thus I think the middle-knowledge view shows much promise.

Although I think we can go *beyond* remaining agnostic on the unevangelized, this is certainly a rationally credible position to hold. Hick contends that Christians such as John Stott who hold to an agnostic position are guilty of evading the problem,[17] but this is a false charge. Hick assumes that if we don't *know* what provision God has made for the unevangelized, then we shouldn't claim that salvation is exclusively through Christ. However, the Christian can confidently affirm that God's attitude toward the unevangelized is wholly just, gracious, and loving. It seems wrongheaded to argue that, given the exclusivism we *all* claim for Christ's work, an all-powerful and all-knowing God has devised *no* plan for or has given *no* thought to the unevangelized in a way that is consistent with his character. Christians can heartily affirm that if something is unjust, God will not do it—even if we don't know the mind of God on the matter.[18] Let us note John Stott's words: "We have to remember too that God does not *want* anybody to perish but *wants* everybody to be saved."[19]

And so we are left with helpful but tentative solutions to explore further. What we can know, though, is that evangelical Christians haven't been silent on the question of the unevangelized. Several views attempt to hold together the twin truths of (a) God's love for all persons and his desire for their repentance and (b) the uniqueness of salvation in Jesus. These attempts to respond to the question of the unevangelized can furnish us with a defense of the character of God in the face of critics' questions. But still we ought to be tentative. Since we began with a citation from William Cowper, we now end with another: "God is His own interpreter, and He will make it plain"—one day!

CHAPTER 24

"Why Can't We Simply Give People the Gospel?"

A GENERATION AGO IN AMERICA, a Christian who cited a Bible verse to a non-Christian most likely would have seen that word taken as authoritative or worthy of respect, even if the hearer didn't want to heed it. But today Christians are told, "Your Bible is nice for you, but what about the Qur'an or the Book of Mormon?" Judeo-Christian assumptions—the existence of a personal Creator, sin, moral accountability, moral absolutes, divine revelation, life after death, sin, and the existence of objective truth—no longer are taken for granted. In fact, these are often explicitly denied.

Before we tell others about the Gospel of Jesus, we almost always have to lay a groundwork that makes our biblical worldview more understandable to non-Christians. This "pre-evangelism"—exposing the inconsistencies of non-Christian belief-systems and answering basic objections to Christianity—is highly necessary. Few people around us will accept the Gospel without substantial preparation.

We see an example of this dynamic in the book of Acts, where two different messages for two distinct audiences meet with two responses. In Acts 2, Peter preached to God-fearing Jews, who shared the same biblical worldview. Peter presupposed the Old Testament's authority, the possibility of a miraculous resurrection, and the coming of the Messiah in fulfillment of prophecy. Peter had far fewer cultural and intellectual barriers to cross than if he had been speaking to pagans. Three thousand believed and were baptized. By contrast, when Paul preached to the Athenians in Acts 17, he spoke in more general terms about the living God and Creator, contrasting him with the Athenian idols. Although what Paul said certainly reflected Old Testament doctrine, he didn't cite the Old Testament. Instead, he quoted notable lines from the Cretan poet Epimenides and the Stoic author Aratus. His reference to the bodily resurrection of Jesus—anathema to Greeks—didn't endear him to his audience, and only a handful responded to his message. A comparison of Jesus' approach to Nicodemus (John 3) with that of the Samaritan woman (John 4) is another reminder that our proclamation of God's saving message should take the context of individuals into account. If Jesus and the apostles found it necessary to adjust the presentation of their message, we can't presume that any evangelistic method we devise will work universally.

Christians must do all they can to foster a Judeo-Christian worldview to make the Gospel more readily understood. Unless our contemporaries are intentionally seeking spiritual answers, they will find it difficult to embrace a message that doesn't readily fit into their philosophical grid. And so as Christians, we should try to help shape that grid as much as possible. The words of theologian J. Gresham Machen ring as true today as they did earlier in this century. He said that *false ideas are the greatest hindrance to the reception of the Gospel.* "We may preach with all the fervor of a reformer and yet succeed only in winning a straggler here and there, if we permit the whole collective thought of the nation to be controlled by ideas which, by the resistless force of logic, prevent Christianity from being regarded as anything more than a harmless delusion."[1] The problem of clashing life philosophies must be attacked at its root—at the level of ideas. Failing to do so will only deter our witness.

As we come to the end of *True for You, But Not for Me,* we will explore strategies for effectively communicating Christ to this generation. From the start, we must realize that a life of love is the Christian's most winsome witness (John 13:35). Our Christian apologetic must be reinforced by a *holy life* lived in *community* with fellow-believers. Although this book has emphasized the shaping of a Christian worldview, defending the Christian faith in light of competing ideas, and changing a cultural mindset to make it more receptive to the Gospel,[2] the challenge lies before us to reach a generation that *hears with its eyes and thinks with its feelings.*[3] Thinkers like Ravi Zacharias are right to emphasize the need for reaching both "heart" and "mind"—to use common metaphors for feelings and intellect.[4] What we communicate to non-Christians must be in the context of relationship and "where they are."

With that in mind, let's look briefly at a half dozen ways we can have a more effective witness in this changing world.

1. *Bringing Together Faith and Life.* Christians need to integrate faith with the vocation or discipline in which God has placed them—to think "Christianly" about all of life. To prepare the soil for the reception of the

Gospel, pre-evangelism best takes place via a number of different avenues—Christian involvement in drama, film-making, journalism, broadcasting, literature, universities, think tanks, intellectual debate, and scholarly books and articles. John Stott writes that there is an "urgent need for more Christian thinkers who will dedicate their minds to Christ" in these areas. "All these can do battle with contemporary non-Christian philosophies and ideologies in a way that resonates with thoughtful, modern men and women, and so at least gain a hearing for the Gospel by the reasonableness of its presentation."[5]

Local churches can encourage study of critical issues by gathering teams of Christian professionals to wrestle with integrating faith with their area of expertise. Medical professionals, for instance, could meet to discuss books on medical ethics in light of genetic engineering or physician-assisted suicide. Adult Sunday school or evening classes can stretch participants intellectually by raising their standard of content and preparation. Pastors and church leaders should model how to grapple with today's prevailing mindset in sermons and teaching. And churches can support Christian scholarship by setting aside money for members to further their education to gain a voice in the marketplace of ideas.

2. *Listening to Christianity's Critics.* Christians must keep an ear open to this ever-changing culture. Christians can be so busy answering that they don't hear the questions correctly, and while criticizing comes easily for many conservative Christians, the more difficult tasks of listening and understanding are all too frequently abandoned. Hearing from people we feel are on the "other side" of the culture war can remind us of neglected biblical truths about ourselves and our culture and about how to relevantly bring Christ to it. And hearing well allows us to affirm common ground with leading cultural thinkers—a starting point for discussion. (Incidentally, postmodernism is much more nuanced than many critics allege. We must, therefore, be careful not to offer black-and-white responses such as "All postmodern writers deny truth, meaning, and morality.")[6]

We can, for example, affirm common ground with postmodernists in three key areas. Like postmodernists, Christians are suspicious of certain modernist *claims of scientific certainty*. Postmodern thinkers have shown how scientific research is often influenced by cultural, economic, and political factors. They remind us that scientists shouldn't be held up as purely objective and unbiased individuals who simply follow the results of their research wherever it may lead. Personal and metaphysical beliefs often shape the nature of investigation, and reason, while reflecting God's image, can often be distorted by sin and used as an instrument to suppress the truth.

For instance, one of the obvious implications of the Big Bang is that the universe had a beginning. This has made physicists who are metaphysical naturalists do a considerable bit of squirming because the universe's beginning smacks of Genesis 1 and the biblical doctrine of creation out of nothing.[7] Nobel Prize winner Stephen Weinberg once remarked that the steady state theory—an eternal, stable universe, as opposed to a finite, expanding one—is philosophically the most attractive theory "because it *least* resembles the account given in Genesis."[8] Like postmodernists, we can point out these presuppositions for what they are: prejudice.

Christians, along with postmoderns, also deny the possibility of possessing a worldview in a *purely objective and neutral fashion*. We are often limited and culture-bound in many ways, like fish surrounded by water, oblivious to the cultural influences such as consumerism or immediate gratification. Of course, this isn't to say that we are *wholly* the products of our culture or environment. (To do so would be making a statement that is wholly the product of our culture or environment!) We are responsible moral agents, and we can by God's grace overcome negative cultural influences and learn to think God's thoughts after him. But postmodernism reminds us, as does Scripture, that we often don't see things as clearly as we ought.

A third area of agreement with postmodernism is our common rejection of the *intrinsic goodness of all knowledge for humans*. It is hard to ignore that the advance and increasing sophistication of technology and scientific knowledge have brought not only benefit but also horror and degradation—Auschwitz, partial-birth abortion, mustard gas, Chernobyl, and Internet smut. No, all knowledge is not necessarily good for finite human beings—as Adam and Eve discovered in Eden. There are certain harmful, soul-destroying matters of which we are better off being ignorant and leaving to God rather than attempting to explore.

3. *Understanding Everyday People.* In our Christian witness, we must understand at an everyday, person-to-person level the characteristics of those around us.[9]

Before he became a Christian, Lee Strobel of Willow Creek Community Church near Chicago was a reporter and a skeptic. Through the relevant yet genuine Gospel witness of Willow Creek and much soul-searching, Strobel eventually became a Christian. He describes the mindset of "unchurched Harry and Mary," which our witness ought to take into account:

- Although "unchurched Harry" has rejected "the church" and hierarchical institutions, that doesn't mean he has the same attitude toward God.
- Although he is morally adrift—and hides behind relativism—he secretly wants an anchor.
- Unchurched Harry or Mary resists *rules* but responds to *reasons*. For instance, the statement "God says that premarital sex is wrong" is cer-

tainly true, but this way of putting matters doesn't reach the postmodern. The same truth can be conveyed by saying, "Premarital sex has harmful psychological, physical, and emotional effects. God lovingly has given us boundaries to protect us."

- The postmodern is often *ignorant* about Christianity. Postmoderns tend to think they are rejecting Christianity when they are only rejecting a *caricature* of it. That fact means that a Christian must listen and give opportunities for the postmodern to speak his views. (Here Christians can gently probe for an explanation of *why* postmodern friends embrace the views they do.)

- The secular postmodern has *legitimate intellectual questions* about God and religion, but Christians are the last people he will ask because he doesn't think they offer thoughtful answers. Believers can use Christian apologetics to defend the intellectual integrity of their faith. This is part of being relevant witnesses.

- In a society that is morally adrift, parents often want their children to have moral training, which Christianity and a church context can provide. Church-based day-care centers, Christian schools, and Sunday schools can offer an attractive alternative to their secular counterparts.

Strobel's points remind us that although postmodernism departs from biblical ideals in many ways, we live in exciting times as Christian witnesses!

4. *Speaking With Clarity*. Christians must speak in terms non-Christians can understand. Too often our talks with non-Christians can be cluttered with "evangelingo." Yet note the *variety* of images or pictures Scripture uses to depict salvation through Christ:[10]

Justification—being declared righteous or "not guilty" before God—reflects the language of the courtroom (Rom. 3:24). It is the opposite of condemnation (Rom. 8:33–34). Jesus' death was a matter of penal substitution, the just taking the punishment of the unjust upon himself.

Another image—*redemption*—is that of the slave market. We are redeemed by the price of Christ's death ("blood") (Eph. 1:7).

A third image comes from the temple—*propitiation* (1 John 2:2), which has to do with turning away God's wrath through some type of offering or sacrifice. By his death on the cross, Jesus became our Passover Lamb (1 Cor. 5:7).

Maybe because Westerners—especially Americans—emphasize rights over responsibility, they don't understand sin well.[11] For instance, as true as this statement is—"We are rebels against a holy God"—many in our society simply can't relate. But this brings us to a fourth biblical image of salvation, the one that seems most relevant and understandable to contemporary people—*reconciliation*, which exhibits the language of *relationship* or *friendship*. The blood/death of Christ has brought us near to God where there once was enmity (Rom. 5:10; Eph. 2:13). This biblical image expresses what our society *can* understand.

If there's anything Westerners can identify with, it is broken relationships. Divorce, prenuptial agreements, dead-beat dads, child abuse, and incest are symptoms of the ruin of healthy, trusting, interpersonal relationships. Most of us can relate to relational failures and to the breach of trust that brings them about. Almost without exception, people feel these failures deeply, and they experience the pain and emotional hunger that alienation brings. This may help provide an understanding of Christ's death, which can bring healing for the most significant broken relationship—with God. This, in turn, provides the basis for reconciliation and forgiveness in the human sphere (Eph. 4:32; 1 John 4:19).

But don't we minimize personal responsibility when we stress our broken relationship with God? Where does *sin* enter the picture? We can explain that the broken relationship we have with God is because we have *done our own thing* and *gone our own way* (Isa. 53:6)—which is *sin*. Instead of living in a God-centered way, we have lived in a self-centered way. This has created a barrier between us and God.

5. *Seeing Evangelism as a Process.* Christians need to adapt their evangelistic methods to this culture. As times change, so will our strategies in reaching people. We need to rethink our approaches to evangelism to connect with a new generation with a new mindset.

In the first place, *evangelism will require more personalized methods that take a long-term approach*. The vast majority of people become Christians through the influence of *friends or relatives*.[12] Many evangelistic strategies have presumed a common understanding of Judeo-Christian ideals between the believer and unbeliever ("God exists, and we are morally accountable to him"; "The Bible is authoritative"; "There is a heaven and a hell") and that the *quest for truth* was of the greatest importance. A generation ago, these were warranted assumptions. Consequently, the personal element in evangelism didn't seem as necessary.

We live in a different era. The personal dimension of the Christian's witness is all the more urgent because secularized persons need more than words to persuade them about the truth of the Gospel. We must observe a life of Christian commitment and integrity in the context of family or work relationships. Love is the ultimate apologetic for the Gospel (John 13:35), as truth can only take us so far.

Second, because we live in a secularized age in which religion is becoming increasingly marginalized, it is probably unrealistic to assume a person with wholly secular ideals would quickly consider Christianity seriously, *unless* he is genuinely seeking. *Evangelism—and even conversion—is a process, not an event*. People need time to process a new worldview so that embedded faulty assumptions can give way to new ones. There is a vast disparity between the biblical worldview and a secularized one.

	Biblical Worldview	Secularized Worldview
Ultimate Reality:	God exists and is concerned with the world. Humans are spiritual—not only physical—beings.	God does not exist. Humans are solely material beings. They create their own reality (anti-realism) or invent morality.
Origins:	Humans are created by a personal God.	Humans are the result of impersonal, materialistic processes.
Authority:	Humans are accountable to God's standards and will be judged accordingly.	Humans are autonomous and generally free to pursue their own course of action.
Morality:	God's character and standards have been violated.	Moral standards tend to be viewed as cultural. People don't "sin," which implies a moral authority.

Given such a marked contrast, and given the deep-rooted nature of worldviews, we can generally assume that any shift from one outlook to another won't be immediate.

While our discussions of evangelism can't overlook the utterly necessary *divine* side—that God's Spirit must first enlighten human minds, which don't naturally seek God (Rom. 3:11–12)—we can't forget the *human* side. Of course, God *can* instantaneously cut through the tangled web of an utterly unbiblical background and worldview with the life-changing message of the Gospel, but more often he chooses to use the gradual process of solid relationships and the ongoing conversations that believers have with non-believers to bring people to faith.

6. *Offering Crucial Answers*. Apologetics should be an integral part of evangelistic training.[13] As never before, all Christians need to be able to give answers to people's sincere objections and clear away caricatures of Christianity—especially when fewer people share our assumptions than a generation ago.

Although a handful of individuals within our churches may be quite effective at "cold-turkey" evangelism by going door-to-door or street-witnessing, we ought to place our emphasis on encouraging *every* member in our congregations to develop relationships with non-Christians—relational evangelism. People today need freedom to process the Christian worldview through loving relationships and conversations that point them toward truth.

As part of a two-year discipleship program I led, participants weren't required to visit a certain number of homes or to "give the Gospel" to a certain number of people. Rather, they were to spend *social time* with non-Christians, cultivating relationships. This allowed discussions about ultimate issues to surface naturally—issues these Christians were trained to address. While this is a "slower" approach, it generally enhances the ongoing discipleship of those who respond to Christ.[14]

A person who wants to learn apologetics needs to be taken by the hand by a more experienced apologist and be given practical experience. For instance, both should go to a Barnes and Noble bookstore—where people book-browse, sit around, and sip coffee—to do an apologetics dialogue with people on, for example, the problem of evil or the reasonableness of Christianity. We need to get out and *do it!*

There are other good nontraditional methods for presenting a biblical worldview to non-Christians. On a couple of occasions I have met with Jehovah's Witnesses who had visited homes of church members. It was an opportunity not only for me to interact with the JWs but for a not-as-experienced Christian to listen in. For a few years, I would speak to a debating society at a nearby college every trimester and bring serious-minded Christian friends who not only listened to my talks and debates but interacted with non-Christian students afterward. Christians in the business world can offer luncheon seminars to corporations on business ethics or even more explicitly religious topics like "Christianity and Religious Pluralism." Their apprentices would accompany the speaker and interact with non-Christians during this time. Xenos Christian Fellowship in Columbus, Ohio, has done this with great success.

This kind of practical involvement can be done at a broader level, however. *All* of the congregation can be involved in apologetics-oriented outreach. Xenos Christian Fellowship regularly sponsors a *Conversation Cuisine*. These gatherings are hosted by small groups, which provide an exotic dinner for their non-Christian friends. A facilitator speaks on a controversial topic (e.g., "Are all religions the same?"), laying out on paper the issues and the Christian position along with about twenty questions to guide the discussion. After a twenty-minute presentation, he encourages anyone to air views without censorship, but respectfully. Christians who have taken friends to this event find that it promotes further conversations. Michael Green has done something similar with his Agnostics Anonymous. In *this* "AA," Christians invite their questioning friends for rap sessions with one or more seasoned apologists on whatever objections they may have to Christianity. These events offer nonthreatening opportunities for Christians—whether they are in a formal training program or not—to engage in important discussions with their non-Christian contacts.

One Step Closer

Because evangelism/conversion today is most often a *process* and not an *event* (John 4:36–38), we may need to redefine our goals. While God's Spirit can still rapidly rearrange human hearts, most of the time it seems that we should attempt—with God's aid—to help non-Christians move in smaller increments.

Instead of trying to budge people from atheism or agnosticism to receiving Christ in twenty minutes, we can encourage non-Christians to move *one step closer* to Christ—*one step closer* to understanding and accepting the Gospel. This is a realistic strategy for communicating the Gospel to a secularized unbeliever.

Quite often Christians feel overwhelmed by skeptics' questions, and for several reasons. The first is that Christians feel they must assemble a mountain of arguments—while putting an atheist or a skeptic under no such burden. This is a misunderstanding. Non-Christians make claims or assumptions—that God or objective moral values don't exist, for example—that need *just as much* justification as our claims.[15]

Second, it may be that a non-Christian demands too high a level of proof—one that implies *mathematical certainty*. And if this standard were consistently applied to other areas of life, precious little could be known! A Christian need only say that there are *good reasons* for believing that Christianity is true, that a *plausible case* can be made for its rationality. Also, a Christian can ask the skeptic, "What *is* your criterion for acceptability?" One time an agnostic college student asked me after a debate, "Prove to me that God exists." I asked, "What would you take as sufficient evidence?" After remaining silent for a time, he replied, "I've never really even thought about it." A Christian can utilize two basic criteria for truth: *rational coherence* (our beliefs are not self-contradictory or irrational) and *experiential relevance* (our beliefs fit the facts of experience and have greater explanatory capacity than rival views).[16]

A third reason Christians can feel intimidated by a skeptic is that they assume there are far too many questions to answer. They think they need to be an expert on history, world religions, philosophy, the Bible, theology, and the natural sciences! But worldviews are limited to only three basic choices—possibly four—and knowing this can make the apologist's task much easier.

There is a three-tiered approach that a number of other apologists and I have, independently, found helpful.[17] The *first* level has to do with *establishing the existence of objective truth (i.e., that which corresponds to reality) and the possibility of knowledge.* If a person doesn't believe in objective *truth*, then the Gospel message will likely fall on deaf ears. So the first tack is talk about truth, employing the arguments of this book.[18]

Having established that objective truth does exist, move to the second level—*the fundamental alternative worldviews*: theism, naturalism, and pantheism (and possibly polytheism). We have already answered some of the claims of naturalism, by far the more common view in the West. Pantheism is the belief that all reality is ultimately one—an impersonal "God" or "Brahman"—and that this physical world is an illusion. A reasonable strategy is to assume that pantheism is unlikely since *there is no good reason to deny the existence of the physical world.* The burden of proof is on the person who denies this common-sense intuition. Polytheism could be eliminated on the basis of *simplicity.* Given a principle of economy, monotheism is the simpler worldview than is polytheism. All things being equal, why suppose a *number* of distinct deities when *one* will suffice?

Having eliminated naturalism and pantheism by exposing their philosophical problems and by using arguments that defend the existence of a personal God,[19] deal with this question: *Which theistic alternative is most plausible—Judaism, Islam, or Christianity?* This is where Christian apologetics comes in—defending the reliability of the Gospels, the evidence for the Resurrection, and the unique self-understanding of Jesus—material covered in the latter part of this book. This is the stage at which a person is more likely to understand the Gospel's assumptions.

So we work from *truth* to *basic worldviews* to *theistic alternatives*:

1. *Truth* level
2. *Worldview* level: theism, naturalism, or pantheism
3. *Theistic* level: Judaism, Islam, or Christianity

This strategy offers a simple but effective framework for pre-evangelism with unbelievers. Knowing that worldview options aren't unlimited can make talking with the inquirer or skeptic far less daunting.[20]

In an age that tells us, "That's true for you, but not for me," evangelism must take a new tack if we are to deflate the slogans that often leave Christians speechless. This is a generation that requires greater personal engagement at a pre-evangelistic level—deeper thinking, more intimate relationships. It is, however, a generation hungering for spiritual reality. If we as Christians are well prepared, we will ably engage our culture's prevailing ideas and articulate the relevance of the Gospel today. Our efforts will take thoughtfulness. They necessitate a long-term strategy. Yet I believe this long-term strategy is a wise investment for God's kingdom.

Appendix

Discussion Questions

These study questions are meant to facilitate discussion in small groups, Sunday school classes, or Christian fellowships on university and college campuses. They have a twofold purpose: (1) to stimulate readers to think through their own experiences with relativism, religious pluralism, and postmodernism; (2) to help review and reinforce the contents of the book. It is my hope that working through this appendix will better equip readers to respond to many of the relativistic and religious pluralistic slogans they hear. (The *best* approach to take in answering these questions is to do so, as best you can, from *memory*. This will only facilitate your discussions with non-Christians.)

Introduction

1. In what ways have you observed relativistic beliefs in our society?
2. Relate a recent encounter or discussion you had with a relativist.
3. What have you found most difficult when discussing your faith with a relativist? What have you found most effective?
4. Do you think that most of the relativists with whom you have spoken are *truly* relativists, or are they absolutists in some sense?

PART I: Absolutely Relative
Chapter 1: "That's True for You, But Not for Me."

1. What does it mean when we say that relativism is self-defeating?
2. When relativists commit the "self-excepting fallacy," what are they doing?

3. In what ways can we respond to the following one-liners?
   "That's true for you, but not for me."
   "Everything is relative."

Chapter 2: "So Many People Disagree——Relativism *Must* Be True."

1. What is flawed in this "diversity-of-beliefs" argument?
2. What two factors contribute to differing beliefs?

Chapter 3: "You're Just Using Western Logic."

1. What did Alan Watts discover?
2. Why is the relativist's claim that we are using "Western logic" problematic?
3. The skeptic claims that "to err is human." How can the existence of error be an argument for truth?
4. Why is it not possible for there to be "opposite truths"?

Chapter 4: "Who Are *You* to Judge Others?"

1. Have you ever been called "judgmental" or "intolerant" by a relativist? Why?
2. What are the terms "judging" and "(in)tolerance" commonly understood to mean?
3. Ephesians 4:13 refers to "speaking the truth in love." How is this appropriate in a relativistic society?
4. Why are the views of a relativist inconsistent with his arguing for "tolerance"?

Chapter 5: "Christians Are *Intolerant* of Other Viewpoints!"

1. What is the *wrong* way to dialogue with those of other religions? What is the *right* way?
2. List the ways in which the relativist is an absolutist.
3. What are some of the dangers of relativism?
4. Christians have often been accused of intolerance. In what ways is this charge accurate?

Chapter 6: "What Right Do *You* Have to Convert Others to Your Views?"

1. Have you ever experienced harassment because you shared your faith with others?

2. Why are the words "proselytize" and "convert" taboo in our culture?
3. How do you respond to the charge "Evangelism is arrogant"?

Part II: The Absolutism of Moral Relativism
Chapter 7: "Your Values Are Right for You, But Not for Me."

1. Make a list of immoral or evil acts that seem to render moral relativism counterintuitive.
2. What place does holy living have when it comes to giving a Christian response to moral relativism?

Chapter 8: "Who Are *You* to Say Another Culture's Values Are Wrong?"

1. What are the mistakes that anthropologists tend to make about moral values?
2. What is the "reformer's dilemma"? How does it relate to moral relativism?
3. In what ways can "political correctness" on university campuses or in the media express relativistic tendencies?
4. How would you respond to the questions "Who are *you* to impose your values on others?" or "*Whose* values are you going to encourage?"

Chapter 9: "You Have the Right to Choose Your Own Values."

1. Where have you encountered the idea of "choosing the values that are right for you"?
2. What is the "is-ought" (descriptive-prescriptive) problem? Explain.
3. When you tell a relativist that a particular culture's moral practices are wrong or deficient in contrast to another culture's, what is good to keep in mind?
4. Why is value-neutrality a myth?

Chapter 10: "We Act Morally Because of Biological Evolution or Social Conditioning."

1. What are the various naturalistically or non-theistically based ethical alternatives we discussed? What are the inadequacies of each?
2. In your view, which of these theories is most difficult to counter? Which ones are easier? Why?

Chapter 11: "To Be Good, We Don't Need God."

1. When a nontheist argues that he can be good without God, what does he mean? What distinction has he failed to make?

2. What moral facts point in the direction of God as the foundation for ethics?

3. What is the connection between personality and morality? Why is grounding ethics in a personal God a more sustainable position than grounding ethics in an impersonal Reality or a naturalistic one?

4. Why is the notion of moral obligation odd if God does not exist?

PART III: The Exclusivism of Religious Pluralism
Chapter 12: "Christianity Is Arrogant and Imperialistic."

1. Why is Christianity often charged with being arrogant and imperialistic?

2. Why is religious pluralism another form of exclusivism?

3. In what ways does religious pluralism end up watering down the tenets of exclusivistic religions?

4. Compare epistemological and moral relativism with religious pluralism. What are some of their similarities and some of their differences? Have you noticed the patterns of "absolutism" or "exclusivism" within these systems?

Chapter 13: "If You Grew Up in India, You'd Be a Hindu."

1. Why does the diversity of religious traditions throughout the world appear to pose a problem for the exclusivist?

2. Why doesn't this diversity *entail* religious pluralism?

3. What can you tell a religious pluralist who argues, "The reason you're a Christian is that you grew up in a predominantly Christian region"?

4. Why are exclusivists charged by religious pluralists with being arbitrary? Why won't the charge stick?

5. What are the problems with Hick's approach "from below"?

Chapter 14: "Mahatma Gandhi Was a Saint If Ever There Was One."

1. Do you think the argument that there are "saints" within other religious traditions has any merit? Why or why not?

2. What negative effects on moral behavior could spring from Hick's views?

3. Why is the "moral fruits" criterion an arbitrary one?

4. List the other problems with Hick's "moral fruits" criterion.

PART IV: The Uniqueness of Jesus Christ: Myth or Reality?
Chapter 15: "You Can't Trust the Gospels. They're Unreliable."

1. What is wrong with starting from the premise that the Gospels are "sacred writings" when talking with a skeptic?

2. How should the Christian respond to sensationalist claims about "Gospels" other than those in the canon?
3. How should you respond to the skeptic who rejects the textual reliability of the Gospels?
4. Who bears the burden of proof regarding the reliability of an ancient historical document? Why is this true?

Chapter 16: "Jesus' Followers *Fabricated* the Stories and Sayings of Jesus."

1. What kinds of criticisms of the Gospels or of the orthodox view of Jesus have you encountered?
2. For what reasons might a skeptic claim that Jesus' followers fabricated stories about him?
3. Respond to the charge that the Gospels are flawed because they are religious testimonials about Jesus.
4. If we want to defend the authoritative claims and miraculous deeds of Jesus when talking with a skeptic, how should we proceed?
5. What is the problem with the following argument: "Jesus' followers put words into the mouth of Jesus to address particular concerns within their community"?
6. What reasons do we have for taking the Gospels and the book of Acts as reliably recorded history?
7. How should we respond to people who point to contradictions or discrepancies in the Gospels?
8. What is the criterion of embarrassment? Why is this apologetically useful?
9. Why is it unlikely that the followers of Jesus fabricated the miracle stories?

Chapter 17: "Jesus Is Just Like Any Other Great Religious Leader."

1. For what reason might people lump Jesus together with other world religious leaders? Why is this an unwarranted assertion?
2. What sets the Christian faith apart from other religious systems?
3. What is the problem with the trilemma articulated by C. S. Lewis?
4. How should we respond to alleged parallels between Jesus' miraculous birth, life, and resurrection with ancient pagan religions?

Chapter 18: "People Claim JFK and Elvis Are Alive, Too!"

1. Why is the bodily resurrection of Jesus of apologetic significance in the context of non-Christian religions?

2. How should we respond to claims that JFK and/or Elvis is alive?
3. What arguments do you find most persuasive for Jesus' bodily resurrection?
4. What are the various alternative (i.e., naturalistic) explanations utilized to dismiss the fact of Jesus' resurrection?

Chapter 19: "But Jesus Never Said, 'I Am God.'"

1. Did Jesus claim to be God? What qualifications need to be made when discussing this question?
2. Why is it a mistake to reduce Jesus' significance to his being a "God-conscious man"?
3. Why did Jesus at times resist being identified as the Messiah? What is the significance of Jesus' identifying himself as the "Son of Man"?
4. How would you make a case for Jesus' uniqueness based on the data of the Gospels?
5. Why is the question "Why did Jesus die?" pertinent to Jesus' identity or self-understanding?
6. What is remarkable about the worship of the early Christian communities? In what way does this fact contribute to the evidence supporting Jesus' deity?
7. Which arguments for Jesus' unique self-understanding do you find most helpful? Why is this so?

PART V: "No Other Name": The Question of the Unevangelized
Chapter 20: "If Jesus Is the Only Way to God, What About Those Who Have Never Heard of Him?"
Response 1: The Accessibilist or Middle-Knowledge Perspective

1. What does "middle knowledge" mean?
2. What reasons are there for believing in other possible worlds?
3. Could God have created a world in which all persons would have freely chosen to respond to his grace?
4. What is "transworld depravity"?

Chapter 21: "If Jesus Is the Only Way..."
Response 2: The Inclusivist or Wider-Hope View

1. In what way does the fate of the unevangelized pose a problem for the Christian? How has this matter been an intellectual difficulty for you?

2. In what way does the issue of justice or fairness have a bearing on the question of the unevangelized? In what way does it not have any bearing?
3. What two important truths does the inclusivist view attempt to keep in balance?
4. Try to summarize the key points of the inclusivist position.
5. What does it mean for God to desire the salvation of all?
6. What are the parallels between Old Testament saints and the unevangelized? What are the differences?
7. For the inclusivist, what does it mean to be saved through Jesus' "name"?
8. Which persons in Scripture seem to fit the picture of the unevangelized person who is receptive to God's revelation?
9. How would the inclusivist respond to the following objection: "Most people in the Old Testament were recipients of God's special revelation"?
10. For the inclusivist, in what way does doctrinal content have a bearing on salvation? In what ways does it not have a bearing?
11. Summarize the similarities between the inclusivist's view and that of the restrictivist or accessibilist. Summarize the differences.
12. Why is the agnostic's view a plausible one?

Chapter 22: "It Doesn't Matter What You Believe—as Long as You're Sincere."

1. When people raise the question about the sincerity of religious non-Christians, how do you respond?
2. What are the problems with the "sincerity" objection? What objections could you add?

Chapter 23: "Who Needs Jesus? And How Are They Going to Find Out About Him?"

1. According to Scripture, what should motivate us to reach those without Christ? List as many motivations as you can.
2. Do you think that the strength of the wider-hope/inclusivist view is diminished by the objection of allegedly removing the "missionary impulse"?
3. Can the wider-hope/inclusivist view actually *strengthen* the motivation for missions?
4. What are the critical weaknesses of inclusivism?

Chapter 24: "Why Can't We Simply Give People the Gospel?"

1. What evangelistic approaches do we typically use, and why are these approaches less likely to be understood by postmoderns than they were by people a generation ago?

2. How can we reach a generation of people who "hears with their eyes and thinks with their feelings"?
3. Why are personal relationships pivotal in reaching postmoderns in particular?
4. Why is it important that the church engage the ideas of the culture? What will this challenge require of the church?
5. Are there Christians you can think of who are role models in holy living and thoughtfulness as well as in cultural engagement?
6. What are the three levels mentioned in the apologetical model? What is the logical progression?
7. List ideas that come to mind about how your church, fellowship, or small group could more effectively penetrate our culture with the Christian message and worldview.

Notes

Acknowledgments

1. The dedication is taken from Paul Johnson's book *The Birth of the Modern: World Society 1815–1830* (New York: HarperCollins, 1991), vii.

Introduction

2. "Pluralism: A Defense of Religious Exclusivism." Paper given at the American Philosophical Association meeting in Portland, Oregon, 26 March 1992. Later published in Thomas D. Senor, ed., *The Rationality of Belief & the Plurality of Faith* FS William P. Alston (Ithaca: Cornell University Press, 1995). I refer to the former.

3. (New York: Simon & Schuster, 1987), 25; see also 31. Richard Rorty, one of today's most noted relativists, says we are stranded in a no-man's land of competing ideologies and interpretations. He expresses contempt for objective foundations or grounds for truth or moral absolutes, arguing that to judge another culture or values of a culture from a different tradition is the mistake of "philosophy." Rorty fiercely opposes basic philosophical ideas such as "essence," "foundation," or "nature"—terms that assume the existence of objective truth. This liberal ironist even doubts his own "final vocabulary," another term for "ideology," "framework," "perspective," "tradition," "worldview," and what others have called "paradigms" (Thomas Kuhn) or "language game" (Ludwig Wittgenstein). See *Contingency, Irony, and Solidarity* (Cambridge: University Press, 1989), 186, and Philip E. Devine, *Relativism, Nihilism, and God* (Notre Dame: University Press, 1989), 113n.

4. George Barna, *What Americans Believe* (Glendale, Calif.: Regal, 1991), 36, 84.

5. George Barna, *Virtual America* (Ventura, Calif.: Regal, 1994), 81–83.

6. Barbara Dafoe Whitehead, "Dan Quayle Was Right," *Atlantic Monthly* (April 1993): 47; David Kupelian, et al., "The Daycare Dilemma," *New Dimensions* (November 1990): 18–34.

7. Cited in Gene Edward Veith, Jr., *Postmodern Times* (Wheaton, Ill.: Crossway Books, 1994), 72.

PART I
Introduction

1. We normally think of *truth* as that which conforms or corresponds to reality and falsity as that which does not. If the statement is true—"Paul Copan married Jacqueline van Tol in December 1988 in Acton, Massachusetts," its truthfulness resides in the fact that it captures the factual who, when, and where of our marriage ceremony; in other words, it *corresponds* to reality. In this book, I am arguing for a *correspondence view* of truth. That is, propositions or ideas correspond to reality, to the facts, to the real world.

There are two main competing views of truth: (a) the *coherence* view (the view that a true proposition is one that belongs to a coherent set of propositions) and (b) the *pragmatic* view (the view that something is true if it is useful to believe it). However, both views face a similar problem: *They unwittingly espouse relativism.*

The pragmatic view would allow for contradictory views to be true based simply on their usefulness. For instance, if an abortionist finds his work satisfying and useful because he thinks he is helping women uphold "freedom of choice," his beliefs are as true as those of women who oppose abortion because of the havoc it wreaks on women. A similar problem exists for the coherence view: It permits opposing beliefs to be true. As philosophers put it, it violates the law of noncontradiction (A cannot equal non-A). The coherence view inadvertently maintains that two people can hold to *opposing* belief systems and—because these systems make sense internally—would *both* be true.

For a more sophisticated criticism of the coherence and pragmatic views of truth and a defense of the correspondence view, see Frederick F. Schmitt, *Truth: A Primer* (Boulder: Westview Press, 1995). For a more popular-level criticism of these views, see Peter Kreeft and Ron Tacelli, *Handbook of Christian Apologetics* (Downers Grove, Ill.: InterVarsity Press, 1994), 364–66.

2. For an excellent study of these two sides, see James Davison Hunter, *Culture Wars: The Struggle To Define America* (New York: Basic Books, 1991).

3. *Theaetetus* 152a. Taken from Edith Hamilton and Huntington Cairns, eds., *The Collected Dialogues of Plato* (Princeton: University Press, 1989). Roger Trigg points out that Protagoras' position could more technically be considered a *subjectivistic* one rather than a *relativistic* one because Protagoras is "thinking in terms of each individual, rather than of societies" (*Reason and Commitment* [Cambridge: University Press, 1973], 3).

4. Patrick Gardiner, "German Philosophy and the Rise of Relativism," *The Monist* 64 (1981): 138.

5. For good analyses of relativism in our society, see William Watkins, *The New Absolutes* (Minneapolis: Bethany House, 1996) and Dennis McCallum, ed., *The Death of Truth* (Minneapolis: Bethany House, 1996).

6. For more on the distinct types of relativism, see Maurice Mandelbaum, "Subjective, Objective, and Conceptual Relativisms," *The Monist* 62 (1979): 403–23.

7. Peter van Inwagen, *Metaphysics* (Boulder, Colo.: Westview Press, 1993), 65.

8. *The Darwinian Paradigm* (London: Routledge, 1989), 232.

9. See Robert Priest, "Cultural Anthropology, Sin, and the Missionary," in D. A. Carson and John D. Woodbridge, eds., *God and Culture* (Grand Rapids: Eerdmans, 1993).

10. Historical *skepticism* is somewhat different from historical *relativism*. It maintains that historical research *cannot* be objective because it is inevitably biased by one's culture and therefore value-laden.

11. For further study of objective standards in art, see Abraham Kaplan, "The Aesthetics of the Popular Arts," *Journal of Aesthetics and Art Criticism* (Spring 1966): 351–64; H. R. Rookmaaker, *Modern Art and the Death of Culture* (Downers Grove, Ill.: InterVarsity Press, 1970); Gene Edward Veith, Jr., *Postmodern Times* (Wheaton, Ill.: Crossway Books, 1994), Part II.

12. Harold Netland, *Dissonant Voices*, 144. See also Lesslie Newbigin, *The Finality of Christ* (Atlanta: John Knox, 1969), 11–12; and Aldous Huxley, *The Perennial Philosophy* (New York: Harper & Row, 1944), 140–141.

13. *The Closing of the American Mind*, 38.

14. "The Gay Science," in *The Portable Nietzsche*, Walter Kaufman, ed. and trans. (New York: Viking, 1954), 95.

15. Cited in Veith, *Postmodern Times*, 163.

16. For example, *Gorgias* 491b. Also, in the *Theaetetus*, the *Sophist*, and the *Statesman* Plato takes aim at relativism, which he despises. The *last* thing he wants to do is equate perception with knowledge, which would mean that falsehood is impossible.

17. Alister McGrath, "The Challenge of Pluralism for the Contemporary Church," *Journal for the Evangelical Theological Society* 35 (September 1992): 363.

Chapter 1

1. "Challenge," 367–8.

2. Note that not all self-referential statements are false (e.g., "This sentence consists of six words").

The problem comes when they are self-referentially *defeating*.
3. The relativist could attempt to evade the self-contradictory argument by claiming that all statements about ultimate reality are true relative to presuppositions of the speaker's own culture. He could *limit* the scope of his claim by asserting that his statement is *not* about the intrinsic nature of ultimate reality. But then the relativist can be challenged to provide a *reason* for *limiting* his claim to such statements about reality. (I owe this point to Larry Lacy.)
4. Maurice Mandelbaum, "Subjective, Objective, and Conceptual Relativisms," 405.

Chapter 2

1. This section is drawn from William J. Wainwright, "Does Disagreement Imply Relativism?" *International Philosophical Quarterly* 26 (March 1986): 47–60.
2. J. P. Moreland, *Christianity and the Nature of Science* (Grand Rapids: Mich., Baker, 1989), 17–58.
3. Michael Polanyi, *Personal Knowledge* (Chicago: University Press, 1958).
4. *An Interpretation of Religion* (New Haven: Yale University Press, 1989), 2.
5. John Hick, "Straightening the Record: Some Responses to Critics," *Modern Theology* 6 (January 1992): 188.
6. McGrath, "Challenge," 370.

Chapter 3

1. David K. Clark, *The Pantheism of Alan Watts* (Downers Grove, Ill.: InterVarsity Press, 1978).
2. In addition, there are plenty of truths that are not observationally demonstrable. For example, we can know with far greater confidence that kindness is a virtue or that murder is evil than that the universe is expanding or that the earth is not the center of the universe.
3. For an excellent, readable resource on the subject of objective truth, see Winfried Corduan, *Reasonable Faith: Basic Christian Apologetics* (Nashville: Broadman & Holman, 1993).
4. See my forthcoming article, "St. Augustine and the Closing of the North African Catholic Mind," *Journal of the Evangelical Theological Society*. Having emerged out of an anti-intellectual environment yet eagerly seeking the truth, St. Augustine (A.D. 354–430) was attracted to the skepticism of the academics in Rome, who taught that it was impossible to attain any sort of certainty. But as his book *Against the Academics* shows, such skepticism is self-refuting (published as *Answers to Skeptics* [New York: CIMA Publishing, n.d.]). Summarized by Frederick Copleston, *History of Philosophy*, vol. 2 (Garden City, N.J.: Doubleday Books, 1985 [reprint ed.]), 52–53.
5. John J. McDermott, ed., "The Possibility of Error," *The Basic Writings of Josiah Royce*, vol. 1 (Chicago: University Press, 1969), 321–353.

Chapter 4

1. For a popular exposition of this passage, see D. A. Carson, *The Sermon on the Mount* (Grand Rapids, Mich.: Baker, 1978), 97ff.
2. See Caroline J. Simon, "Judgmentalism," *Faith and Philosophy* 6 (July 1989): 275–287.
3. Mother Teresa, "We Must Give Until It Hurts," *World* (12 February 1994): 22, 24. See also her amicus brief concerning abortion ("Recalling America") in *First Things* (May 1994): 9–10.
4. Harold Netland, "Professor Hick on Religious Pluralism," *Religious Studies* 22 (1986): 76.
5. Richard Mouw, *Uncommon Decency: Christian Civility in an Uncivilized World* (Downers Grove, Ill.: InterVarsity Press, 1992).
6. Ibid., cited on 12.
7. Ibid., 55.
8. Plantinga, "Pluralism."
9. Taken from a booklet—whereabouts unknown—recounting this speech.

Chapter 5

1. Klass Runia, "The Gospel and Religious Pluralism," *Evangelical Review of Theology* 14 (October 1990): 344.

2. Although I am aware of the slippery concept of "religion" (see chapter 4), I am here assuming that religion primarily refers to theistic belief systems—Judaism, Christianity, and Islam.

3. Maurice Cranston, "Toleration," in Paul Edwards, ed., *Encyclopedia of Philosophy*, vol. 8 (New York: Macmillan/Free Press, 1967), 143. Cranston maintains that toleration "implies the existence of something believed to be disagreeable"; it "has an element of condemnation built into its meaning."

4. Alister McGrath, "The Christian Church's Response to Pluralism," *Journal for the Evangelical Theological Society* 35 (December 1992): 490.

5. Clark Pinnock, *Set Forth Your Case* (Chicago: Moody Press, 1971), 55. See chapter 6 for a fuller discussion.

6. Richard John Neuhaus, "A Voice in the Relativistic Wilderness," *Christianity Today* (7 February 1994): 35.

7. Philip E. Devine, *Relativism, Nihilism, and God* (Notre Dame: University Press, 1989), xii.

Chapter 6

1. Some non-Christians may be unwilling to discuss religion because they believe it is a *private* issue. The Christian could helpfully point out that religious views may be *personal*, but they shouldn't be considered private—especially if they are of vital or life-changing importance.

2. (Philadelphia: Temple University Press, 1991), 75. John Hospers says something similar: "We usually profess to make our choice of action depend on prior *reasons*, but in practice we are likely *first* to decide what we want to do and *then* think up reasons for doing it. We find reasons for doing what we would have done anyway without reasons" (*Human Conduct* [New York: Harcourt, Brace, & World, 1961], 19).

3. Cited in Richard John Neuhaus, "Joshing Richard Rorty," *First Things* (December 1990): 14.

PART II
Introduction

1. For instance, see Paul V. Mankowski, "What I Saw at the American Academy of Religion," *First Things* (March 1992): 36–41.

2. William Lane Craig, *Reasonable Faith* (Wheaton, Ill.: Crossway Books, 1994), 73–74.

3. Gilbert Harman, "Moral Relativism Defended," in Jack Meiland and Michael Krausz, eds., *Relativism: Cognitive and Moral* (Notre Dame: University Press, 1982), 189.

4. "Wilding: Evil in the Park," in *Suddenly* (New York: Free Press, 1990), 27.

5. Jean Bethke Elshtain, "Judge Not?" *First Things* 46 (October 1994): 39.

6. Richard Taylor argues in this fashion in *Ethics, Faith, and Reason* (Englewood Cliffs, N.J.: Prentice-Hall, Inc., 1985). Other accounts of virtue ethics do not eliminate considerations of obligation, however. For selected readings in virtue ethics, see Joram Graf Haber, *Doing and Being: Selected Readings in Moral Philosophy* (New York: Macmillan, 1993), Part II.

7. See Terry Christlieb's fine critique of Richard Taylor in *Faith and Philosophy* 5 (July 1988): 323–327.

8. See William Lane Craig, "The Indispensability of Theological Meta-Ethical Foundations for Morality," *Foundations* 5 (Spring 1997): 9–12.

9. See Clyde Kluckhohn, "Ethical Relativity: *Sic et non*," *Journal of Philosophy* 52 (November 1955): 663–77. I would add that the same point could be made with regard to epistemological relativism. Context plays an important part in the discussion of relativism.

10. This point is taken from Stuart C. Hackett's on-line ethics book, *The Rediscovery of the Highest Good: A Philosophical and Critical Ethic*, 34.

Chapter 7

1. Michael Ruse, *The Darwinian Paradigm* (London: Routledge, 1989), 268.

2. Ibid.

3. Ibid., 232.

4. I came across a similar story in Mark Ashton's booklet, *Absolute Truth?* (Downers Grove, Ill.: InterVarsity Press, 1996), 9–10. In this account, Robert Wengert, a philosophy professor at the

University of Illinois, would ask his ethics class if his students thought truth was relative. The majority of students typically raise their hands. Then he tells them that short students get A's while tall students fail. When his students protest that his grading system is not fair and that he ought not or should not grade in that fashion, Wengert points out to his class that when they use words like *ought* or *should*, they betray a belief in an objective moral standard; they really *don't* believe that morality is relative.

5. As we saw in the previous section, moral relativists reveal their inconsistency when they ask, "Who are *you* to judge?" This question itself is a judgment about the person who is being judged. When we are accused of allegedly "playing God" for making a moral judgment about a person's wrong actions, our accusers are themselves "playing God" by making a moral judgment about us—which is either self-defeating or special pleading. Anyone who accuses another of making moral judgments is playing the part of an absolutist. For further discussion on judgmentalism, see Thomas L. Carson, "Who Are We to Judge?" *Teaching Philosophy* 11 (March 1988): 3–14. The glibly used paraphrase of Jesus' words "Let him who is without sin cast the first stone" (John 8:7), is often used to support the idea that morally imperfect people are not allowed to point out sin in others. Of course, Jesus had no intention of prohibiting *all* moral judgments, but merely *hypocritical* judgment. The Jews trying to frame Jesus were hardly interested in justice. Jesus refers to Deuteronomy 13:9 and 17:7, where those who are the first to throw stones must be witnesses of the crime and *not participants in that crime itself* (in this case, adultery)— even if they are not morally perfect (see D. A. Carson's discussion, *The Gospel According to John* [Leicester, England/Grand Rapids, Mich.: InterVarsity Press/Eerdmans, 1991], 333–337).

Chapter 8

1. Robert Priest, a Christian anthropologist, has documented and analyzed the typical anthropologist's relativistic assumptions in "Anthropologists and Missionaries: Moral Roots of Conflict," in Karl J. Franklin, ed., *Current Concerns of Anthropologists and Missionaries* (Dallas: International Museum of Cultures, 1987), 13–40. For instance, he cites Sol Tax: "Whatever propensities and values may unite and distinguish anthropologists, first among them is a view of life that is relativistic and pluralistic . . . we are the only profession, or even community, for which this view of life is definitive" (17).
2. The Stanford incident is taken from Dinesh D'Souza, *Illiberal Education: The Politics of Race and Sex on Campus* (New York: Free Press, 1991).
3. I am indebted to Doug Geivett on this point.

Chapter 9

1. Robert Hatcher, et al., *The Quest for Excellence* (Decatur, Ga.: Bridging the Gap, 1993), 3.
2. Ibid., 59.
3. Cited in W. S. F. Pickering, ed., *Durkheim: Essays on Morals and Education*, trans. H. L. Sutcliffe (London: Routledge & Kegan Paul, 1979), 12–13.
4. Nicholas Rescher, *Moral Absolutes: An Essay on the Nature and Rationale of Morality*, Studies in Moral Philosophy, vol. 2 (New York: Peter Lang, 1989), 43.
5. Robert Priest, "Anthropologists and Missionaries," 23, 31.

Chapter 10

1. Arthur Allen Leff, "Unspeakable Ethics, Unnatural Law," *Duke Law Journal* 6 (December 1979): 1249.
2. *The Darwinian Paradigm* (London: Routledge, 1989), 231.
3. John Hick, *Arguments for the Existence of God* (London: Macmillan, 1970), 63.
4. Arthur Holmes, *Ethics: Approaching Moral Decisions* (Downers Grove, Ill.: InterVarsity Press, 1984), 73.
5. *The Virtue of Selfishness* (New York: New American Library, 1961).
6. Louis Pojman, "A Critique of Contemporary Egalitarianism: A Christian Perspective," *Faith and Philosophy* 8 (October 1991): 496.
7. An advocate of this view is John Leslie. See his book *Universes* (New York: Routledge, 1989).

8. *Moral Values and the Idea of God* (Cambridge: University Press, 1918).
9. Peter van Inwagen notes, ". . . the thesis that ethical requiredness can, in itself, be *effective* [i.e., causal], remains as puzzling as the thesis that the beauty and sublimity of gothic architecture (considered simply as a *possible* system of architectural design) could bring about the existence of cathedrals and colleges and guild halls without the mediation of the action of conscious, purposive beings" ("Review of John Leslie, *Universes*," *Faith and Philosophy* 10 [July 1993]: 443).
10. William Lane Craig argues against this Neoplatonism in "The Teleological Argument and the Anthropic Principle," in William Lane Craig and Mark McLeod, eds., *The Logic of Rational Theism* (Lewiston, N.Y.: Edwin Mellen Press, 1990): "How can there be morality without the previsioning of a moral Being? Personal agents, not impersonal principles, display morality" (151).
11. Kai Nielsen, "Why Should I Be Moral? Revisited," *American Philosophical Quarterly* 21 (January 1984): 90.

Chapter 11

1. See William Sorley, *Moral Values and the Idea of God* (Cambridge: University Press, 1918).
2. "The Mirror of Evil," in Thomas V. Morris, ed., *God and the Philosophers* (New York: Oxford University Press, 1994), 238. Some of the above thoughts on moral intuitions are taken from Stump's essay.
3. Arguing for the objectivity and correctness of our basic moral intuitions is *not* committing the naturalistic (or the is/ought) fallacy mentioned earlier (which pertains to deriving obligation from *natural* states of affairs such as biological impulses or social contracts). Rather, these intuitions are *evidence* that objective, transcendentally given moral duties exist.
4. As James Q. Wilson writes in *The Moral Sense*, "When we think about it, we realize that the aversion we feel to baby torturing for fun not only springs from deeply held sentiments whose truth we find self-evident, it also has important practical value" (New York: Free Press, 1993), 240. Wilson discusses these sentiments in detail.
5. A surprising number of people deny the existence of any objective evil in the world. For example, Oxford zoologist Richard Dawkins asserts, "In a universe of blind physical forces and genetic replication, some people are going to get hurt, other people are going to get lucky, and you won't find any rhyme or reason in it, nor any justice." For a metaphysical naturalist like Dawkins, there can be "no evil and no good" in this universe—nothing but "blind, pitiless indifference." *River out of Eden: A Darwinian View of Life* (New York: Basic Books, 1995), 133. Although we can't respond to the views of naturalism here, it can probably be safely said that most people (even self-pronounced moral relativists) *do* believe that evil exists. For a fine *theological* defense of the problem of evil, see D. A. Carson, *How Long, O Lord? Reflections on Suffering and Evil* (Grand Rapids: Baker, 1991). For a more *philosophical* defense of the problem of evil, see William Lane Craig's popular-level discussion on "Suffering and Evil" and "Hell" in *No Easy Answers* (Chicago: Moody Press, 1990), 73–116. For a more advanced-level exploration of the topic, see Peter van Inwagen, "The Magnitude, Duration, and Distribution of Evil: A Theodicy," *Philosophical Topics* 16, 2 (1988): 161–87.
6. Kai Nielsen in a debate with William Craig, 6 February 1991, at the University of Western Ontario.
7. George Mavrodes, "Religion and the Queerness of Morality," in Robert Audi and William Wainwright, eds., *Rationality, Religious Belief, and Moral Commitment* (Ithaca, N.Y.: Cornell University Press, 1986), 219.
8. It would be an error, however, to state—as Hugo Grotius (1583–1645) did—that natural law is independent of God, that it would be valid and binding even if God did not exist. Rather, if God didn't exist, there would simply be no standard of goodness by which actions should be judged. The origin of morality, as we have already argued, is *supernatural*. Carl Henry, "Natural Law in a Nihilistic Culture," *First Things* 49 (January 1995): 54–60.
9. A well-documented example of the evils of Soviet collectivization is Robert Conquest's *Harvest of Sorrow: Soviet Collectivization and the Terror-Famine* (New York: Oxford University Press, 1986).
10. Nicholas Rescher, *Moral Absolutes*, 84–89.
11. Devine, *Relativism, Nihilism, and God*, 78.

12. Incidentally (though not unimportantly), we are not obligated to act morally simply because God *commands* certain things and not others (what is called the divine-command theory of ethics)—a view that notables like Martin Luther and René Descartes maintained (Robert M. Adams would be the noted contemporary proponent of this view). If this were the case, God could have commanded the exact *opposite* of what he does, and it would still be right because he commanded it. (In an episode of *M.A.S.H.*, Father Mulcahy was horrified to find that the new Bibles given to the *M.A.S.H.* unit contained a significant typographical error in Exodus 20:14: "Thou *shalt* commit adultery." But under the divine command theory, this command could have been permissible.) *Such a view, however, leaves us with no way of distinguishing between God and Satan.* The source of goodness, rather, springs from the very *character of God*; moral principles and commands are rooted in his nature.

God does not comply with or obey some independently existing moral law. God neither *obeys* nor *creates* the moral law, as C. S. Lewis said. He merely *acts*, and it is good. And since we are created in God's image, God's will can never be in conflict with our best moral intuitions. For further reading on this subject, see Mark D. Linville, "On Goodness: Human and Divine," *American Philosophical Quarterly* 27 (Apr. 1990): 1430–52; Thomas V. Morris, "Duty and Divine Goodness," in *Anselmian Explorations* (Notre Dame: University Press, 1987); William Alston, "Some Suggestions for Divine Command Theorists," in Michael D. Beaty, ed., *Christian Theism and the Problems of Philosophy* (Notre Dame: University Press, 1990), 304–320.

PART III
Introduction

1. Corduan, *Reasonable Faith*, 37.
2. The following synopsis of John Hick's pilgrimage is adapted from Paul Eddy, "John Hick's Theological Pilgrimage," *Proceedings of the Wheaton Theology Conference* (Wheaton, Ill.: Wheaton Theology Conference, 1992).
3. When we refer to "pluralism," we should remember that this word has different uses. *Religious pluralism* (in which all religions are capable of bringing humans to "salvation") is distinct from *pluralism as a fact of life* (that is, the fact that we live in a pluralistic or diversified society, which in itself is *not* a bad thing) and from *ideological pluralism* (the belief that any system that claims to be true over other views is imperialistic and narrow-minded) (McGrath, "Challenge," 361).
4. Since the end of the Second World War, which brought an end to colonialism, the West experienced a new cultural shift away from a stance of clear superiority to being roughly equal with formerly dominated nations. A new attitude toward non-Christian religions has come with this shift.
5. *The Contemporary Christian: Applying God's Word to Today's World* (Downers Grove, Ill.: InterVarsity Press, 1992), 298–300.
6. For example, religious pluralism was presumed at the Parliament of the World Religions in 1993, which convened again in Chicago for the first time since 1893. The conference's themes were on the unity of religions and the importance of "tolerance," the condemnation of "fundamentalism" (which was vaguely defined as dogmatically believing that one's own religion is true), the fatherhood of "God," and the brotherhood of man. In fact, the documents signed by the Parliament's delegates lacked virtually all religious overtones so that *atheists* could easily have signed on (D. A. Carson, *The Gagging of God: Christianity Confronts Pluralism* [Grand Rapids, Mich.: Zondervan, 1996], 30). On the Parliament itself, see Elliot Miller, "The 1993 Parliament of the World Religions," (Parts I and II) *Christian Research Journal* (Fall 1993/Winter 1994).
7. Cited in Klaas Runia, "The Gospel and Religious Pluralism," 342.
8. Lesslie Newbigin, *Foolishness to the Greeks* (Grand Rapids, Mich.: Eerdmans, 1986), 16.
9. Gotthold Ephraim Lessing, *Laocoon, Nathan the Wise, Minna von Barnhelm*, William A. Steel, ed. (New York: Dutton, 1967 repr.). The story is recounted on 166–169.
10. Lessing writes,
    "For base not all [religions] their creeds on history,
    Written or handed down? And history
    Must be received in faith implicitly.
    Is't not so? Then on whom rest we this faith
    Implicit, doubting not? Surely on our own?

Them from whose blood we spring. Surely on them
Who from our childhood gave us proofs of love"(167–168).

11. John Hick, "Response to Alister E. McGrath," in Dennis L. Ockholm and Timothy R. Phillips, eds., *More Than One Way?* (Grand Rapids, Mich.: Zondervan, 1995), 181.
12. John Hick, "A Concluding Comment," *Faith and Philosophy* 5 (Oct. 1988): 453. Hick states that the Ultimate Reality itself does not have incompatible, self-contradictory properties (453).
13. Hick, *An Interpretation of Religion: Human Responses to the Transcendent* (New Haven: Yale University Press, 1989), 242.
14. "Copernican Revolution of Theology," in *God and the Universe of Faiths: Essays in the Philosophy of Religion* (London: Macmillan, 1973), 120–32.
15. "Straightening the Record: Some Response to Critics," *Modern Theology* 6 (Jan. 1990): 187.
16. Ibid., 189.
17. Hick's view, although not following Kant, parallels Kant's distinction between the *noumenal* realm (Ultimate Reality, of which we have no knowledge) and the observable *phenomenal* realm (the way things *appear* to humans). Hick, however, applies Kant's distinction in epistemology (i.e., how we come to know what we do) to human religious experience. See Paul R. Eddy, "Religious Pluralism and the Divine: Another Look at John Hick's Neo-Kantian Proposal," *Religious Studies* 30 (Dec. 1994): 468.
18. John Hick, "Review of Peter Byrne, *Prolegomena to Religious Pluralism: Reference and Realism in Religion*" in *Religious Studies* 32 (June 1996): 291.
19. The "different and incompatible beliefs remain, but they are beliefs about different and perhaps equally salvific manifestations of the Real." See Hick, "A Concluding Comment," 453.
20. John Hick, *The Second Christianity* (London: SCM Press, 1983), 86.
21. Gavin D'Costa, "The Impossibility of a Pluralist View of Religions," *Religious Studies* 32 (June 1996): 227.
22. John Hick, "The Pluralist View," in *More Than One Way?*, 44.
23. "The Philosophy of World Religions," *Scottish Journal of Theology* 37 (1984): 231. Although taking a more pragmatic approach than Hick, the pluralist Paul Knitter also believes that all religions have roughly equal soteriological (saving) value since they are all in touch with the same transcendent Reality. For a good discussion of Knitter's views, see Paul Eddy, "Paul Knitter's Theology of Religions: A Survey and Response," *Evangelical Quarterly* 65 (1993); Timothy D. Westergren, "Do All Roads Lead to Heaven? An Examination of Unitive Pluralism," in William V. Crockett and James G. Sigountos, eds., *Through No Fault of Their Own? The Fate of Those Who Have Never Heard* (Grand Rapids, Mich.: Baker, 1991), 169–182.
24. Cited in C. S. Lewis, ed., *George MacDonald: An Anthology* (New York: Macmillan, 1978), 7.
25. Stott, *The Contemporary Christian*, 299–300.

Chapter 12

1. This point is made in the excellent analysis of religious pluralism by Gavin D'Costa, "The Impossibility of a Pluralist View of Religions," 223–232.
2. Ibid., 226.
3. In John Hick and Paul F. Knitter, eds., *The Myth of Christian Uniqueness* (London: SCM Press, 1987), 141.
4. Plantinga, "Pluralism," 8.
5. "Dialogue and Liberation," *Drew Gateway* 58 (1987): 1–53.
6. D'Costa, "Impossibility," 232.
7. Peter Donovan, "The Intolerance of Religious Pluralism," *Religious Studies* 29 (1993): 218.
8. "Challenge," 371–372.
9. (London: SCM Press, 1977), ix.
10. *God Has Many Names* (Philadelphia: Westminster Press, 1982), 58–59.
11. McGrath, "Challenge," 372.
12. Taken from Harold Netland, "Professor Hick on Religious Pluralism," *Religious Studies* 22 (1986): 255–56.
13. Netland, *Dissonant Voices*, 153.
14. See Hick's *Problems of Religious Pluralism* (New York: St. Martin's Press, 1985), 43, 96.
15. "Response to McGrath," in *More Than One Way?*, 183. Hick views the elephant and the blind

men analogy to be "inadequate," claiming he begins from the ground level to explain human experience.

16. George Mavrodes, "The Gods Above the Gods: Can the High Gods Survive?" Eleonore Stump, ed., *Reasoned Faith* (Ithaca, N.Y.: Cornell University Press, 1993), 202.

17. Peter van Inwagen, "*Non Est Hick,*" in *God, Knowledge, & Mystery* (Ithaca, N.Y.: Cornell University Press, 1995), 214 (my emphasis).

18. Peter van Inwagen, "A Reply to Professor Hick," 300.

Chapter 13

1. *An Interpretation of Religion,* 2.

2. Van Inwagen, "*Non Est Hick,*" 213–214.

3. John Hick's reply to this analogy is inadequate, thus leaving the traditional Christian view open to the charge of arrogance: "The Church's claim is not about the relative merits of different political systems, but about the eternal fate of the entire human race" ("The Epistemological Challenge of Religious Pluralism," *Faith and Philosophy* 14 [July 1997]: 282). Peter van Inwagen responds by saying that Hick's accusation is *irrelevant* to the charge of arrogance. Whether in the political or religious realm, I still must figure out which beliefs to hold among a number of options. So if I adopt a certain set of beliefs, then "I have to believe that I and those who agree with me are right and that the rest of the world is wrong. . . . What hangs on one's accepting a certain set of beliefs, or what follows from their truth, *doesn't enter into the question of whether it is arrogant to accept them*" ("A Reply to Professor Hick," *Faith and Philosophy* 14 [July 1997]: 299–300).

4. "Pluralism," 23–24.

5. This citation is from a personal letter from John Hick to Alvin Plantinga. See Alvin Plantinga's article, "Ad Hick," *Faith and Philosophy* 14 (July 1997): 295. The critique of Hick in this paragraph is taken from Plantinga's article in *Faith and Philosophy* (295–302).

6. D'Costa, "The Impossibility of a Pluralist View of Religions," 229.

7. Hick has claimed that he does not *know* but merely presents a "hypothesis" (see his rather unilluminating essay "The Possibility of Religious Pluralism," *Religious Studies* 33 [1997]: 161–166). However, his claims that exclusivism is "arbitrary" or has "morally or religiously revolting" consequences (in *More Than One Way?*, 246) betrays his certainty.

8. This and the following paragraphs are based on Paul R. Eddy's argument in "Religious Pluralism and the Divine," 470–78.

9. "Religious Pluralism and Conflicting Truth Claims," in Gavin D'Costa, ed., *Christian Uniqueness Reconsidered: The Myth of a Pluralistic Theology of Religions* (Maryknoll, N.Y.: Orbis Books, 1990), 102.

10. On this point, I draw much from D. A. Carson, *The Gagging of God,* 182–189.

11. *Summa Theologiae* I.2.3c.

12. Two fine popular-level apologetics books are William Lane Craig, *Reasonable Faith* (Wheaton, Ill.: Crossway Books, 1994) and J. P. Moreland, *Scaling the Secular City* (Grand Rapids, Mich.: Baker Book House, 1987). A bit more rigorous but rewarding is Stuart C. Hackett, *The Reconstruction of the Christian Revelation Claim* (Grand Rapids, Mich.: Baker, 1984). Three other apologetics books worth noting are Peter Kreeft and Ronald K. Tacelli, *Handbook of Christian Apologetics* (Downers Grove, Ill.: InterVarsity Press, 1994); Norman Geisler, *Christian Apologetics* (Grand Rapids, Mich.: Baker, 1976); and Winfried Corduan, *Reasonable Faith.*

13. Some well-meaning Christians have minimized the place of Christian apologetics for a number of reasons. But their reasons, discussed by C. Stephen Evans, tend to be inadequate: (1) "Human reason has been damaged by sin," but reason is not worthless, only defective. (2) "Trying to use general revelation is presumptuous": Seeking to persuade a person with arguments from general revelation doesn't assume unassisted and autonomous reason (after all, reason is a gift from God); any such approach ought to rely upon God—just as presenting the gospel message should. (3) "Natural revelation is unnecessary since special revelation is sufficient": This argument wrongly assumes that God cannot use the world he created and the reason he gave us to interpret that creation to draw people to himself. (4) "The arguments for God's existence aren't very good": The Christian apologist should recognize that God has made the world in such a way that if a person is looking for loopholes to avoid God's existence, he may do so, but it is not due to a

lack of evidence. It seems that God would permit evidence for his existence to be *resistible* and *discountable* so that humans do not look like utter nitwits if they reject God. There is more to belief than mere *intellectual* reasons; people often have *moral* reasons for rejecting God. (See Evans' fine essay, "Apologetics in a New Key," in Craig and McLeod, *The Logic of Rational Theism*, 65–75.)

Chapter 14

1. "Response to McGrath," 183.
2. For a scholarly treatment of the Resurrection, see William Lane Craig, *Assessing the New Testament Evidence for the Resurrection of Jesus* (Lewiston, N.Y.: Edwin Mellen, 1989). See Craig's popular treatment of the Resurrection, *Knowing the Truth About the Resurrection* (Ann Arbor, Mich.: Servant, 1988).
3. This point and the next are taken from Kelly James Clark's essay, "The Perils of Pluralism," *Faith and Philosophy* 14 (July 1997): 303–320. While Clark's points are not an attempt to *refute* Hick, they show that Hick shouldn't try to speak with any definitiveness about his religious pluralism.
4. Peter Byrne (who has since embraced pluralism) makes this valid point in "John Hick's Philosophy of World Religions," *Scottish Journal of Theology* 35 (1982): 299.
5. See the discussion of Stuart C. Hackett, *Oriental Philosophy*, 201–203.
6. Physicist Fred Hoyle declared that the universe was once "shrunk down to nothing at all" (*Astronomy and Cosmology* [San Francisco: W. H. Freeman, 1975], 658). A brief but helpful discussion on the initial singularity is William Lane Craig, "God's Non-Existence: a Criticism," in *Theism, Atheism, and Big Bang Cosmology* (Oxford: University Press, 1993), 258–260.
7. The steady-state theory was refuted through the discovery of the universe's microwave background radiation—the "echo of the Big Bang itself" (John Gribbin, *In the Beginning: The Birth of the Living Universe* [Boston: Little, Brown and Company, 1993], x). The oscillating model suffers from the following problem: "By what mechanism does the Universe 'bounce back' from each contraction? No satisfactory mechanism has ever been proposed" (Edward B. Tryon, "Is the Universe a Vacuum Fluctuation?" *Nature* 246 [14 December 1973]: 396). See also Alan H. Guth and Marc Sher, "The Impossibility of a Bouncing Universe," *Nature* 302 (7 April 1983): 505–506.
8. For a technical philosophical (and scientific) defense of the universe's necessary beginning, see William Lane Craig, *The Kalâm Cosmological Argument* (New York: Macmillan, 1972). See also William Craig's third chapter in *Reasonable Faith* and J. P. Moreland's first chapter in *Scaling the Secular City*. For a popular discussion of Creation and contemporary science, see Hugh Ross, *The Creator and the Cosmos* (Colorado Springs: Navpress, 1993).
9. The metaphysical view of monism, common in Eastern religions, maintains that no differences exist at all. Johann Sebastian Bach, Notre Dame Cathedral, and the Bunker Hill monument are One (i.e., *Brahman*). The monism of Eastern religions denies any individuality, rejecting it as illusory. However, we can offer some responses to this: First, at least the *illusion* that the external world exists would be real, which would mean that something besides *Brahman* exists. Second, we normally follow a common-sense intuition to accept what appears to be true unless there is good reason to reject it (such as rejecting the earth's flatness, for example, because of the overwhelming evidence of its sphericity). To believe what doesn't even *seem* to be true when we know of no good reason to accept it (such as the physical world's being an illusion) or even to believe what seems to be *false* when we have no good reason to accept this makes no sense. See Peter van Inwagen, *Metaphysics* (Boulder, Co.: WestviewPress, 1993), 31.
10. For documentation of the fraudulent, dishonest "scholarship" of the Watchtower/Jehovah's Witnesses, see Robert J. Bowman, Jr., *Why You Should Believe in the Trinity* (Grand Rapids, Mich.: Baker, 1989); regarding the problems of Mormonism, see Gerald and Sandra Tanner, *The Changing World of Mormonism* (Chicago: Moody Press, 1980); Linda Newell and Valeen Avery (who are both Mormons), *Mormon Enigma: Emma Hale Smith: Prophet's Wife, "Elect Lady," Polygamy's Foe, 1804–1879* (Garden City, N.Y.: Doubleday, 1984); D. Michael Quinn, *The Mormon Hierarchy: Origins of Power* (Salt Lake City: Signature Books, 1994).
11. George Mavrodes, "Polytheism," in Thomas D. Senor, ed., *The Rationality of Belief & the*

Plurality of Faith FS William P. Alston (Ithaca, N.Y.: Cornell University Press, 1995), 286.

12. "Straightening the Record: Some Responses to Critics," 189.

PART IV
Introduction

1. "Jesus and the World Religions," in John Hick, ed., *The Myth of God Incarnate* (London: SCM Press, 1977), 180.
2. John Hick, "A Pluralist View," in *More Than One Way?*, 52.
3. John Hick, "Jesus and the World Religions," 167.
4. Ibid., 168–169.
5. Ibid., 170–171.
6. Ibid., 172.
7. Ibid., 178.
8. Hick, "A Pluralist View," in *More Than One Way?*, 52–54.
9. The options of "liar" and "lunatic" are utterly implausible in light of the portrait the Gospels paint of Jesus. We see there a psychologically whole and utterly sincere person—not a trickster or an unbalanced man. On the other hand, a "good teacher" does not merely make the kinds of extraordinary claims Jesus did. See C. S. Lewis, *Mere Christianity* (New York: Macmillan, 1952), 55–56.
10. See William Craig, *Reasonable Faith*, 253.
11. Craig Evans documents this in his "Life-of-Jesus Research and the Eclipse of Mythology," *Theological Studies* 54 (1993): 3–36, esp. 14. Martin Hengel offers a helpful summary of his assessment regarding "the historical-critical method" in his *Acts and the History of Earliest Christianity* (Philadelphia: Fortress Press, 1980), 129–136; see also Craig A. Evans, "Source, Form, and Redaction Criticism: The 'Traditional' Methods of Synoptic Interpretation," in Stanley E. Porter and David Tombs, eds., *Approaches to New Testament Study*, JSNT Supplement Series 120 (Sheffield: JSOT Press, 1995), 17–45.
12. See my forthcoming book, *Will the Real Jesus Please Stand Up? A Debate Between William Lane Craig and John Dominic Crossan* (Grand Rapids, Mich.: Baker, 1998). Note especially William Craig's final response.
13. See Craig A. Evans, *Life of Jesus Research: An Annotated Bibliography* (Leiden: E. J. Brill, 1989). Also, see N. T. Wright's two outstanding volumes, *The New Testament and the People of God* (Minneapolis, Minn.: Fortress Press, 1992) and *Jesus and the Victory of God* (Minneapolis, Minn.: Fortress Press, 1997).
14. *Essay on Criticism II*, 438–439.
15. Recounted in Paul Johnson's *Intellectuals* (New York: Harper & Row, 1988), 283.
16. David Hackett Fischer, *Historians' Fallacies: Toward a Logic of Historical Thought* (New York: Harper & Row, 1970), 42–43n. See also Maurice Mandelbaum's criticism of historical relativism in *The Problem of Historical Knowledge: An Answer to Relativism* (New York: Harper & Row, 1938).
17. R. T. France, *The Evidence for Jesus* (Downers Grove, Ill.: InterVarsity Press, 1986). The four Gospels should be treated as *independent* historical sources for Jesus—not to mention Acts and the epistles. In terms of extrabiblical attestation, Josephus refers to his being a wise man, doing "astonishing deeds," and being crucified (*Antiquities* 18.63–64). (Regarding later embellishments added by Christian interpolators [e.g., "He was the Christ"], which don't negate the basic description of Jesus, see John P. Meier, *A Marginal Jew*, vol. 1 [New York: Doubleday, 1991], chap. 3). Other extrabiblical attestation includes Tacitus (*Annals* 15.44), Pliny the Younger (*Epistles* 10.6), Suetonius (*Lives*: Nero, 16.2), and the Babylonian Talmud (*Sanhedrin* 43a).
18. (Buffalo: Prometheus Books, 1975).
19. See John P. Meier's brief discussion in *A Marginal Jew*, 87n.
20. See N. T. Wright's criticisms in chap. 3 of *Jesus and the Victory of God*.
21. "A Historian Looks at Jesus," (Washington, D.C.: Wilberforce Forum/Prison Fellowship, 1991). This booklet is an excellent, popular-level defense of the reliability of the biblical record in light of historical, textual, and archaeological considerations.

Chapter 15

1. A concise, first-rate defense of the New Testament's reliability is Craig L. Blomberg's essay, "The Historical Reliability of the New Testament," in William Craig, *Reasonable Faith*, chap. 6. See also an expanded argumentation in Blomberg's *The Historical Reliability of the Gospels* (Downers Grove, Ill.: InterVarsity Press, 1987).
2. For a discussion of criteria of historicity, see C. Behan McCullagh, *Justifying Historical Descriptions* (Cambridge: University Press, 1984). William Lane Craig discusses these in his chapter "Did Jesus Rise from the Dead?" in Michael J. Wilkins and J. P. Moreland, eds., *Jesus Under Fire: Modern Scholarship Reinvents the Historical Jesus* (Grand Rapids, Mich.: Zondervan, 1995), 143–146.
3. See John Meier's discussion of *The Gospel of Thomas* in *A Marginal Jew*, 1:123–141. For a concise argument, see Craig L. Blomberg, "Where Do We Start Studying Jesus?" in Wilkins and Moreland, eds., *Jesus Under Fire*, 22–25.
4. On the status of *Thomas*, see Craig L. Blomberg, "Where Do We Start Studying Jesus?" 22–25.
5. For example, Jacob Neusner, *A Rabbi Talks With Jesus: An Intermillennial, Interfaith Interchange* (New York: Doubleday, 1993), 11. Jesus' tone sounds more like that of the Old Testament prophets (e.g., Isa. 1:4, 10; Amos 5:21–24) than an anti-Semite.
6. D. A. Hagner, *The Jewish Reclamation of Jesus* (Grand Rapids, Mich.: Zondervan, 1984).
7. See Carl F. H. Henry's comments in "The Identity of Jesus of Nazareth," *Criswell Theological Review* 6 (1992): 92.
8. D. A. Hagner, *The Jewish Reclamation of Jesus*, 288–292.
9. Stephen T. Davis discusses this matter in "Can We Know That Jesus Rose From the Dead?" *Faith and Philosophy* 1 (1984): 147–159.
10. For extensive documentation of this, see Kurt Aland and Barbara Aland, *The Text of the New Testament*, 2nd ed. (Grand Rapids, Mich.: Eerdmans, 1989). See also Craig Blomberg, "Gospels (Historical Reliability)," Joel B. Green, Scot McKnight and I. Howard Marshall, eds., *Dictionary of Jesus and the Gospels* (Downers Grove, Ill.: InterVarsity Press, 1992): 292.
11. Kurt Aland and Barbara Aland, *The Text of the New Testament*: "The actual number of New Testament manuscripts in existence today is probably closer to 5,000" (74).
12. See F. F. Bruce, *The New Testament Documents: Are They Reliable?* (Grand Rapids, Mich.: Eerdmans, 1960 repr.), 16.
13. Ibid., 14–20. Note the comparative chart in Josh McDowell, *Evidence That Demands a Verdict* (San Bernardino, Calif.: Here's Life Publishers, 1972), 48.
14. Some of these thoughts are developed further in Stewart Goetz and Craig Blomberg, "The Burden of Proof," *Journal for the Study of the New Testament* 11 (1981): 39–63.
15. Taking a mediating position between the historical skeptics and those who assume a text's reliability until proved otherwise, Craig Evans claims that the burden of proof rests on *all* who argue a case ("Authenticity Criteria in Life of Jesus Research," *Christian Scholar's Review* 19 [Sept. 1989]: 30–31). However, perhaps it is helpful to distinguish between the *strategic* and the *ideal* approaches. *Strategically*, we may need to take Evans' perspective since a number of critical scholars don't assume the Gospels' historical trustworthiness. This would show that we can argue from *their* starting point and still arrive at a conservative conclusion. On the other hand, the more *consistent* method is the *ideal* approach since applying Evans' approach to other ancient texts would *wipe out large amounts of ancient history* from our textbooks. We would have to resort to a total agnosticism about purportedly historical documents if we assumed they were *in*authentic unless proved otherwise. Thanks to Craig Blomberg for his comments through personal correspondence, 7 August 1996.

Chapter 16

1. (New York: Random House, 1986), 5.
2. *The First Coming*, 6.
3. "A Pluralist View," in *More Than One Way?*, 35. (The Jesus Seminar takes a similar approach.)
4. Goetz and Blomberg, "The Burden of Proof," 42–45.
5. Blomberg, "Where Do We Start Studying Jesus?" 36–37.
6. William Craig, *Assessing the New Testament Evidence*, xvi–xvii.

7. Thomas D. Lea, "The Reliability of History in John's Gospel," *Journal of the Evangelical Theological Society* 38 (Sept. 1995): 387–402.
8. Admittedly, historical and archaeological support provide *partial* evidence for reliability. In some cases, one may be warranted in arguing for a very restricted reliability claim (limited to a specific passage).
9. "Gospels (Historical Reliability)," 297.
10. At a popular level, see Robert Stein's *The Synoptic Problem: An Introduction* (Grand Rapids, Mich.: Baker, 1987).
11. See Colin J. Hemer's defense of this date in his *The Book of Acts in the Setting of Hellenistic History*, Conrad H. Gempf, ed. (Tübingen: Mohr, 1989), 365–410.
12. Some conservative scholars, however, would take a later date for certain theological reasons. See David John Williams, *Acts* NIBC (Peabody, Mass.: Hendrickson, 1990), 11–13.
13. See Hemer, *The Book of Acts in the Setting of Hellenistic History*, 308–364. See also Blomberg, "Where Do We Start Studying Jesus?" in *Jesus Under Fire*, 29. For an introduction to the issues surrounding the dating of the Gospels, note D. A. Carson, Douglas J. Moo, and Leon Morris, *An Introduction to the New Testament* (Grand Rapids, Mich.: Zondervan, 1992).
14. Carson, Moo, and Morris, *An Introduction to the New Testament*, 25: "The importance of memorization in first-century Jewish society is undeniable, and we are justified in thinking that this provides a sufficient basis for the careful and accurate oral tradition of gospel material." The German evangelical from Tübingen, Rainer Riesner, has documented this in his "Jüdische Elementarbildung und Evangelienüberlieferung," in R. T. France and David Wenham, eds., *Gospel Perspectives* I (Sheffield: JSOT Press, 1980): 209–223. He has expanded upon this in his *Jesus als Lehrer* (Tübingen: Mohr, 1981).
15. This dating is more disputed, however.
16. For a wealth of documentation on the many connections between Jesus and Paul, see David Wenham, *Paul: Follower of Jesus or Founder of Christianity?* (Grand Rapids, Mich.: Eerdmans, 1995); also, Gary Habermas, "The Resurrection Appearances of Jesus," in Gary R. Habermas and R. Douglas Geivett, eds., *In Defense of Miracles* (Downers Grove, Ill.: InterVarsity Press, 1997).
17. R. T. France, "The Gospels as Historical Sources for Jesus, the Founder of Christianity," *Truth* 1 (1985): 86.
18. *Roman Society and Roman Law* (Grand Rapids, Mich.: Baker, 1978 repr.), 187.
19. For plausible harmonizations of the Resurrection narratives, see George Eldon Ladd, *I Believe in the Resurrection of Jesus* (Grand Rapids, Mich.: Eerdmans, 1975), 91–93; Murray Harris, *Three Crucial Questions About Jesus*, 107–109; William Craig, *Assessing the New Testament Evidence for the Resurrection of Jesus*, 307–309; John Wenham, *Easter Enigma* 2nd ed. (Grand Rapids, Mich.: Baker, 1992).
20. *Gospel Fictions* (Buffalo, N.Y.: Prometheus, 1989), 133.
21. A. T. Lincoln, "The Promise and the Failure: Mark 16:7–8," *Journal of Biblical Literature* 108 (1989): 283–300.
22. See John P. Meier, *A Marginal Jew*, 168–171. See Meier's discussion on the merits of other criteria such as discontinuity, multiple attestation, coherence, and rejection and execution.
23. See "Jesus the Baptist?" by R. T. France in Joel B. Green and Max Turner, eds., *Jesus of Nazareth: Lord and Christ* (Grand Rapids, Mich.: Eerdmans, 1994), 94–111.
24. Craig Evans, "Life-of-Jesus Research and the Eclipse of Mythology," *Theological Studies* 54 (1993): 28.
25. Ibid., 29. Mark's language *explicitly* suggests this!

Chapter 17

1. John Hick, "A Pluralist View," 52.
2. Cited in Margaret Chatterjee, *Gandhi's Religious Thought* (Notre Dame: University Press, 1983), 55.
3. Ibid., 53.
4. Ibid.
5. Ibid., 34.
6. However, their followers at times did exalt their masters even to divinity—a charge leveled

against the Gospel tradition. But we saw in chapter 15 and in this chapter that such a fabrication about Jesus by his followers is unlikely.

7. See his fine book, *Oriental Philosophy: A Westerner's Guide to Eastern Thought* (Madison: University of Wisconsin Press, 1979).
8. Stuart C. Hackett, *Reconstruction of the Christian Revelation Claim* (Grand Rapids, Mich.: Baker, 1984), 250–251.
9. "What Are We to Make of Jesus Christ?" in *God in the Dock: Essays on Theology and Ethics* (Grand Rapids, Mich.: Eerdmans, 1970), 158–159.
10. John Hick says this of Jesus as "the son of God": "Emperors, pharaohs, and great philosophers and religious figures were sometimes called 'son of God' and regarded as divine in the broad sense that 'divine' then had" ("A Pluralist View," 35). Hick concludes that theology is "a human creation" (36).
11. John Dominic Crossan, *Jesus: A Revolutionary Biography* (San Francisco: HarperCollins, 1994), chap. 1.
12. See Samuel Sandmel, "Parallelomania," *Journal of Biblical Literature* 81 (1962): 1–13.
13. Martin Hengel argues that the history of religions school failed to get at the *origin* of the New Testament's exalted view of Jesus. See *The Son of God: The Origin of Christology and the History of Jewish-Hellenistic Religion*, trans. John Bowden (Philadelphia: Fortress, 1976), chap. 5.

Chapter 18

1. Gary Habermas, "Resurrection Claims in Non-Christian Religions," *Religious Studies* 25 (1989): 167–177. See L. D. Hurst, "New Testament Theological Analysis," in Scot McKnight, ed., *Introducing New Testament Interpretation* (Grand Rapids, Mich.: Baker, 1989). Jesus did, however, acknowledge his messiahship in certain contexts such as his trial before Caiaphas (Matt. 26:62–64) and his encounter with the Samaritan woman (John 4:25–26). When John the Baptist asked him if he was "the coming one" (the Messiah), Jesus responded with messianic references from Isaiah (33:5–6; 61:1–2; see Matthew 11:2–6), indicating that Jesus believed he was fulfilling the role of Messiah. Further, his temptation in the wilderness, transfiguration, triumphal entry into Jerusalem, and death as "King of the Jews" are fraught with messianic overtones (Richard Longenecker, "The Messianic Secret in Light of Recent Discoveries," *Evangelical Quarterly* 41 [1969]: 207–215).
2. See Douglas Geivett's chapter, "The Evidential Value of Miracles" in Geivett and Habermas, eds., *In Defense of Miracles*.
3. For a summary of these arguments, see William Craig's *Reasonable Faith*, chap. 8.
4. William Lane Craig, *Assessing the New Testament Evidence for the Resurrection of Jesus*; see Craig's less-technical, popular-level book, *Knowing the Truth About the Resurrection*; Stephen T. Davis, *Risen Indeed* (Grand Rapids, Mich.: Eerdmans, 1994); John Wenham, *Easter Enigma*.
5. See Martin Hengel's *Crucifixion in the Ancient World and the Folly of the Message of the Cross* (London: SCM Press, 1977).
6. A recent "resurrection" of this view has been offered by Gerd Lüdemann. See, for example, his *The Resurrection of Jesus*, trans. John Bowden (London: SCM Press, 1994).
7. Stephen T. Davis, "Doubting the Resurrection: A Reply to James A. Keller," *Faith and Philosophy* 7 (Jan. 1990): 106.
8. Pinchas Lapide, an orthodox Jewish New Testament scholar, argues that the historical evidence points to the bodily resurrection of Jesus. Even though Lapide believes that Jesus was not the Messiah, Lapide believes Jesus was God's instrument of bringing salvation to the Gentiles. See his *The Resurrection of Jesus: A Jewish Perspective* (Minneapolis, Minn.: Augsburg, 1983).

Chapter 19

1. *The Metaphor of God Incarnate* (London: SCM Press, 1993), 27.
2. "The Uniqueness of Jesus," *Evangelical Review of Theology* 17 (Jan. 1993): 15–16.
3. In Mark's gospel, this phenomenon has been called the "messianic secret" or, better, the "messianic *misunderstanding*." Up until Mark's turning point in 8:29 (at Peter's confession, "You are the Christ"), Jesus silences those who identify him overtly and publicly. Immediately after this point, Jesus warns his disciples to tell no one but proceeds to *educate* his disciples about what

the mission of the Messiah should be: He must be rejected by the Jewish leaders, be killed, and rise again: "Having at last got over to them the message *that* He is Messiah, He must now explain *what kind* of Messiah" (James D. G. Dunn, "The Messianic Secret in Mark," *Tyndale Bulletin* 21 [1970]: 105). Three times Jesus predicts his crucifixion (8:31–32a; 9:30–32; 10:32–34). Three times the disciples make a misjudgment about the nature of Jesus' messiahship (8:32b–33; 9:33–34; 10:35–41). And three times Jesus uses this misunderstanding to show how the Messiah's followers must also experience hardship (8:34–9:1; 9:35–10:31; 10:42–45).

4. Murray Harris, *Three Crucial Questions About Jesus*, 99–100.
5. Raymond Brown, "Did Jesus Know He Was God?" *Biblical Theology Bulletin* 15 (1985): 77.
6. France, "The Uniqueness of Christ," 18.
7. Jesus' response in Mark is clear enough: "I am [*egô eimi*]." And although some have doubted that Jesus is admitting anything at all, for example, in Matthew's gospel by saying, "It is as you say [*su eipas*]" (26:64), Jesus is speaking *affirmatively*. This is borne out by the fact that Jesus previously issued the same response to Judas Iscariot, who asked if he was the betrayer: "Yes, it is you [*su eipas*]" (Matt. 26:25).
8. Ben Witherington III, *The Jesus Quest: The Third Search for the Jew of Nazareth* (Downers Grove, Ill.: InterVarsity Press, 1995), 95.
9. See D. A. Carson's concise discussion of the term "Son of Man" (*bar enasha*) in "Matthew" EBC 8, Frank Gaebelein, ed. (Grand Rapids, Mich.: Zondervan), 209–213. C.F.D. Moule offers a more technical discussion in *The Origin of Christology* (Cambridge: University Press, 1977), 11–22. Incidentally, Moule notes that we should think in terms of the *development* rather than the *evolution* of viewing Jesus as God. Whereas *evolution* implies mythical ideas being attached to the human Jesus, *development* implies an outworking of something already implicit at the outset (2). Astonishingly, John Hick *ignores* this when citing Moule to support the opposite point ("A Pluralist View," 53).
10. See Seyoon Kim's *The Son of Man as the Son of God* (Grand Rapids, Mich.: Eerdmans, 1985).
11. Ben Witherington, III, *Jesus the Sage: The Pilgrimage of Wisdom* (Minneapolis, Minn.: Augsburg Fortress, 1994). For a succinct summary of this perspective, see Witherington's *The Jesus Quest*, 185–96.
12. R. T. France, "Development in New Testament Christology," 6.
13. Craig Evans makes this point in an unpublished essay.
14. John Meier, *A Marginal Jew*, 177.
15. Scot McKnight, "Who Is Jesus? An Introduction to Jesus Studies," in *Jesus Under Fire*, 61–62.
16. These features (listed on 268) are argued for in Ben Witherington, III, *The Christology of Jesus* (Minneapolis, Minn.: Fortress Press, 1990).
17. Ibid., 267.
18. Martin Hengel, *The Son of God*, 1.
19. In this section, I am indebted to some of the remarks made by Larry Hurtado in *One God, One Lord: Early Christian Devotion and Ancient Jewish Monotheism* (Philadelphia: Fortress Press, 1988) and his "The Origins of the Worship of Christ," *Themelios* 19 (Jan. 1994): 4–7.
20. Hurtado, "The Origins," 4.
21. Hurtado, *One God, One Lord*, 2.
22. Moule, *The Origin of Christology*, 41.
23. Hurtado, "The Origins," 5.
24. For instance, it was detestable to offer worship to mere human beings (Acts 10:25–26; 14:11–15).
25. Hurtado, "The Origins," 5. Also, Hurtado notes, given their Jewish loyalty to ancestral traditions—remember Paul's having persecuted early Christians almost from the outset because of such loyalty!—and avoidance of syncretism with paganism, the earliest Christians' supreme exaltation of Jesus (e.g., Phil. 2:9–11) cannot be accounted for by pagan influences of certain "god-men" or heroes ("The Origins," 5).
26. Taken from Hurtado, *One God, One Lord*, chaps. 2–4.
27. Paul Johnson, "A Historian Looks at Jesus."

PART V
Introduction

1. Source unknown.
2. This isn't meant to be a derogatory or pejorative term, but rather a *descriptive* one.

3. "A Pluralist View" in *More Than One Way?*, 45.
4. "Response by McGrath," in *More Than One Way?*, 257.
5. When speaking of "justice," one need not assume that God *owes* salvation to anyone. So for the inclusivist to speak of God's justice toward the unevangelized, he must *qualify* what aspect of justice is meant (distributive versus retributive). I explore this issue of justice or fairness below.

Chapter 20

1. This view has been most prominently defended by William Lane Craig, "No Other Name: A Middle Knowledge Perspective on the Exclusivity of Salvation Through Christ," *Faith and Philosophy* 6 (April 1989): 172–88; *The Only Wise God: The Compatibility of Divine Foreknowledge and Human Freedom* (Grand Rapids, Mich.: Baker, 1996), 127–151; *No Easy Answers* (Chicago: Moody, 1990), 105–16; "Politically Incorrect Salvation," in Timothy R. Phillips and Dennis L. Ockholm, eds., *Christian Apologetics in the Postmodern World* (Downers Grove, Ill.: InterVarsity Press, 1995), 75–97. I shall follow his arguments here without significant addition. Unfortunately, I am attempting to do much synthesizing and summarizing.
2. William Craig makes these distinctions in "Politically Incorrect Salvation," 84.
3. For an argument opposing the middle-knowledge view, see Robert M. Adams, "Middle Knowledge and the Problem of Evil," *American Philosophical Quarterly* 20 (1983): 225–64. But also see Craig's concise response to this and a later piece by Adams: "Robert Adams's New Anti-Molinist Argument," *Philosophy and Phenomenological Research* 54 (Dec. 1994): 857–61. Although William Hasker has written a response to Craig ("Explanatory Priority: Transitive and Unequivocal: a Reply to William Craig," *Philosophy and Phenomenological Research* 57 [June 1997]: 389–93), William Craig has also issued a forthcoming response ("Hasker on Explanatory Priority") in *Faith and Philosophy*, which points out certain problems in Hasker's essay.
4. Louis Molina first wrote of middle knowledge in 1588. (*Harmony of Free Will With the Gifts of Grace*) in an attempt to harmonize divine foreknowledge and human freedom. (The description of the three aspects of God's knowledge is taken from Craig, *The Only Wise God*, 131).
5. *The Problem of Pain* (New York: Macmillan, 1962), 127.
6. Ibid., 124.
7. William Craig, *The Only Wise God*, 134–5. God's foreknowledge of a future event doesn't necessitate the conclusion that it *must* happen, only that it *will* happen. For instance, the fact that God foreknows that my children are going to pick mulberries tomorrow does not necessitate that they *must* pick them tomorrow. God's foreknowledge of this event entails only that they *will* pick mulberries tomorrow. And if they were desirous of picking mulberries the day after tomorrow instead, then God's foreknowledge would be different. (See Craig, *The Only Wise God*, chap. 5.) After all, most theists wouldn't maintain that because God *knows* what he will do in the future, necessitates that he *must* do it!
8. *No Easy Answers*, 112.
9. Craig, "Politically Incorrect Salvation," 92.
10. Ibid., 115.
11. Ibid.
12. William Lane Craig, "Should Peter Go to the Mission Field?" *Faith and Philosophy* 10 (April 1993): 262, 264.
13. Thanks to William Craig for his suggestions for this and the following chapter.

Chapter 21

1. This event is recounted in Walter Schweitzer's book *Out of Europe's Night* (Brooklyn: Bible Christian Union, 1968), 13–14.
2. This view is also called the "implicit-faith" view (as in David K. Clark, "Is Special Revelation Necessary for Salvation?" in Crockett and Sigountos, eds., *Through No Fault of Their Own* (Grand Rapids, Mich.: Baker, 1991), 35–43. For a balanced discussion of the question of the fate of the unevangelized, see Millard J. Erickson, *How Shall They Be Saved? The Destiny of Those Who Do Not Hear of Jesus* (Grand Rapids, Mich.: Baker, 1996).
3. From a phone conversation on 19 August 1997.
4. Don Richardson also knew of a couple of Sawi men (in Irian Jaya) who were examples of persons

who, despite their responsiveness to the one true God, never heard the Gospel.

5. John Sanders, *No Other Name: An Investigation Into the Destiny of the Unevangelized* (Grand Rapids, Mich.: Eerdmans, 1992), 25.

6. Jesus is in some way the Savior of all—potentially, though not actually (1 Tim. 4:10: ". . . the Savior of all men, and especially of those who believe.") First John 2:2 reminds us that Jesus died not merely for an exclusive few but for "the whole world" (the very same phrase that is used in 1 John 5:19: ". . . the *whole world* is under the control of the evil one").

7. Cited in Netland, *Dissonant Voices*, 265.

8. The inclusivist argues that Romans 10:14–17, which is frequently cited at missions conferences ("how can they hear without a preacher?"), *continues on* in verse 18 but tends to be overlooked by restrictivists: "Indeed they have [heard]." Paul then cites the "general revelation" passage from Psalm 19. The "sound" of general revelation is available to all; it has gone to the "ends of the earth."

9. R. C. Sproul, *Reason to Believe* (Grand Rapids, Mich.: Zondervan, 1982), 56.

10. John Stott (with David Edwards), *Evangelical Essentials* (Downers Grove, Ill.: InterVarsity Press, 1988), 327.

11. The point of Romans 1:18–3:20 is that the power of sin is universal, affecting both Jews and Gentiles (Douglas Moo, *Romans 1–8* WEC (Chicago: Moody Press, 1991), 88–90.

12. Just as a passage like Romans 5:12 (which refers to death's coming into the world to all through Adam's sin) assumes the general category of those who consciously, personally sin and does not take into consideration mentally restricted human beings (Moo, 343); so passages that speak of the necessity of believing on or confessing Christ (e.g., Rom. 10:9–10) imply that the Gospel *has* been proclaimed. But this does not, Douglas Moo asserts, address the different question of the unevangelized.

13. *The Second Epistle of Peter and the Epistle of Jude*, Tyndale NT Commentary Series 18 (Grand Rapids, Mich.: Eerdmans, 1982 repr.), 136.

14. See I. Howard Marshall's discussion, "Universal Grace and Atonement in the Pastoral Epistles," in Clark Pinnock, ed., *The Grace of God and the Will of Man* (Minneapolis, Minn.: Bethany House Publishers, 1995), 51–69. Gordon Fee, commenting on 1 Timothy 2:5–6, writes that "the Gospel, therefore, potentially provides salvation for all people, because Christ's death was 'in behalf of' (*hyper*) *all* people. Effectually, of course, it ends up being 'especially [for] those who believe' (4:10)" (*1 and 2 Timothy, Titus* NIBC 2nd ed. [Peabody, Mass.: Hendricksen, 1988], 66). Millard Erickson comments on 1 Timothy 4:10: "Apparently the Savior has done something for all persons, though it is less in degree than what he has done for those who believe" (*Christian Theology* [Grand Rapids, Mich.: Baker, 1985], 834).

15. John Sanders, "Response to Nash," in John Sanders, ed., *What About Those Who Have Never Heard?* (Downers Grove, Ill.: InterVarsity Press, 1995), 148.

16. See Douglas Stuart's comments on Jonah in *Hosea-Jonah* WBC 31 (Waco: 1987).

17. *No Other Name*, 61.

18. *The Reconstruction of the Christian Revelation Claim* (Grand Rapids, Mich.: Baker, 1984), 244.

19. John Sanders, "Evangelical Responses to Salvation Outside the Church," *Christian Scholar's Review* 24 (September 1994), 57–58.

20. Some may argue that this distinction is overwrought; that is, the belief-condition for salvation isn't only a matter of knowledge (epistemology). However, the inclusivist would reply that there is an *actual* (ontological) connection with the God who redeems as the source of salvation. The *same* God is involved in salvation—even if the historical Jesus is not known. Moreover, there must be an *epistemological* connection with the one true God as a belief condition.

Furthermore, the restrictivist will ask, "Does *anyone* have to believe in Jesus to be saved?" To this, the inclusivist responds, "Saints in the Old Testament didn't. They were saved by faith in God. Why couldn't this apply to the unevangelized?" In addition, the inclusivist would add that anyone who hears and understands the Gospel *must* receive it in order to be saved.

21. Bruce A. Demarest, *General Revelation* (Grand Rapids, Mich.: Zondervan, 1982), 233. God may use cultural traditions and ancient stories (*not* religious systems) of tribal or people groups who have a remote awareness of the supreme God in order to prepare them for a large-scale reception of the Gospel. Don Richardson has documented this preparation in *Eternity in Their Hearts* (Ventura, Calif.: Regal Books, 1981).

22. These thoughts are taken from Peter Forrest, *God Without the Supernatural: A Defense of Sci-*

entific Theism (Ithaca, N.Y.: Cornell University Press, 1996), 129, 133–135.

23. This list is taken from Demarest, *General Revelation*, 243.

24. See D. K. Clark's succinct, helpful comments in "Is Special Revelation Necessary for Salvation?" 44–45. These commitments run on two continua: one between God's transcendence and immanence and the other between human sinfulness and God-likeness. For instance, those who downplay the immanence and God-likeness pole also downplay general revelation.

25. The restrictivist may ask, "Where in the Bible do you find that someone is saved apart from becoming part of Israel or hearing of Jesus?" However, the inclusivist would reply that the Bible is *explicitly about* Israel and Jesus! And so it does not specifically deal with the matter of the unevangelized. Hence, the inclusivist believes that this question may not be as forceful as it first appears. Also, inclusivists claim that restrictivists seem to disallow any type of *continuum* in the process of conversion. They tend to see the issue of the unevangelized as an either-or proposition (*either* there is direct biblical evidence for it *or* such a position is unwarranted).

26. Sanders, *No Other Name*, 69.

27. For examples of misuse (such as Matt. 25:31–46 and John 1:9), see D. A. Carson, *The Gagging of God*, 300–313.

28. R. Douglas Geivett and W. Gary Phillips, "A Particularist View," in *More Than One Way?*, 240.

29. As Carson, a restrictivist, describes them, they are people who "though they live this side of the decisive events connected with the life, ministry, death, and resurrection of Jesus, have never heard of them, and are therefore very much in the place of those who came before Jesus, and who consequently never heard of him" (*The Gagging of God*, 298).

30. Although Acts 11:14 speaks of Cornelius' being saved as a future event, one could view salvation as being a much more extensive concept than "becoming a Christian." James Dunn writes, "Luke would by no means wish to question the spiritual standing of an Old Testament saint or of a pious Jew before God (e.g., Luke 18:14). Cornelius came up to the highest standards of Jewish piety.... But, for Luke, what made a man a Christian and brought him into the salvation of the new [covenant] age ... was belief in Jesus and the gift of the Holy Spirit" (*Baptism in the Holy Spirit* [Philadelphia: Westminster, 1970], 79–80).

Stott, however, views Cornelius' deeds as being "accepted" (Acts 10:35), as having the comparative sense of "acceptable" (*The Spirit, the Church, and the World: The Message of Acts* [Downers Grove, Ill.: InterVarsity Press, 1990], 199). Erickson raises some questions about the status of Cornelius as well, indicating that Cornelius' case may be a good deal less clear-cut than inclusivists argue (*How Shall They Be Saved?* 155–56).

31. Carson, *The Gagging of God*, 298.

32. John Sanders, "Response to Nash," in *What About Those Who Have Never Heard?* 142.

33. John Sanders, "Is Belief in Christ Necessary for Salvation?" *Evangelical Quarterly* 60 (1988): 252–253.

34. Carson, *The Gagging of God*, 296.

35. Ibid., 312–313.

36. Millard Erickson, *How Shall They Be Saved?*, 194–195 (my emphasis).

37. Klaas Runia, "The Gospel and Religious Pluralism," 375.

38. Geivett and Phillips, "A Particularist View," in *More Than One Way?*, 238. See also Erickson's analysis, *How Shall They Be Saved?*, chap. 11.

39. *Evangelical Essentials*, 328. Norman Anderson offers the suggestion that Matthew 7:14 refers to the difficult road of self-denial that Christ's disciples must travel, which is often lonely and arduous (*Christianity and World Religions*, 162–163). See also Kreeft and Tacelli, *Handbook of Christian Apologetics*, 330.

40. McGrath, "A Particularist View," in *More Than One Way?*, 179.

Chapter 22

1. Winfried Corduan, *Reasonable Faith*, 33.

2. Peter Kreeft and Ronald Tacelli, *Handbook of Christian Apologetics*, 323.

3. *God's Words* (Downers Grove, Ill.: InterVarsity Press, 1981), 210. See also J. I. Packer, " 'Good Pagans' and God's Kingdom," *Christianity Today* (17 Jan. 1986): 22–26.

Chapter 23

1. *The Reformed Doctrine of Predestination* (Grand Rapids, Mich.: Eerdmans, 1936, repr.), 119.
2. It would be *political* in the sense that some Christian leaders may be reluctant to openly espouse the inclusivist view because they would appear to be diminishing missionary urgency or discouraging missionary activity.
3. In a personal letter (28 Sept. 1991), Marshall wrote: "About the fate of the unevangelized, you are right to conclude that I share the view of Norman Anderson."
4. Phone conversation on 15 July 1997.
5. Netland, *Dissonant Voices*, 275.
6. Evert D. Osburn, "Those Who Have Never Heard: Have They No Hope?" *Journal for the Evangelical Theological Society* 32 (Sept. 1989): 372.
7. Personal correspondence from 19 November 1989.
8. Norman Anderson, *Christianity and World Religions* (Downers Grove, Ill.: InterVarsity Press, 1984), 155.
9. William Crockett, *Through No Fault of Their Own*, 260.
10. *Handbook of Christian Apologetics*, 329.
11. *Evangelical Essentials*, 327.
12. *The Contemporary Christian: Applying God's Word to Today's World* (Downers Grove, Ill.: InterVarsity Press, 1992), 319.
    I would add here special thanks to Stuart Hackett, Don Richardson, and John Sanders for their discussing some aspects of this chapter.
13. William Craig, personal correspondence from 17 November 1997.
14. Walter M. Abbott, S.J., ed., (New York: Guild Press, 1966), 34–35. The emphasis in the citations above is mine.
15. Cited in William Lane Craig, "Politically Incorrect Salvation," 85.
16. For documentation of the grievous deterioration of Christian missions in light of religious pluralism, see Grant Wacker, "The Protestant Awakening to World Religions," in William R. Hutchison, ed., *Between the Times: The Travail of the Protestant Establishment in America, 1900–1960* (Cambridge: Cambridge University Press, 1989), 253–277.
17. John Hick, "The Epistemological Challenge of Religious Pluralism," *Faith and Philosophy* 14 (July 1997): 283.
18. This response to Hick is taken from Peter van Inwagen, "A Reply to Professor Hick," 300–301.
19. *Evangelical Essentials*, 328.

Chapter 24

1. "Christianity and Culture," *Princeton Theological Review* 11 (1913): 7.
2. On this topic, see J. P. Moreland's *Love Your God With All Your Mind* (Colorado Springs: NavPress, 1997).
3. I am grateful to Ravi Zacharias for this aptly stated point.
4. I recommend his writings and taped messages as a model effort to bring the two together. See Ravi Zacharias' *Can Man Live Without God?* (Dallas: Word Books, 1994); *Deliver Us From Evil* (Dallas: Word Books, 1996; *Cries of the Heart* (Dallas: Word Books, 1998); and *A Shattered Visage: The Real Face of Atheism* (Grand Rapids, Mich: Baker Books, 1993). For further information, contact RZIM, 4725 Peachtree Corners Circle, Suite 250, Norcross, GA. 30092; (770) 449–6766.
5. *The Spirit, the Church, and the World*, 281.
6. For an example of a nuanced approach to postmodern thinkers like Jacques Derrida, see Andrew Gustafson, "Apologetically Listening to Derrida," *Philosophia Christi* 20 (Winter 1997): 15–42.
7. On this doctrine, see Paul Copan, "Is *Creatio ex Nihilo* a Post-Biblical Invention? A Critical Review of Gerhard May's Thesis," *Trinity Journal* 17 NS (Spring 1996).
8. Cited in John D. Barrow, *The World Within the World* (Oxford: Clarendon Press, 1988), 226.
9. This is somewhat adapted from Lee Strobel, *Inside the Mind of Unchurched Harry and Mary* (Grand Rapids, Mich.: Zondervan, 1993). Note that in this chapter I am not equating *secularized* persons (i.e., those whose lives have little or no religious influences) with *postmoderns*, although these terms frequently overlap.
10. John Stott has a useful discussion of these images in *The Cross of Christ* (Downers Grove, Ill.: InterVarsity Press, 1986).

11. This point on interpersonal relationships is taken from William A. Dyrness, *How Does America Hear the Gospel?* (Grand Rapids, Mich.: Eerdmans, 1989), chap. 7.
12. See Win Arn and Charles Arn, *The Master's Plan for Making Disciples* (Pasadena: Church Growth Press, 1982).
13. See J. P. Moreland's sage advice in his "Philosophical Apologetics, the Church, and Contemporary Culture," *Journal of the Evangelical Theological Society* 39 (March 1996): 123–140.
14. For further documentation on this, see Win Arn and Charles Arn, *The Master's Plan for Making Disciples*.
15. For a brief assessment of the burden-of-proof issue, see my article "The Presumptuousness of Atheism," *Christian Research Journal* (Spring 1996): 8.
16. See William Craig's discussion of these criteria in chap. 1 of *Reasonable Faith*.
17. I am assuming that *no* one can be reasoned into God's kingdom. Intellectual arguments or methods by themselves will not persuade people to embrace Christ. In fact, people can use intellectual arguments to suppress truth. However, the apologetic endeavor can be carried out in dependence upon God's Spirit. He can use rational arguments—as he can the reading of Scripture, a crisis experience, or an evangelistic sermon—to draw people closer to Christ.
18. For an excellent, readable resource on objective truth, see Winfried Corduan, *Reasonable Faith: Basic Christian Apologetics*. Peter Kreeft and Ron Tacelli briefly discuss various theories of truth in their *Handbook of Christian Apologetics*, 361–383. For a more technical defense, see Frederick F. Schmitt, *Truth: A Primer*.
19. These arguments are nicely presented in William Craig, *Reasonable Faith* and J. P. Moreland, *Scaling the Secular City*.
20. A book that deals more specifically with the reliability of the Gospels and the resurrection of Jesus is William Craig, *Reasonable Faith*. A standard defense of the New Testament's reliability is F. F. Bruce, *The New Testament Documents: Are They Reliable?*